32 boroughs

32 boroughs
LONDON
2013–2021

HARRIET TURNEY

Contents

Introduction 6

32 boroughs 8

Map of London's 32 boroughs 192

Q&A with Harriet Turney & Seetal Solanki 194

Acknowledgements 207

Introduction

London is the kind of city that is constantly screaming out for a love letter. It's full of history and culture and architecture and landmarks and all those things that make people start spouting romantic lists that trail off into breathless ellipses . . .

If you've been, you'll also know that London is full of people. About 8.9 million of them if you want to talk numbers, all packed into a capital city that somehow is overcrowded but manages to keep offering standing room for all, at the same time. How? Because one of the biggest clichés about London is also one of the truest - that it's not actually one place. It's an experiment in multidimensional social physics, with communities that overlap and intersect in an impossible logical palimpsest.

Like any jigsaw, it's hard to know exactly where to start. I mean, how do you begin to define the identity, singular of a place that is made up of so many identities, plural? How do you make sense of the confusion and energy and history and potential all at the same time?

Funnily enough, these aren't rhetorical questions. I actually have an answer.
And here's the big reveal: to make sense of London you grow with London.
And to grow with London you have to be young in London.

32 boroughs is a portrait of youth in London. It might even be a love letter to that most enigmatic of realities - modern, urban adolescence. This is the London that doesn't always get the love letter, or the whispered, breathless words of wonder. This is the real London, lived in by the very real young people who call the city home, with biographies set in stone. Or brick, at least. Every picture in this book is a reminder of the stories that don't always get told, the realities that don't always get seen, rooted in the concrete or reaching out far across oceans and deep into cultural histories - multicultural, multiethnic and unmistakably London.

There's a lot to be fascinated by and, arguably, even more to celebrate. For me, Harriet Turney has compiled something historic and momentous in the truest sense of the word, in that it captures a moment of what it means to grow up now in the 32 boroughs of London city. You can see the tribes, the trends and the traditions, but more than that, you can see the pride and the empowerment too. Harriet has done that most human of things: going beyond the stereotypes to reveal the human hearts of kids in the city. Capturing the shades of childhood intermingling with the shadows of maturity, those moments that come and go so quickly in the seasons of life, especially when the city is forcing you to be grown before your time. Harriet has gone 'click' and stripped that all away. Empathy. Connection. Honesty. This is what cameras are made for.

This is also what makes this book so special. It isn't just a snapshot of modern Britain from the ground up. It's also a repositioning, shifting the focus so that the margins become the centre. For someone like me, a teacher who grew up as a black boy in one of these boroughs (Lambeth), went on to teach inner city kids in a few others (Ealing, Newham), recently moved away from the capital (bye bye) and is now officially too old to fully understand the generations who came after him, *32 boroughs* has a warm familiarity that feels a lot like home.

So, consider yourself invited. Turn the page, take a tour, and meet each young face with your own warm smile. It's impossible not to.

Jeffrey Boakye

"I'm gonna get
them baby blue
pointy nails
with the diamonds"

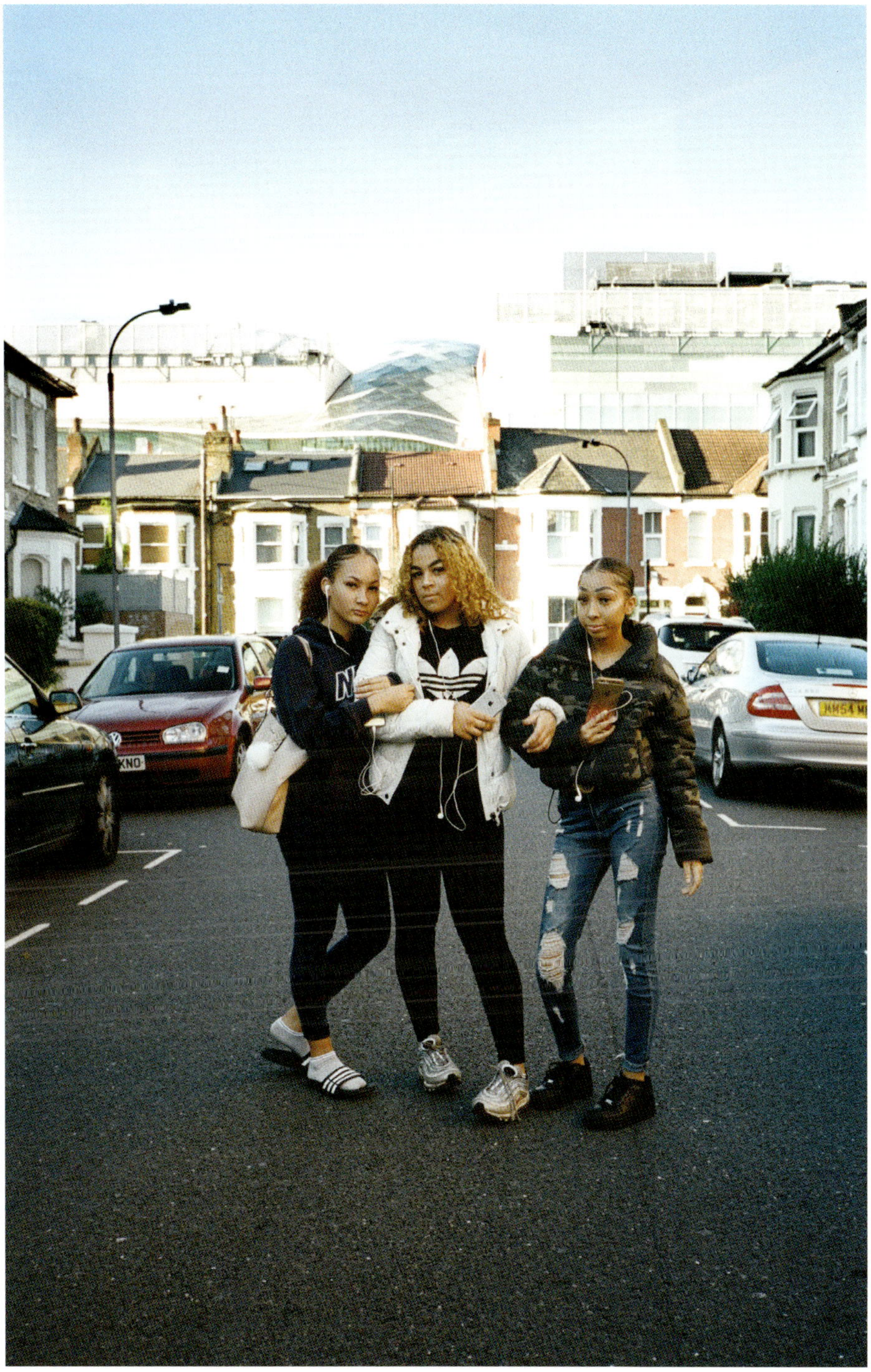

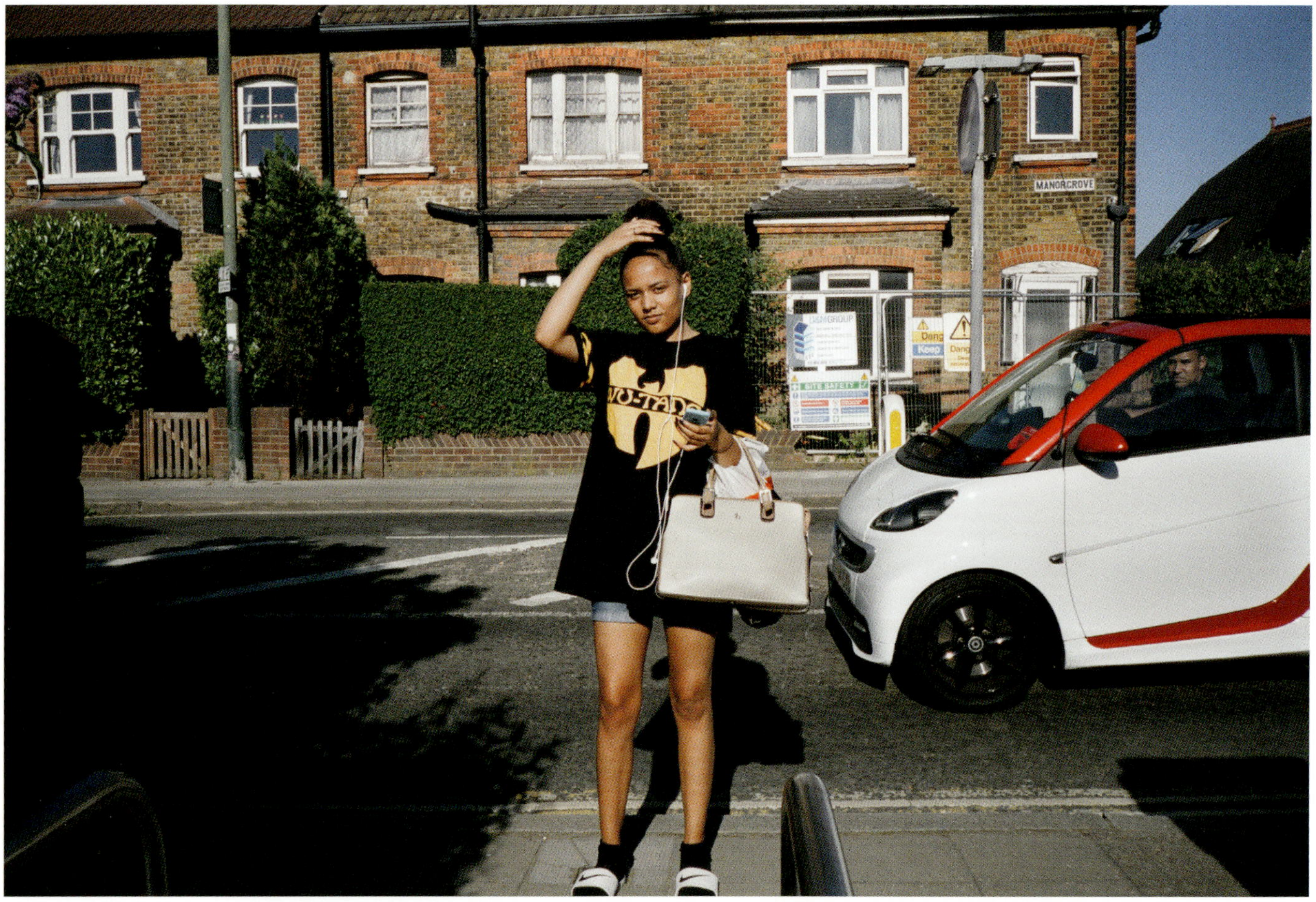
MANORGROVE

"My bus will be here
in eight minutes,
I'm just on the phone
to a mate,
I got some time"

*"It's good growing up in London.
Some parts are wild, some good.
You need good guidance,
elders, a mentor, social worker.
My parents don't always
understand how it is out here,
they are from a different place"*

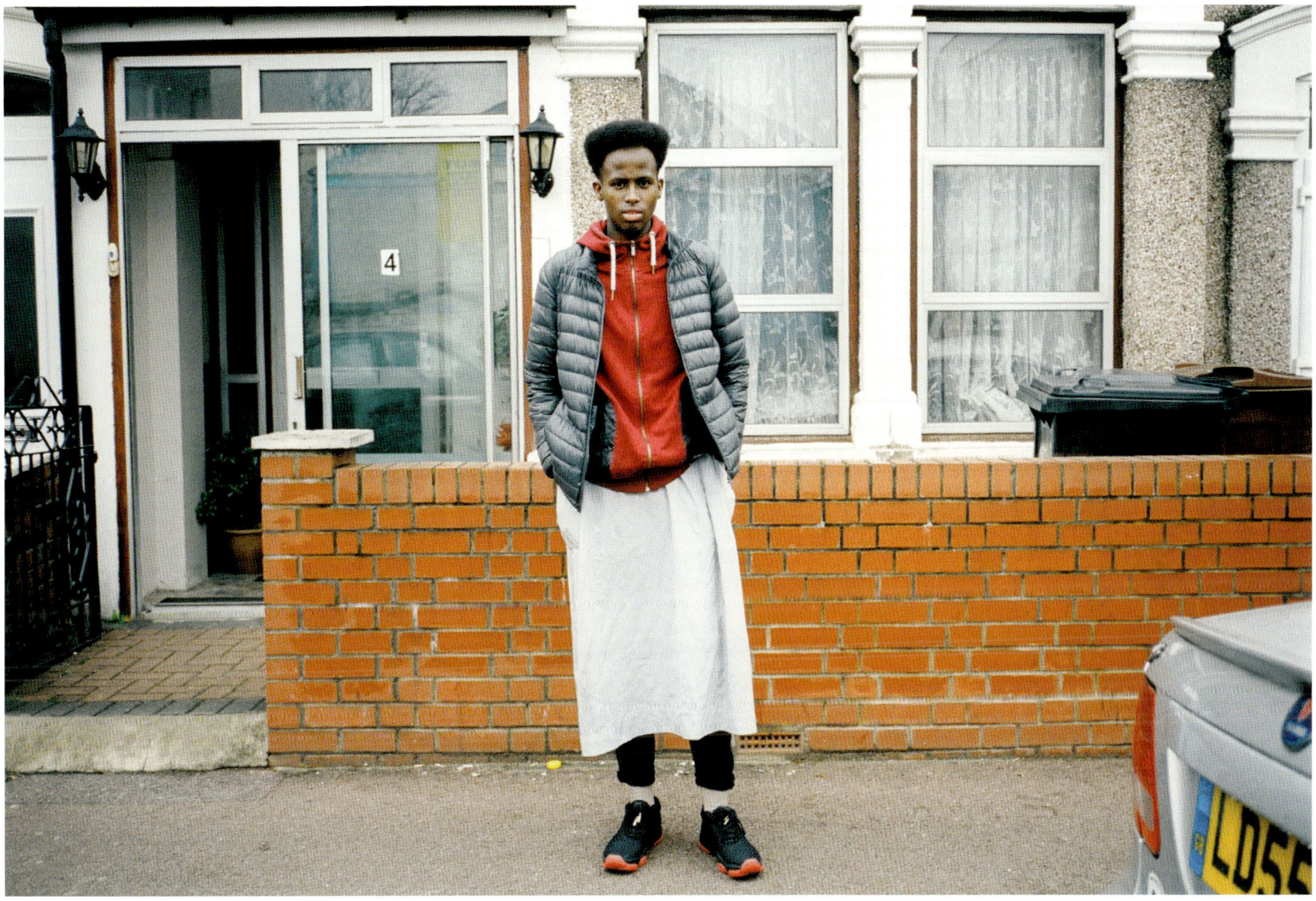
4

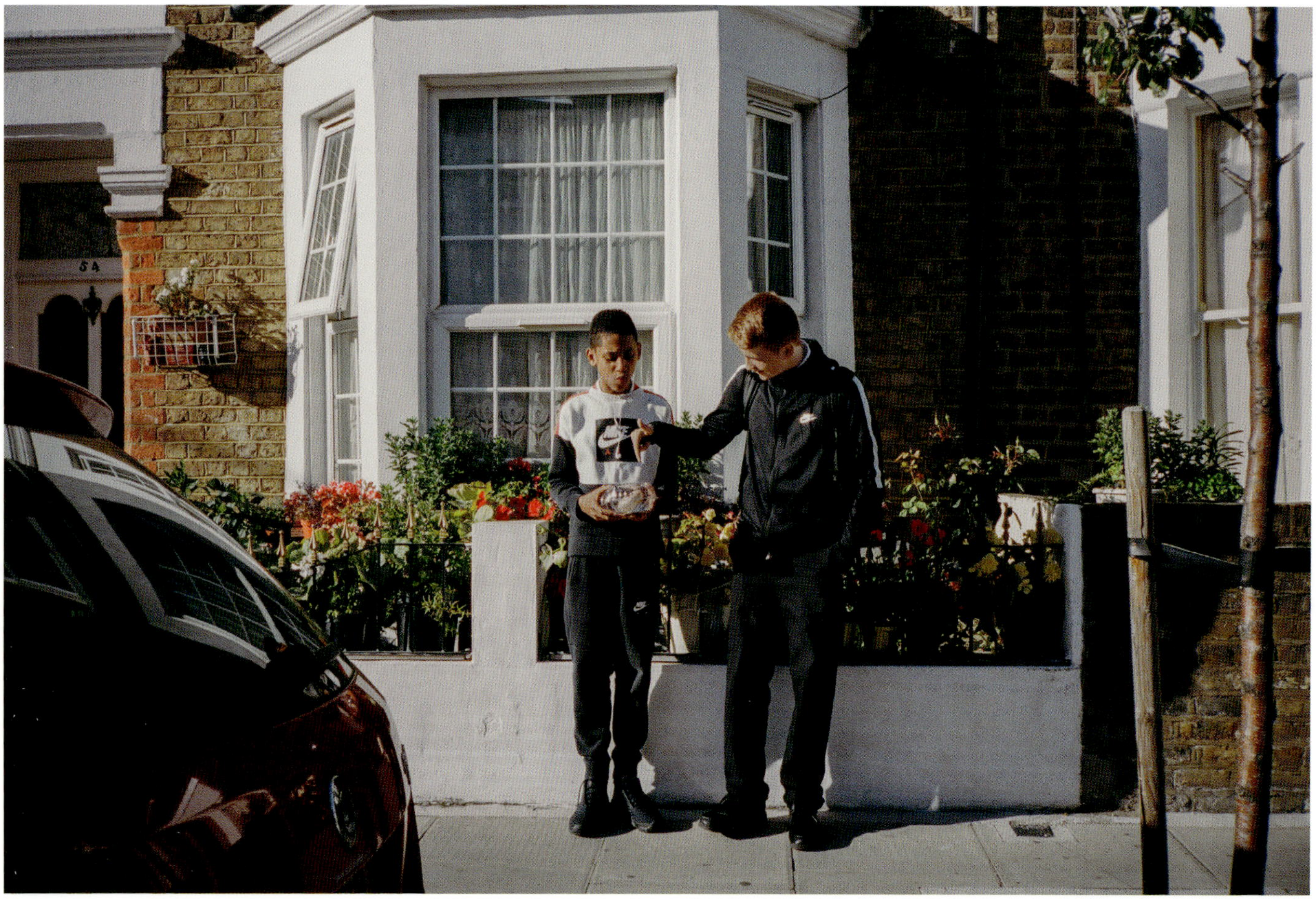

"That's his
third
doughnut today"

"Carnival was
full of
greatness"

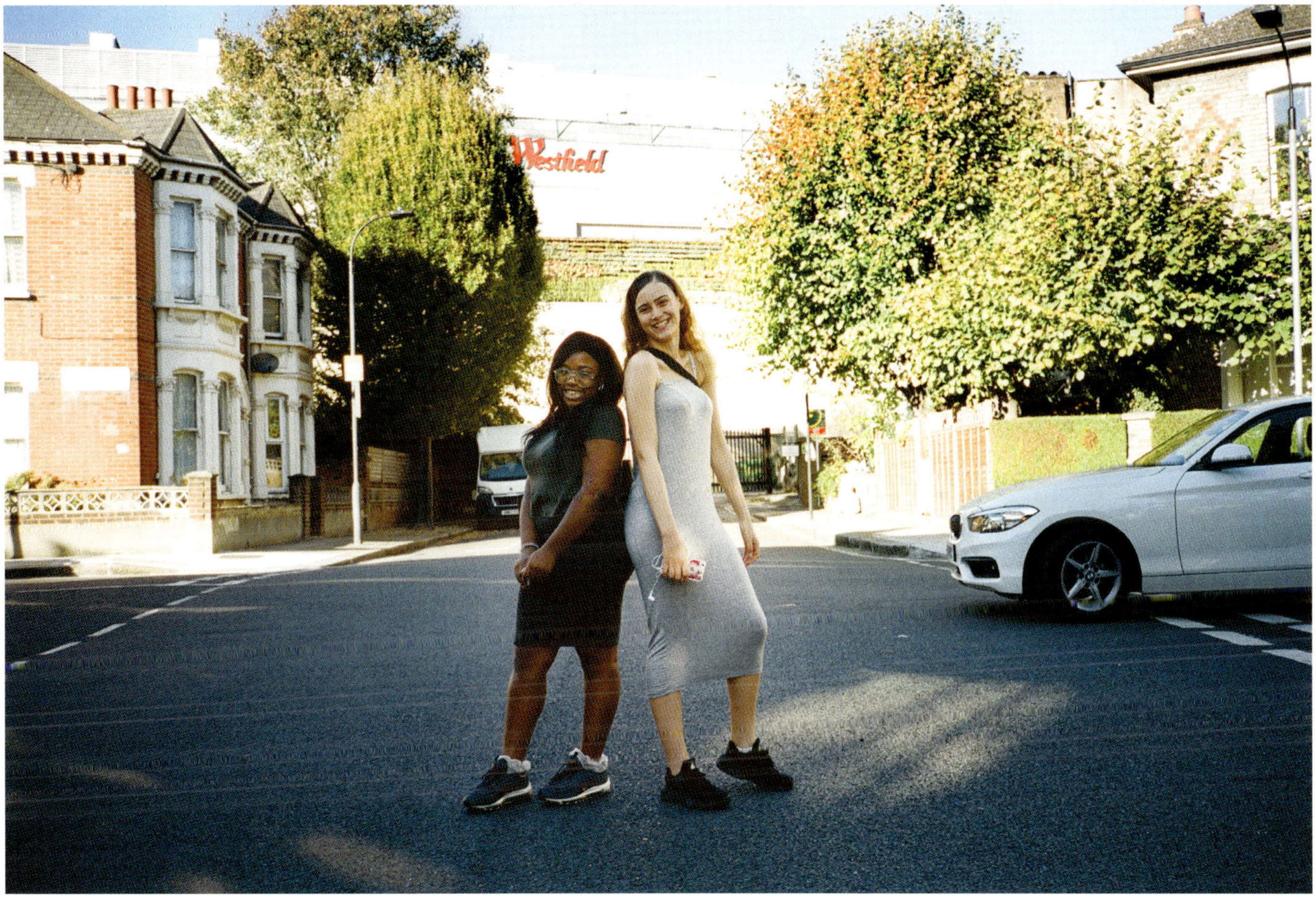
Westfield

"We ride with
Bike Life,
with the
South-East
London lot"

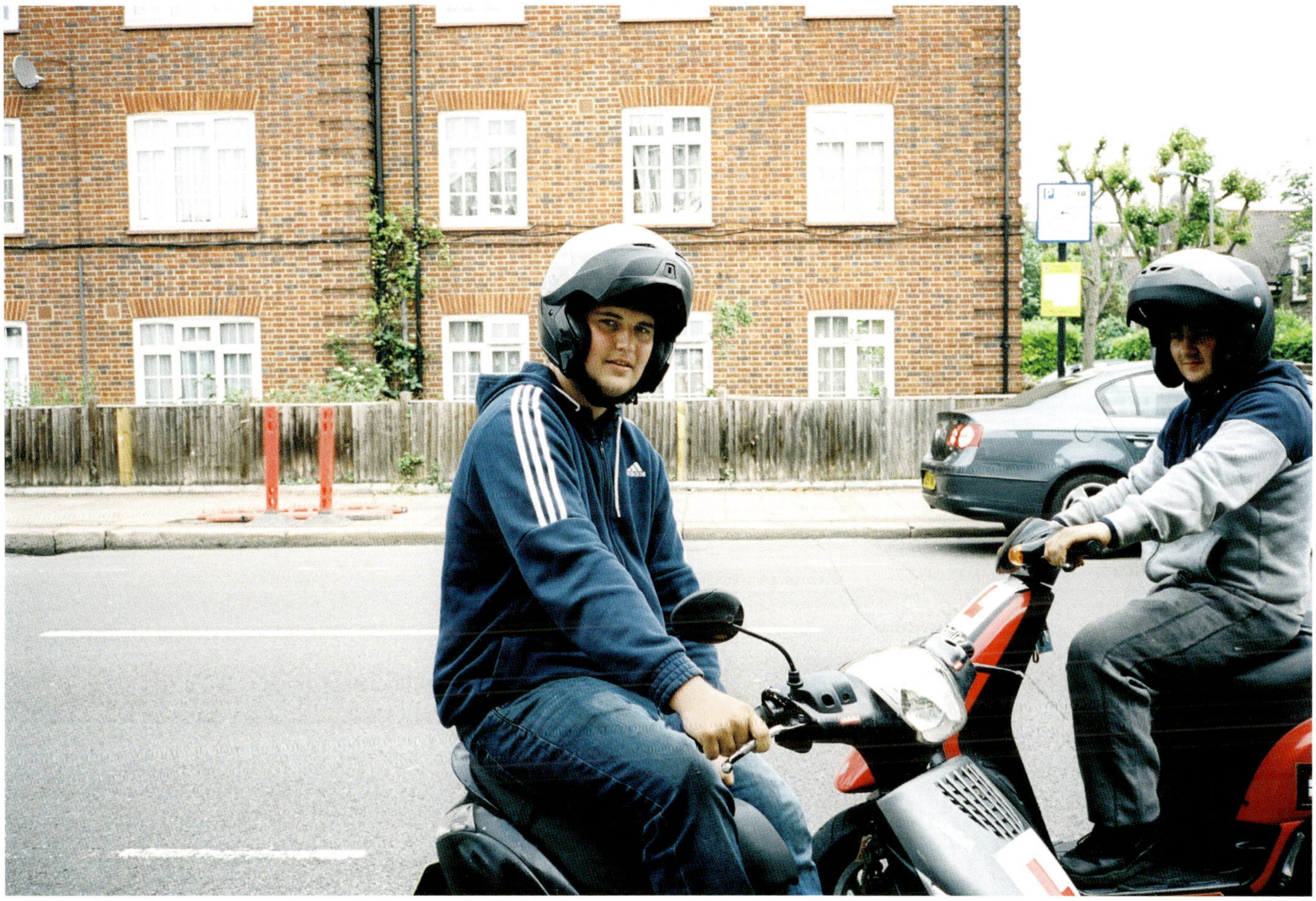

"I'm taking P.E.,
wait,
sshhh,
we're just about to go
past my nan's house,
it's all good,
I saw her
this morning"

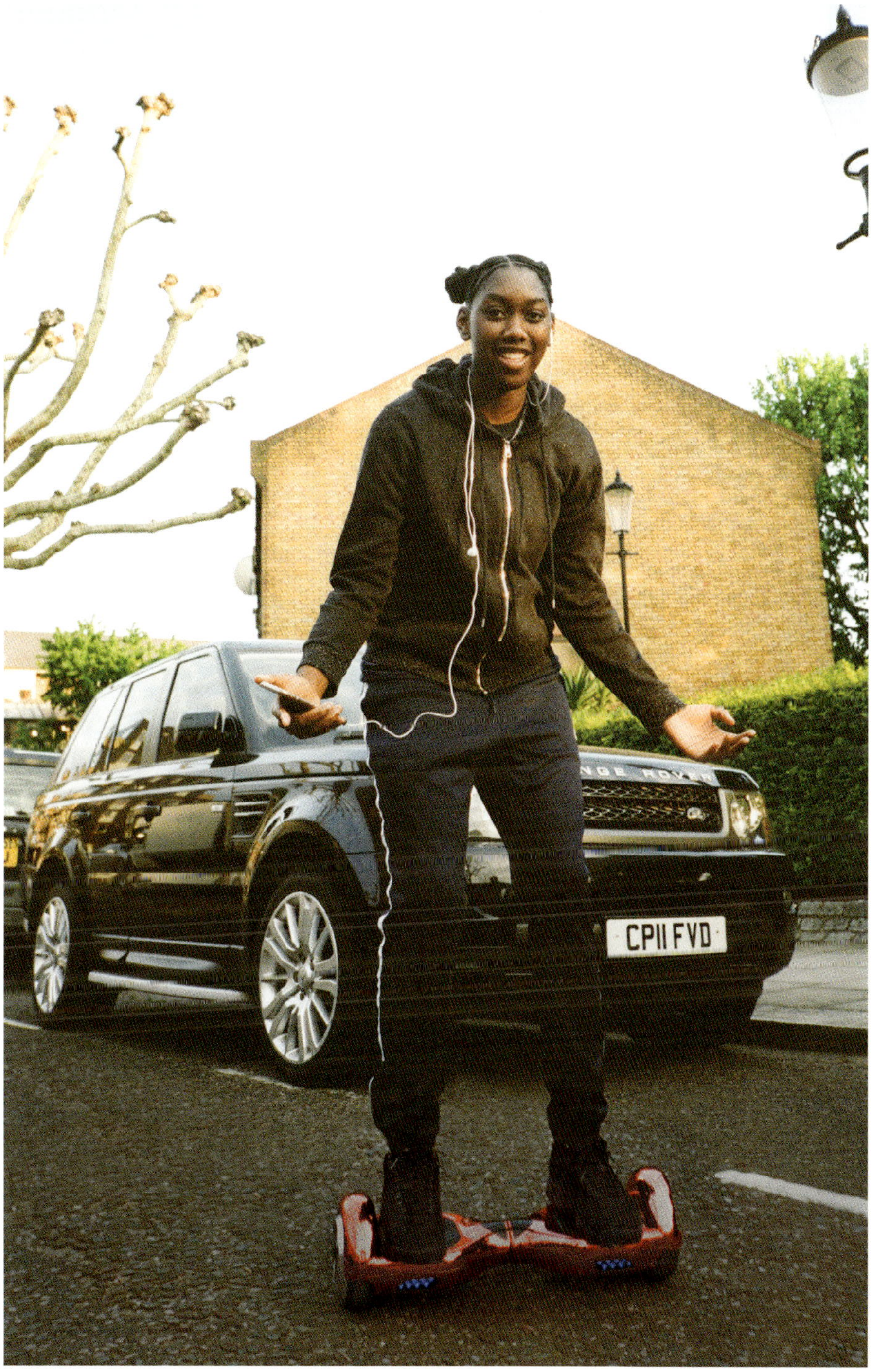
CP11 FVD

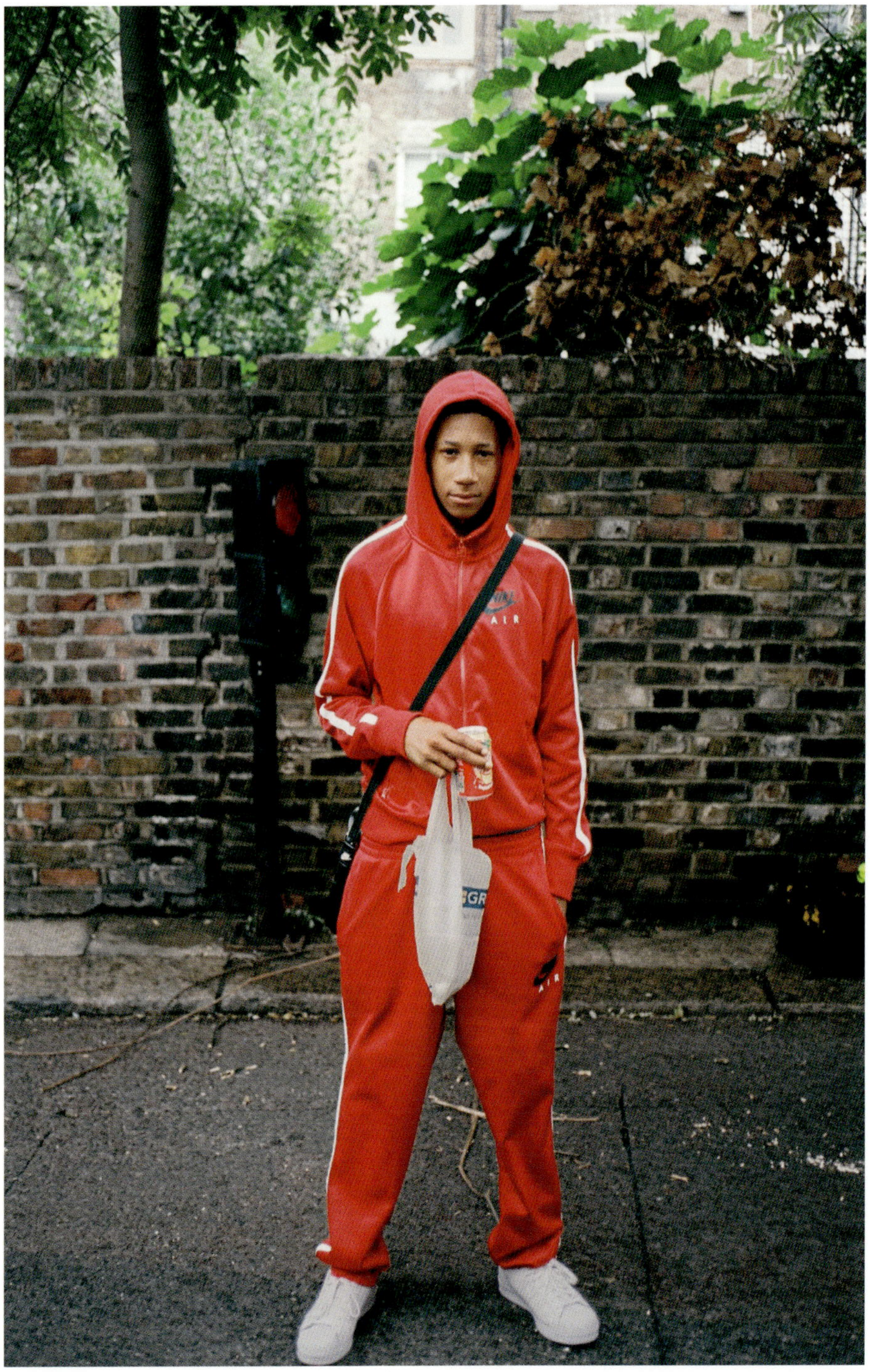

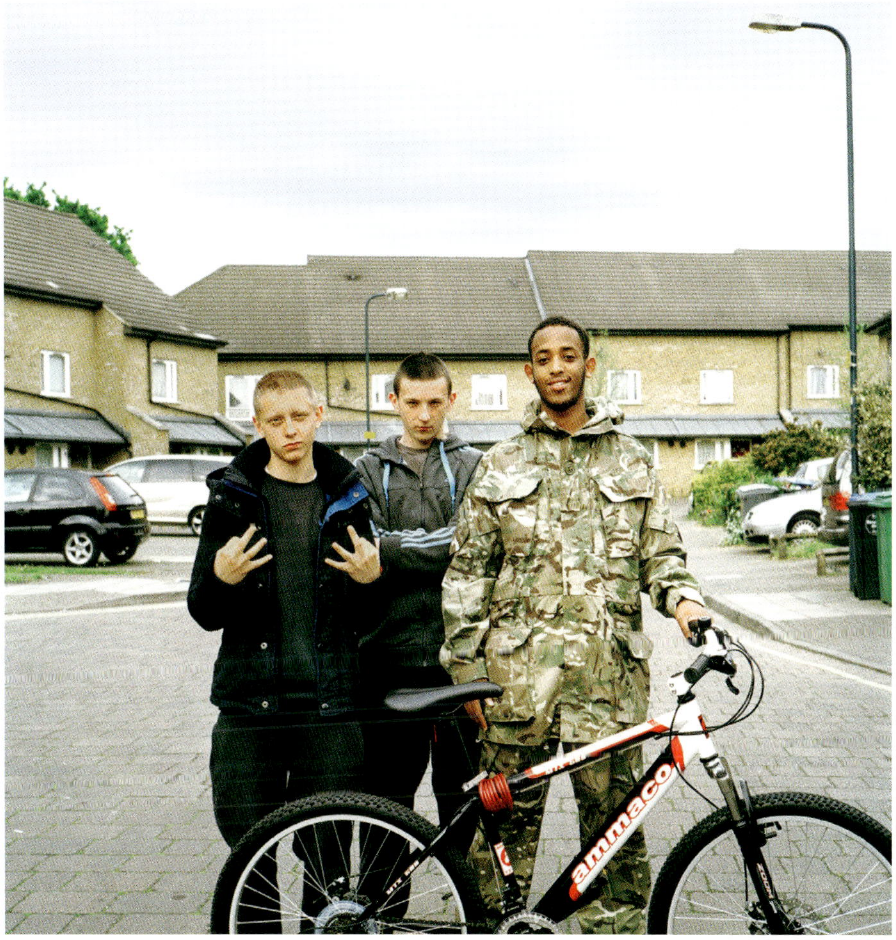
ammaco

"I'm training
to be a
Bricklayer"

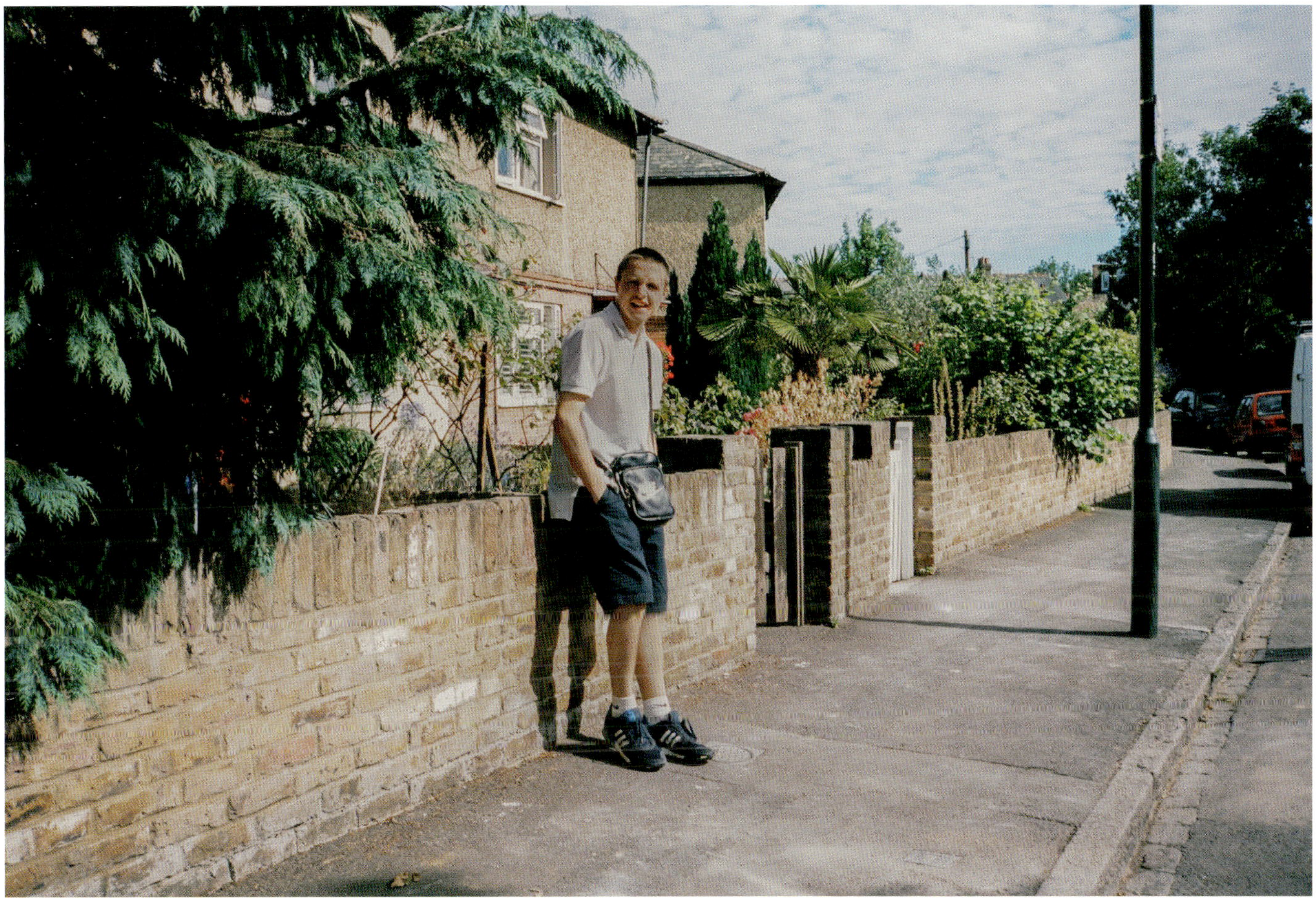

"I'm mainly into dance,
so this is
my little sister
Reniyah,
she's not smiling
at all though"

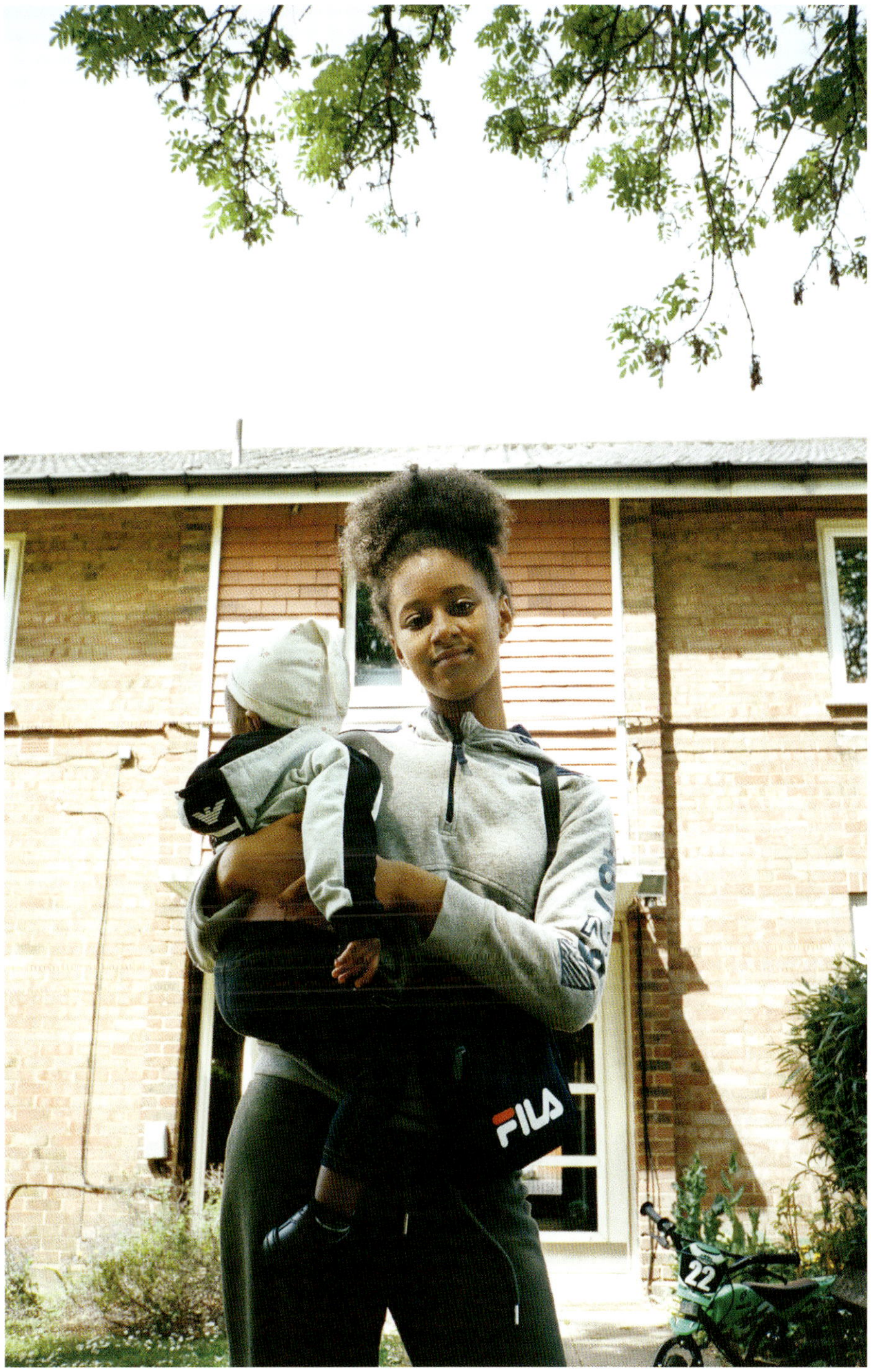
FILA
22

"Back
in a
minute"

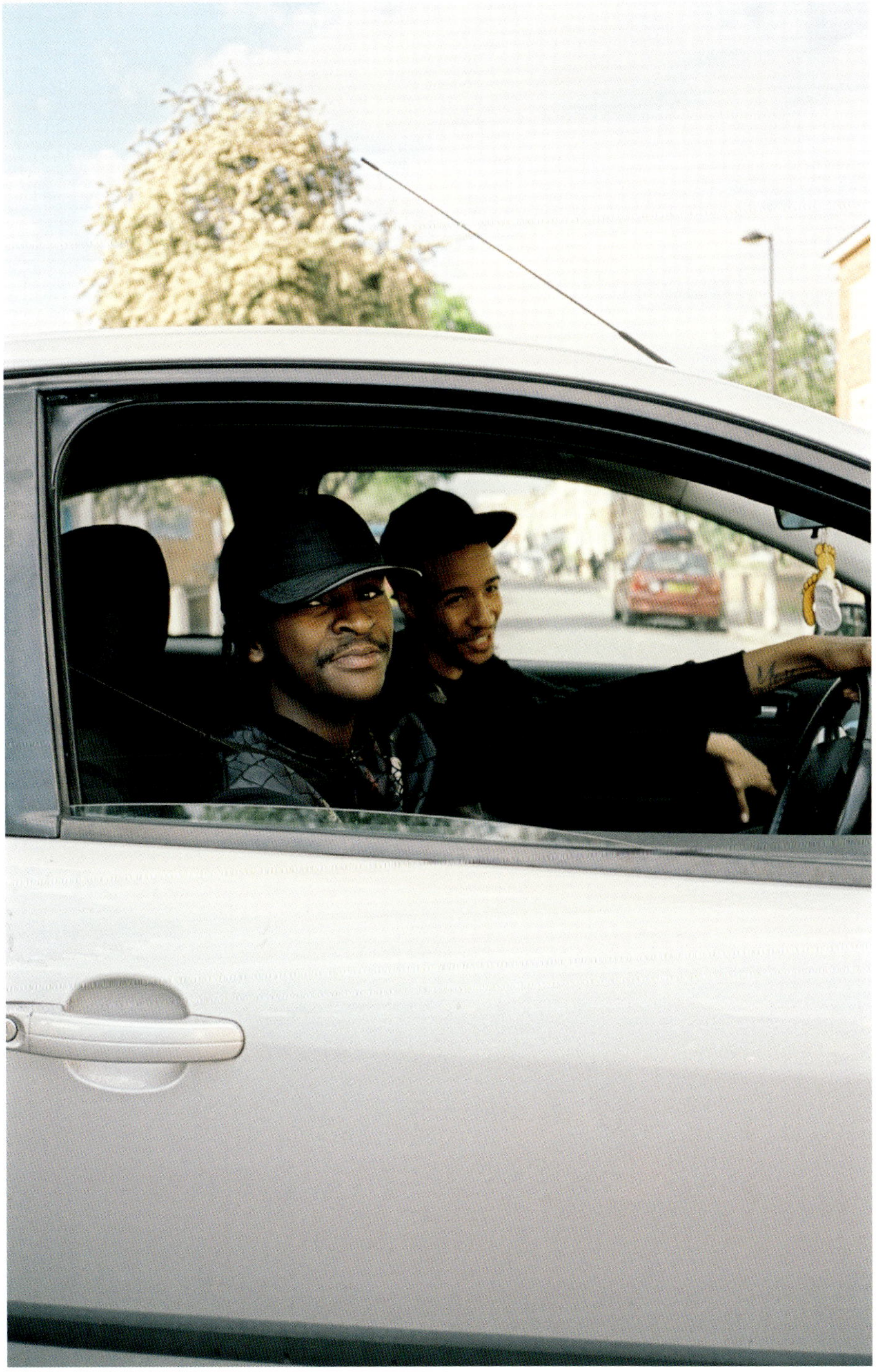

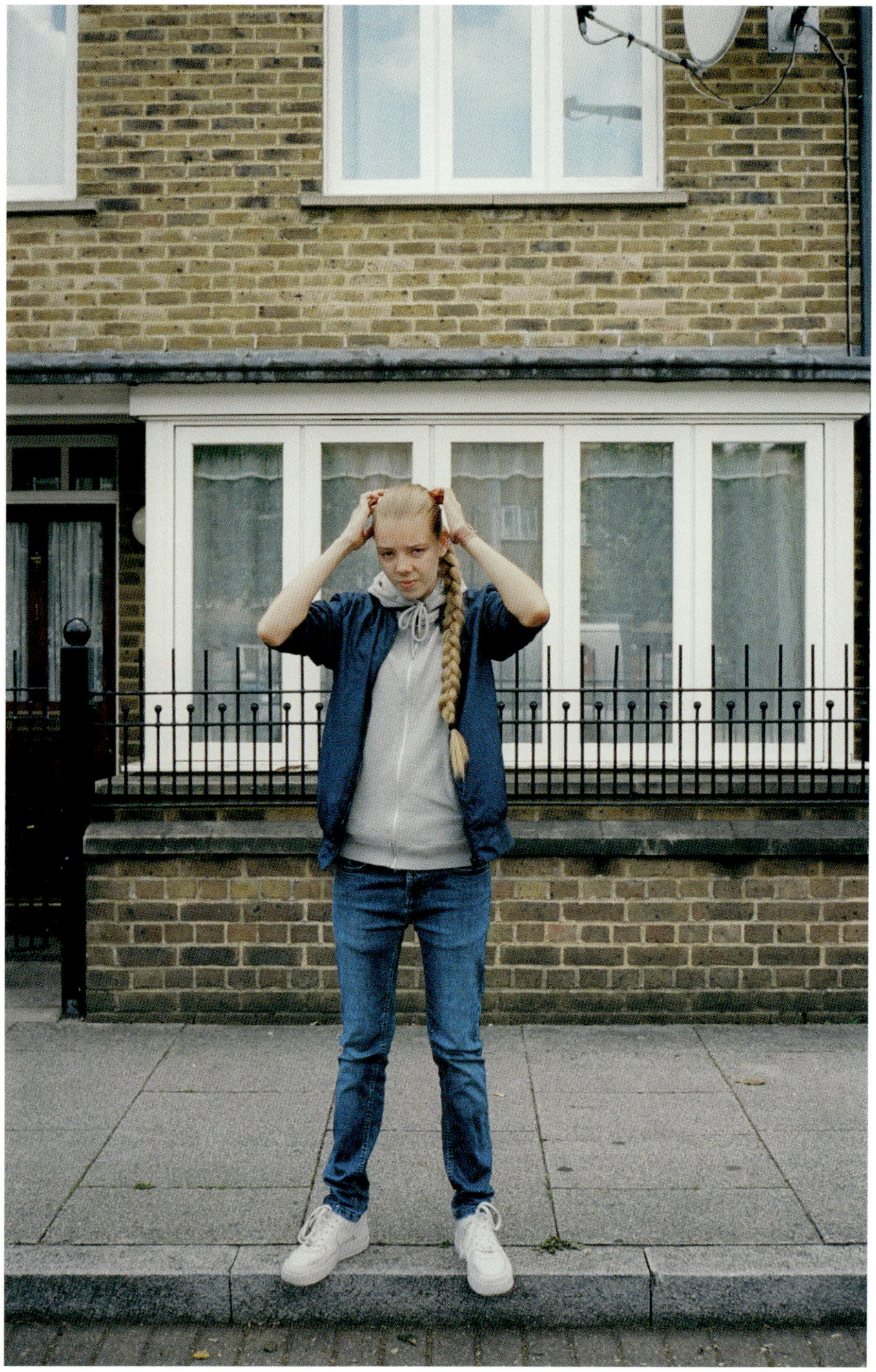

"I'm 18,
I work at a shoe shop
trying to get that overtime shift,
get the money in.
I wanna be a youth worker,
we had youth workers out here
helping us on the street,
talking to us, they helped us.
There's nowhere for us to go,
the youth centres got
shut down,
they're all closed"

"I'm studying Psychology,
just up the road from here,
yeah I know that author,
he came to my school,
the book and his talk
was so good"

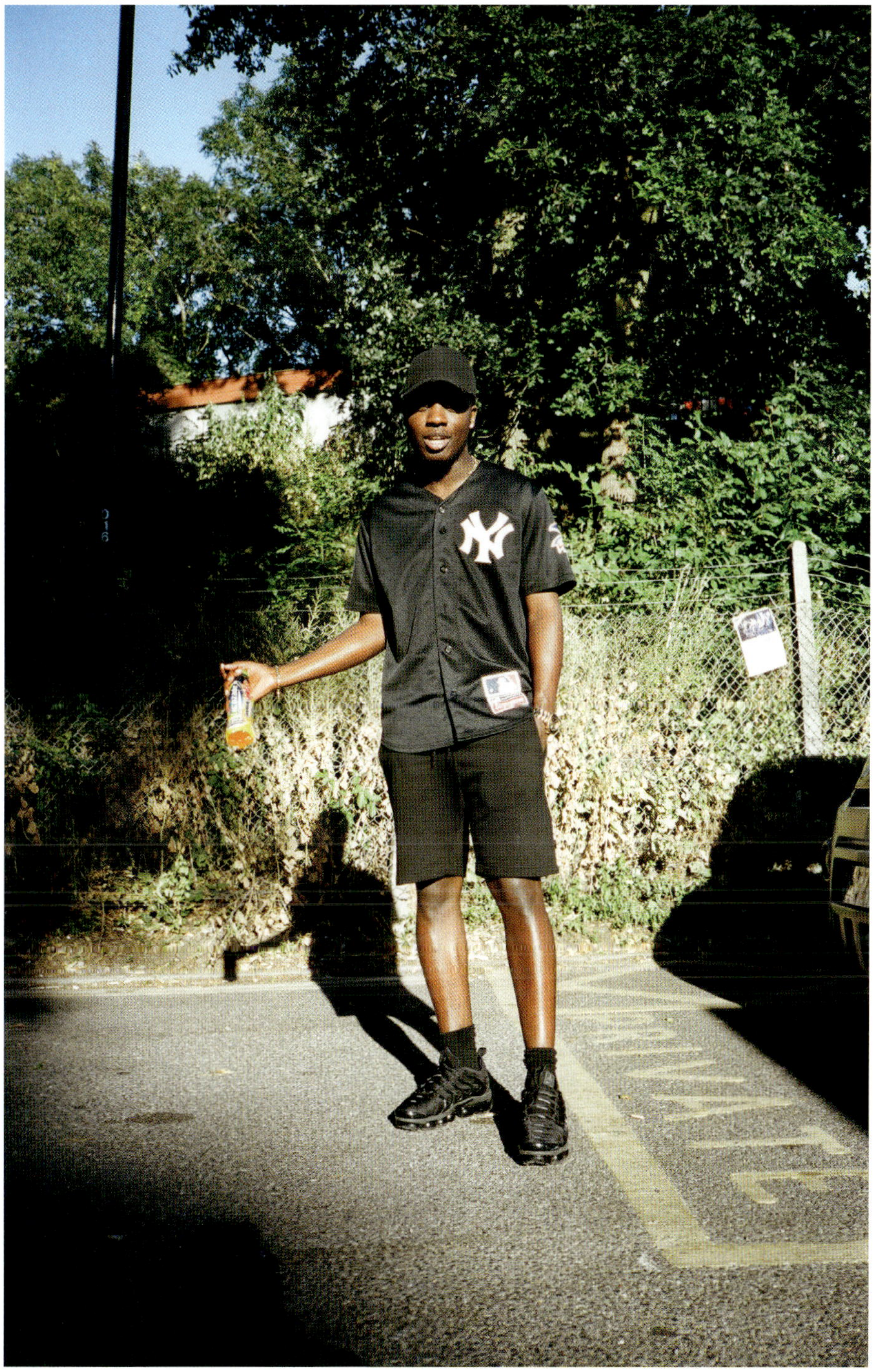

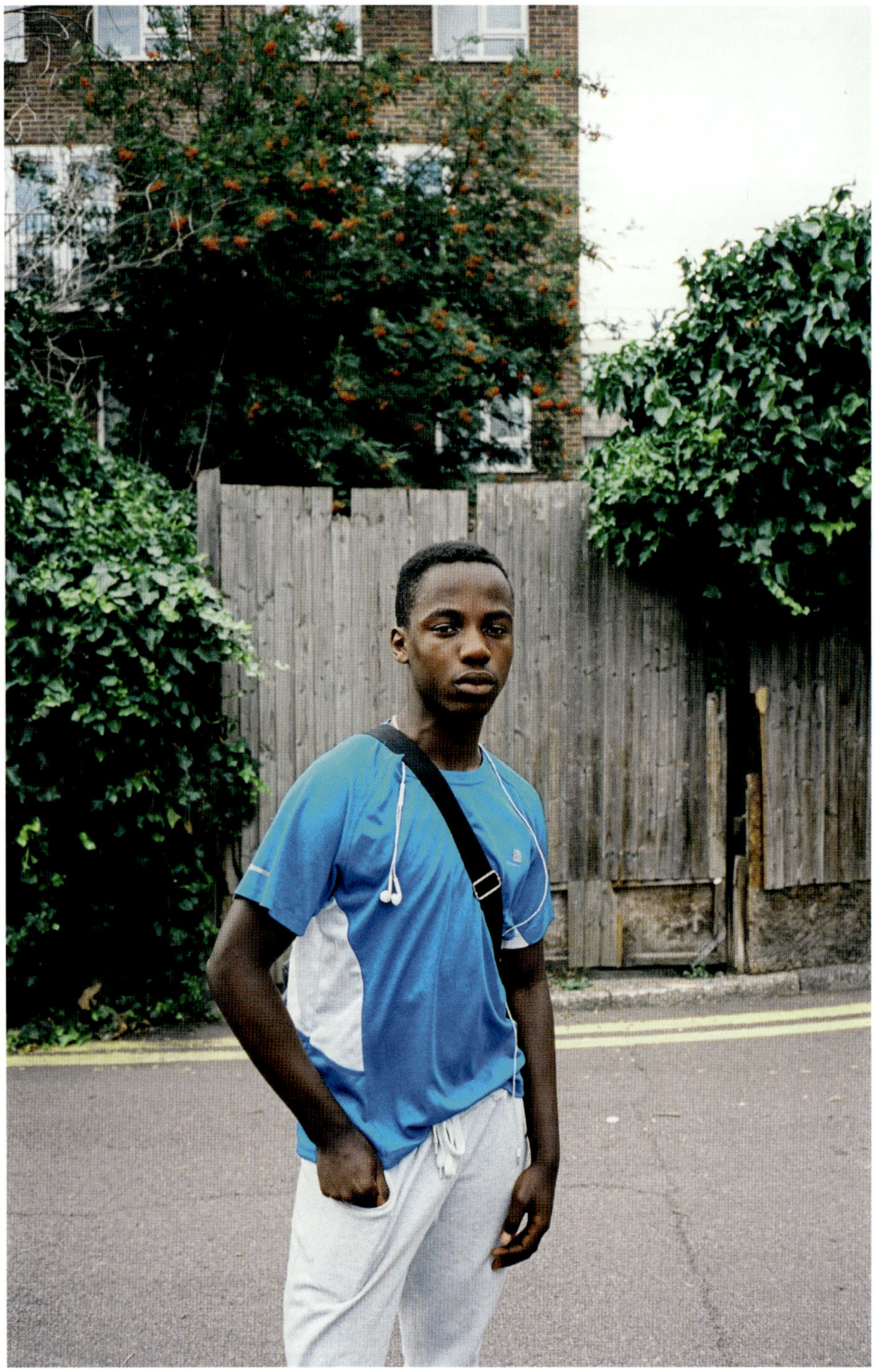

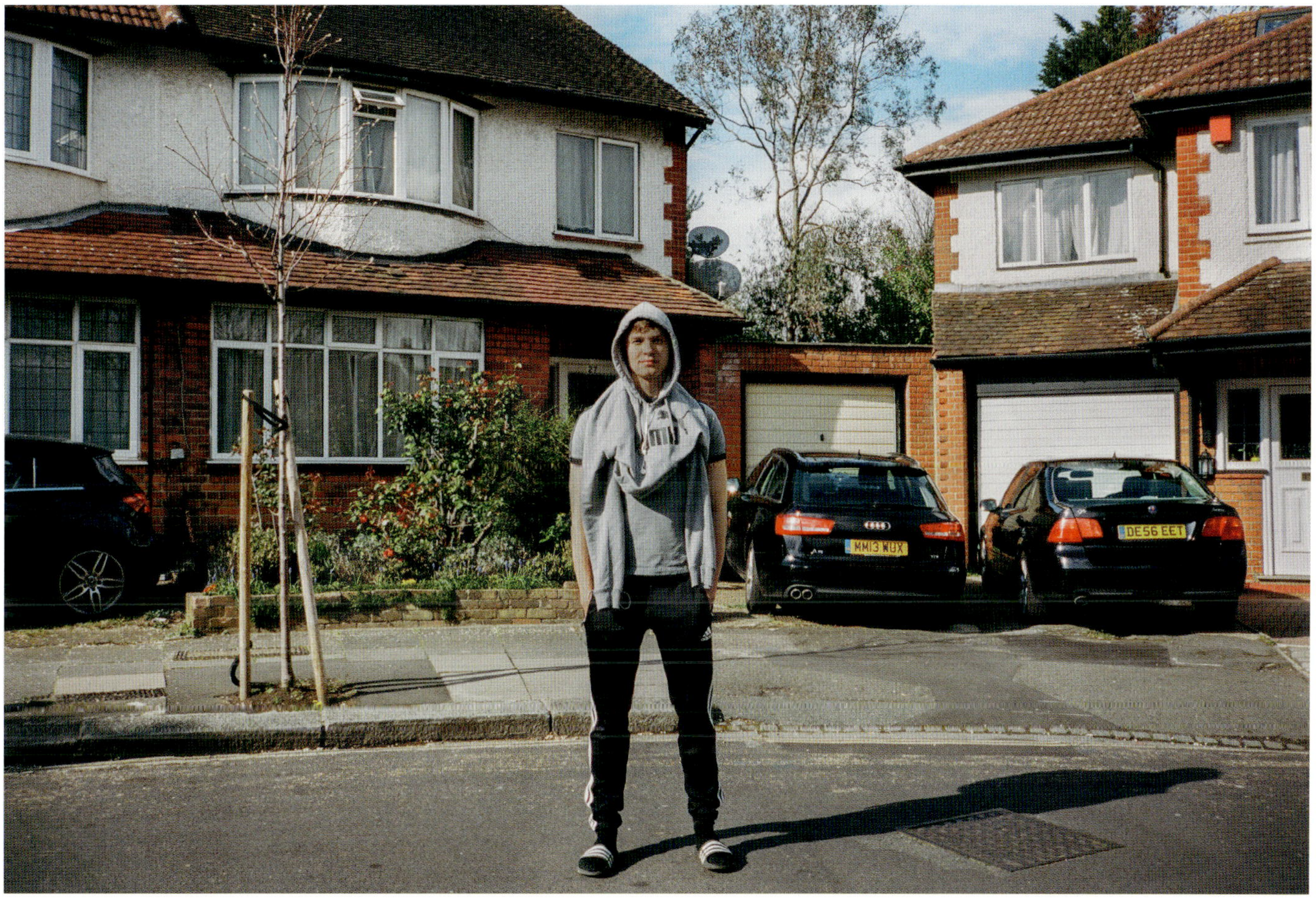
MM13 WUX
DE56 EET

"You getting
the watch?"

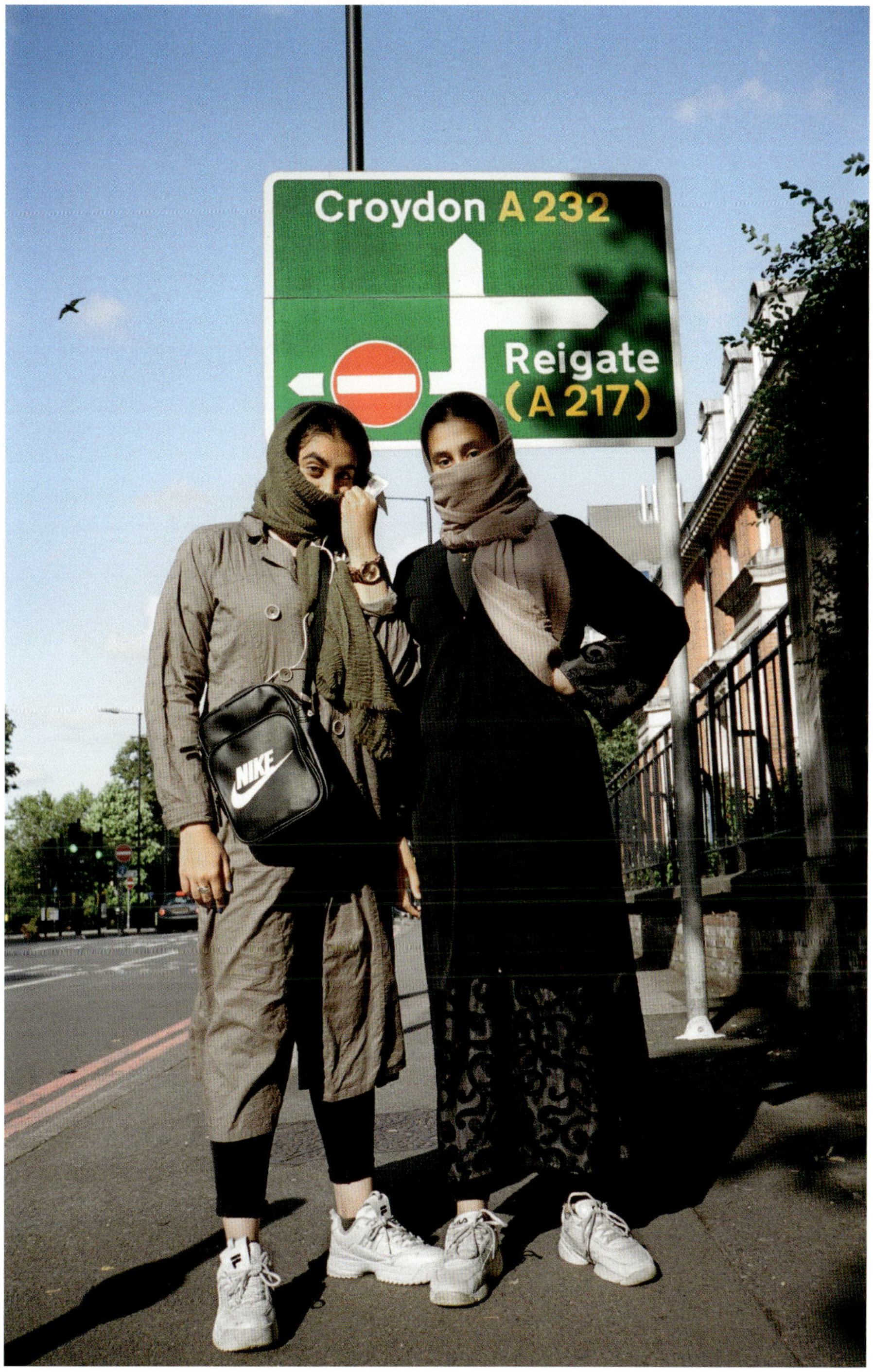
Croydon A 232
Reigate
(A 217)
NIKE

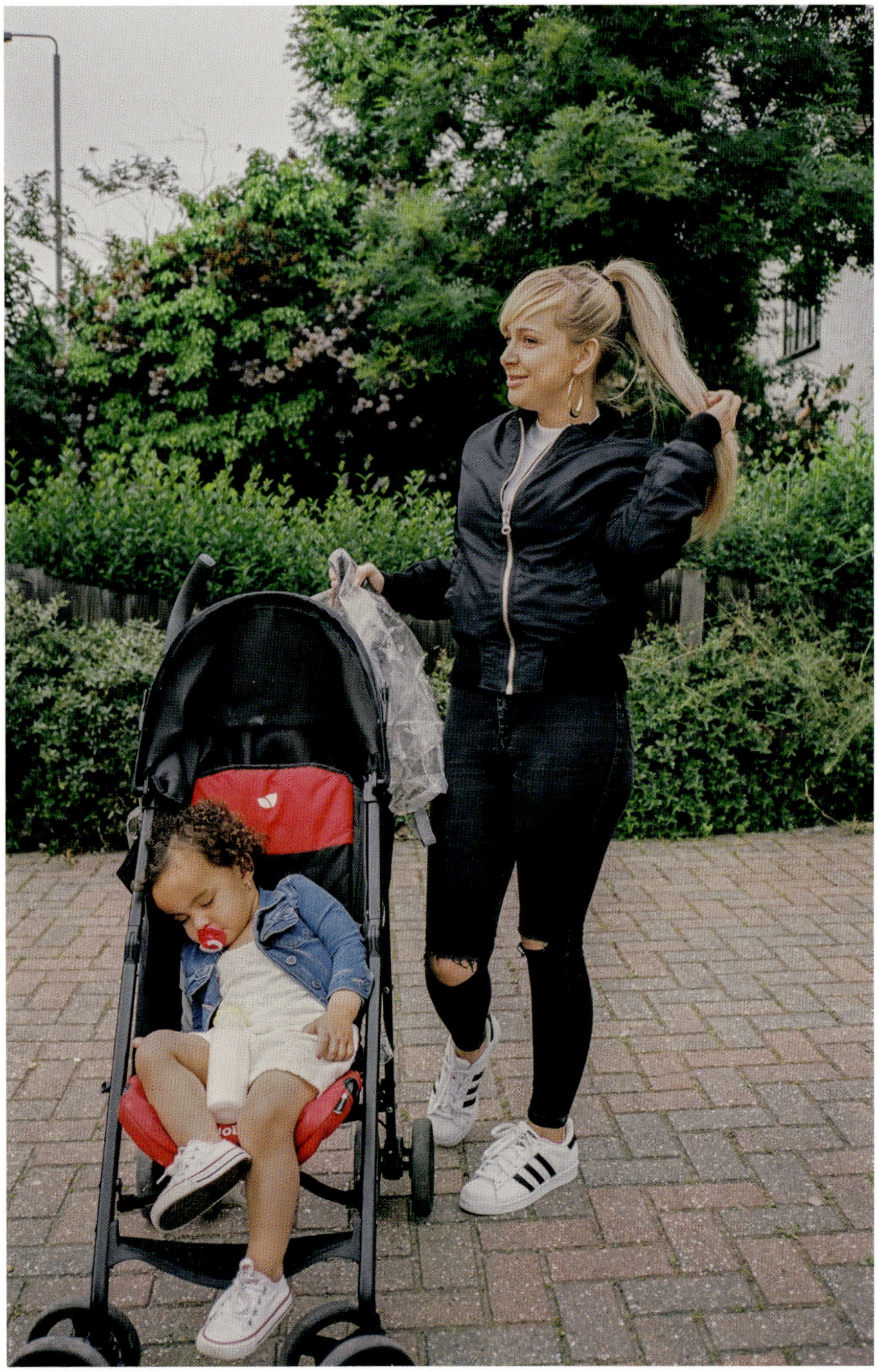

"This is
baby girl
Aaliyah"

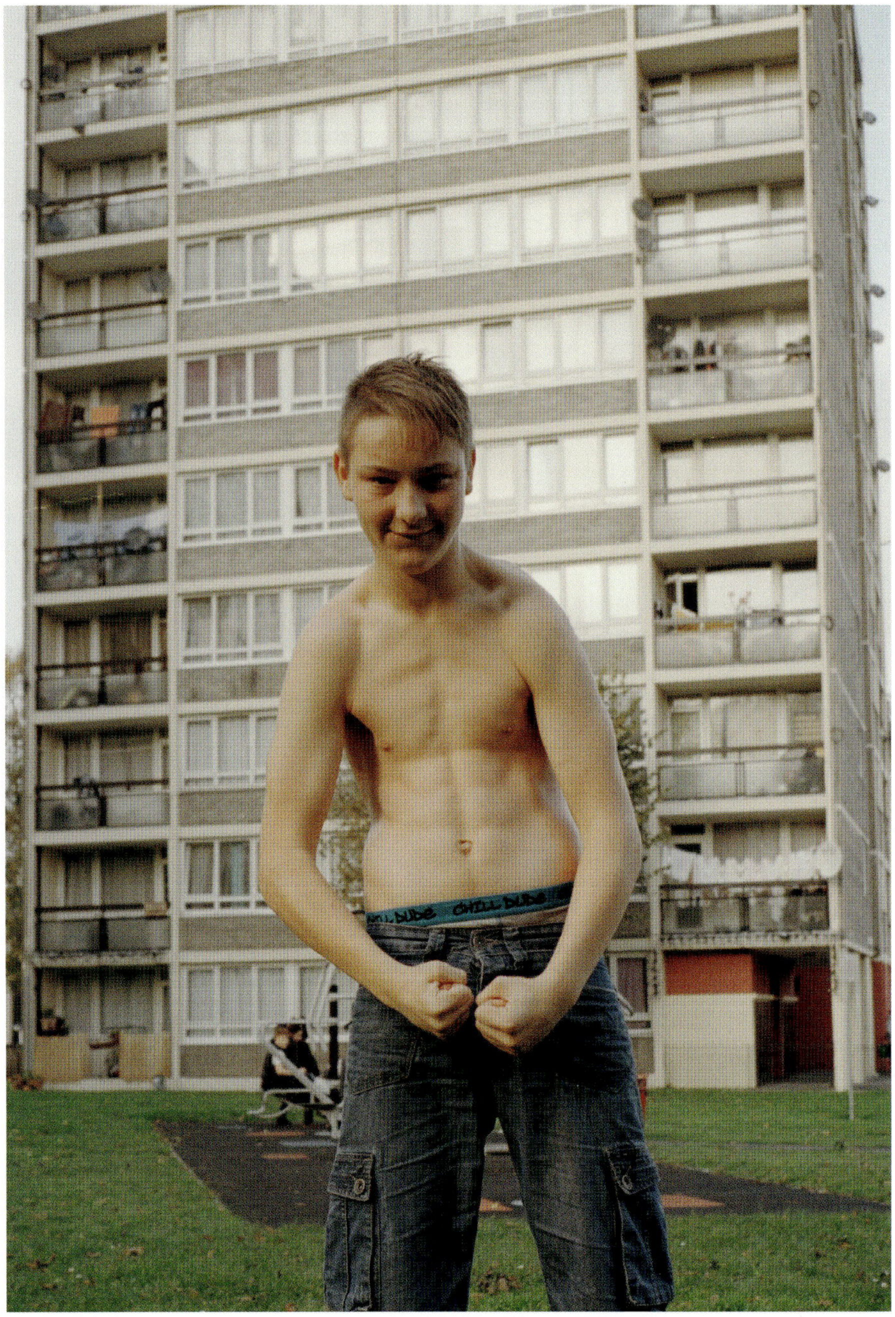
CHILL DUDE

"Oi"

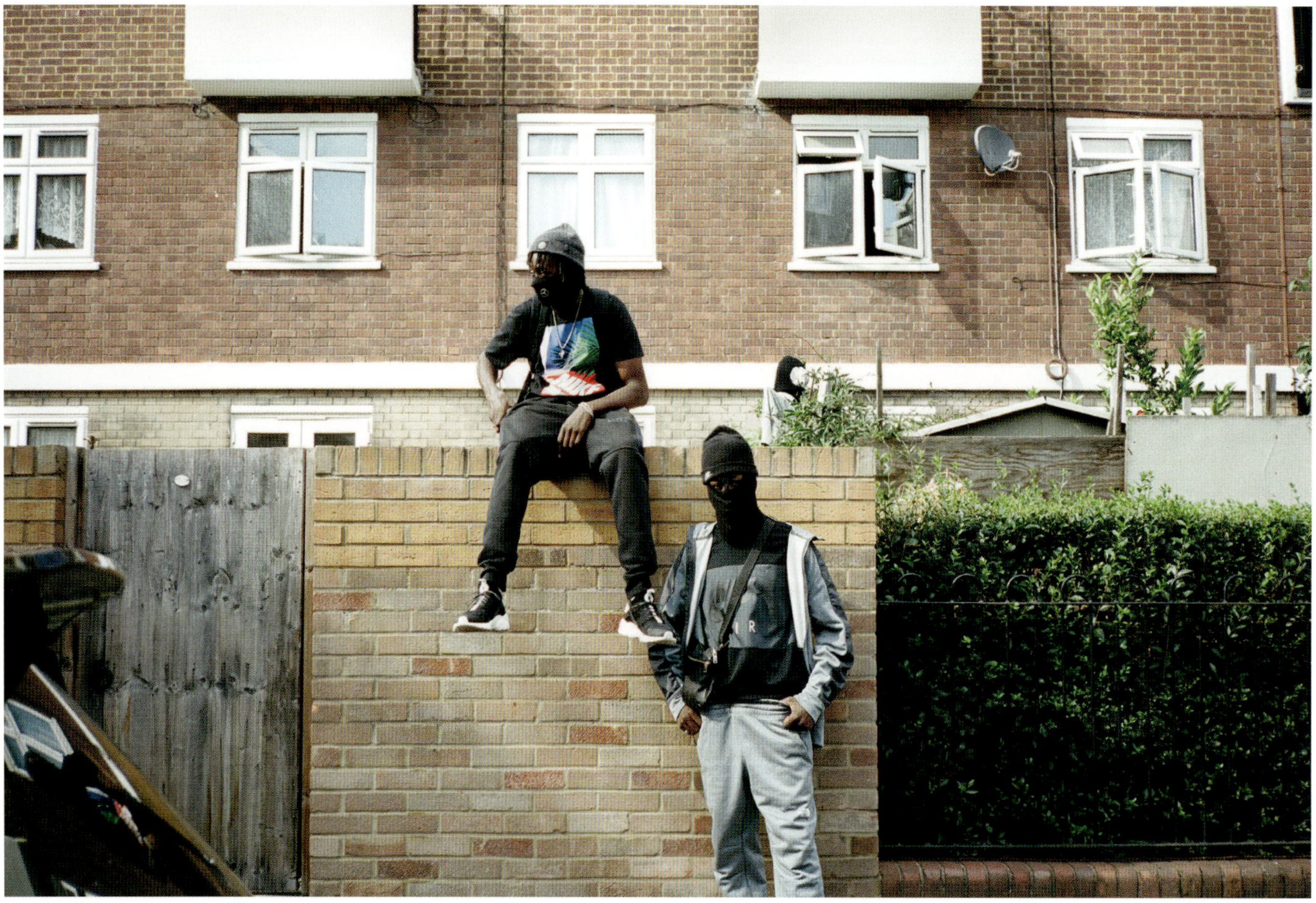

"How's my bally?"

"Exams are done,
I'm heading home"

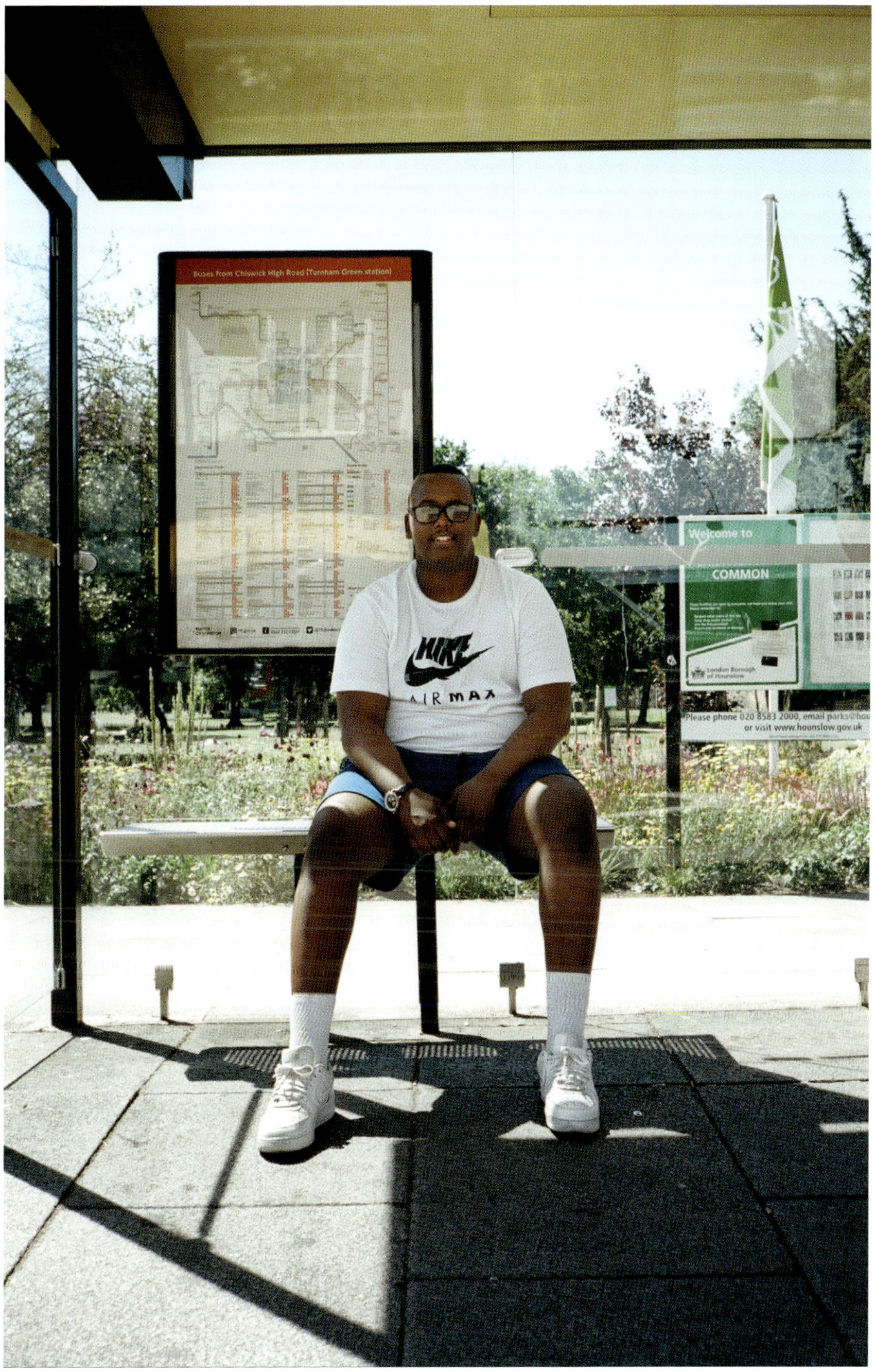
Buses from Chiswick High Road (Turnham Green station)
NIKE
AIR MAX
Welcome to
COMMON
London Borough of Hounslow
Please phone 020 8583 2000, email parks@hou
or visit www.hounslow.gov.uk

"We been

playing football"

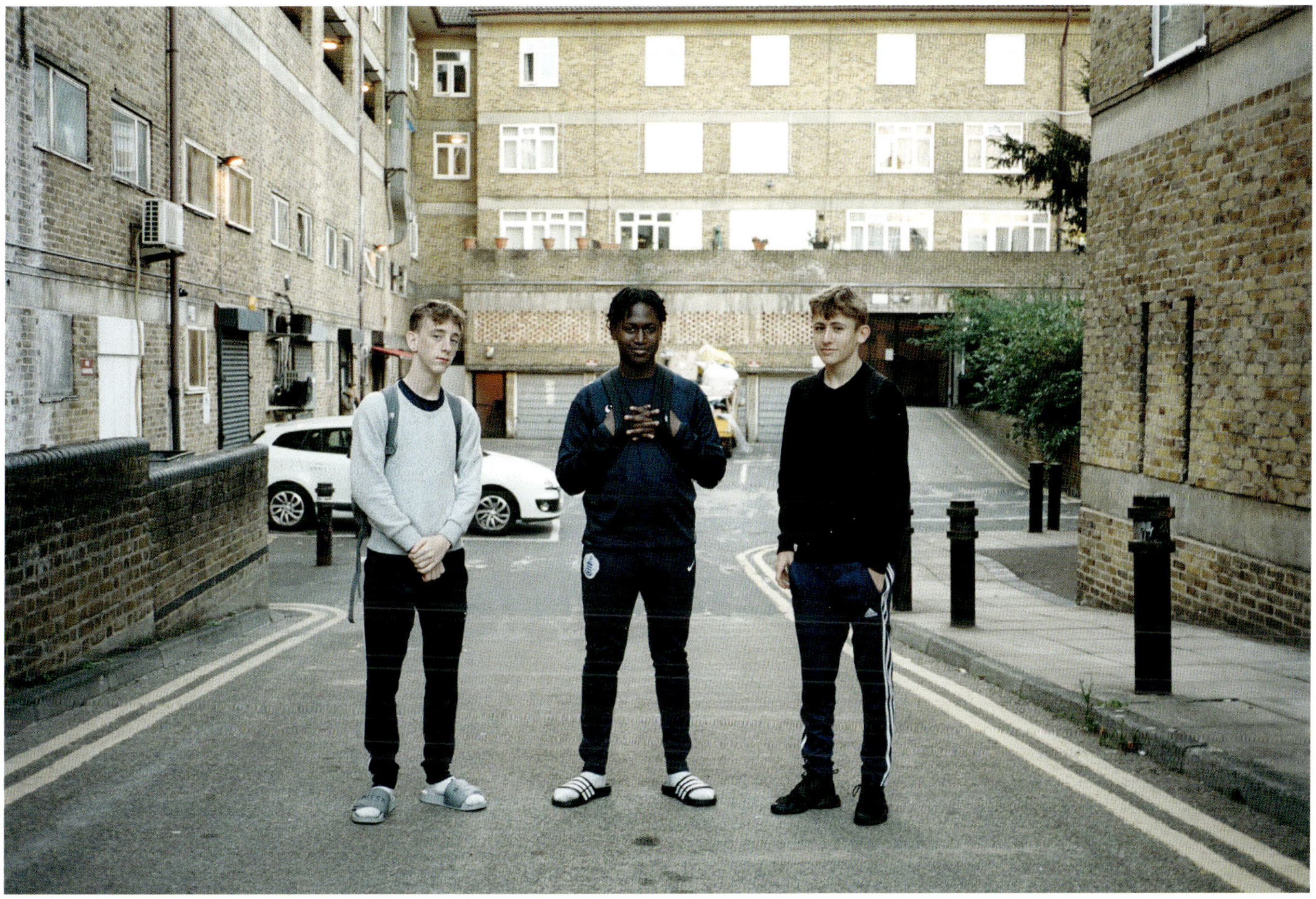

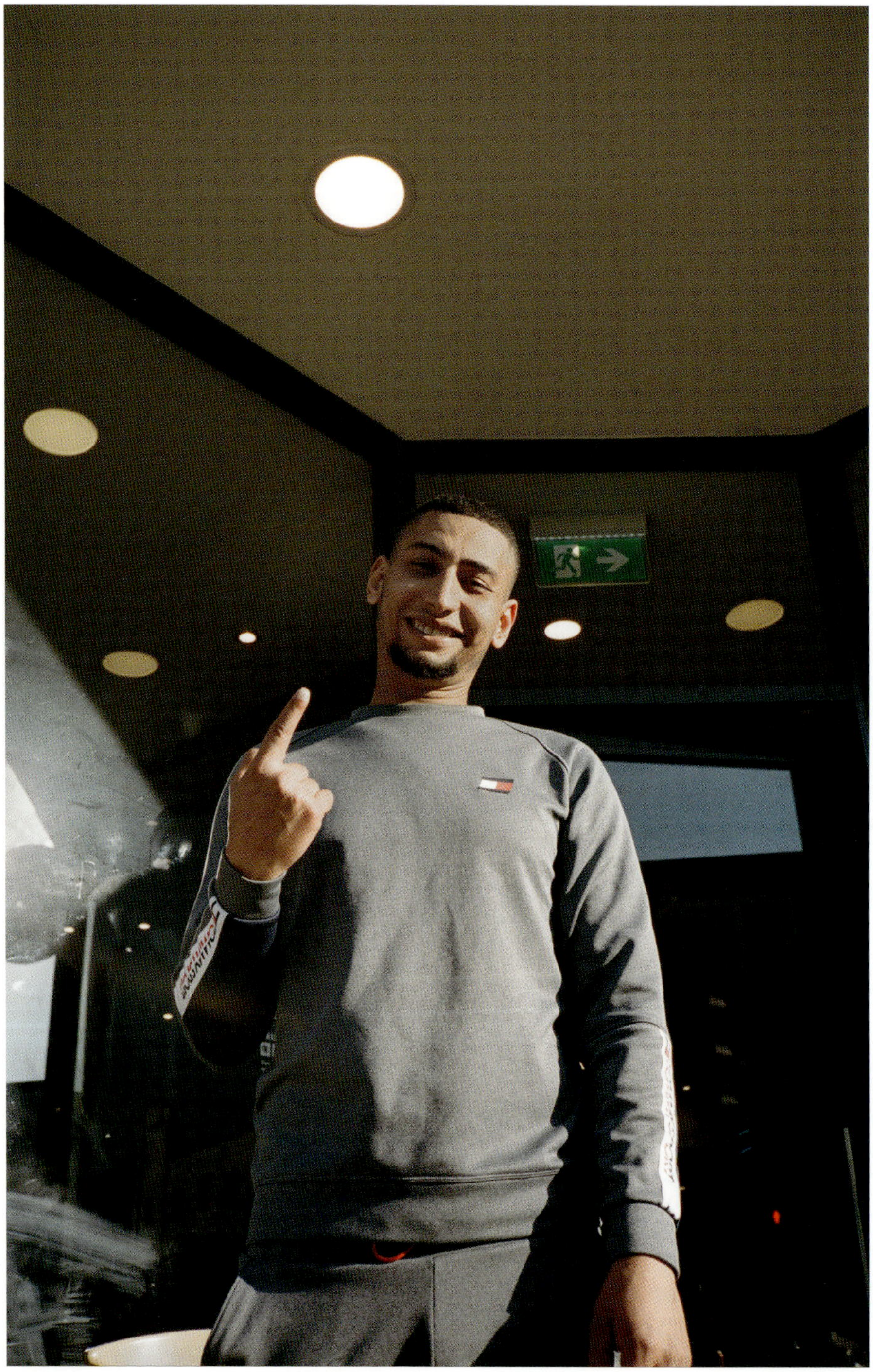

"You speak Arabic?"

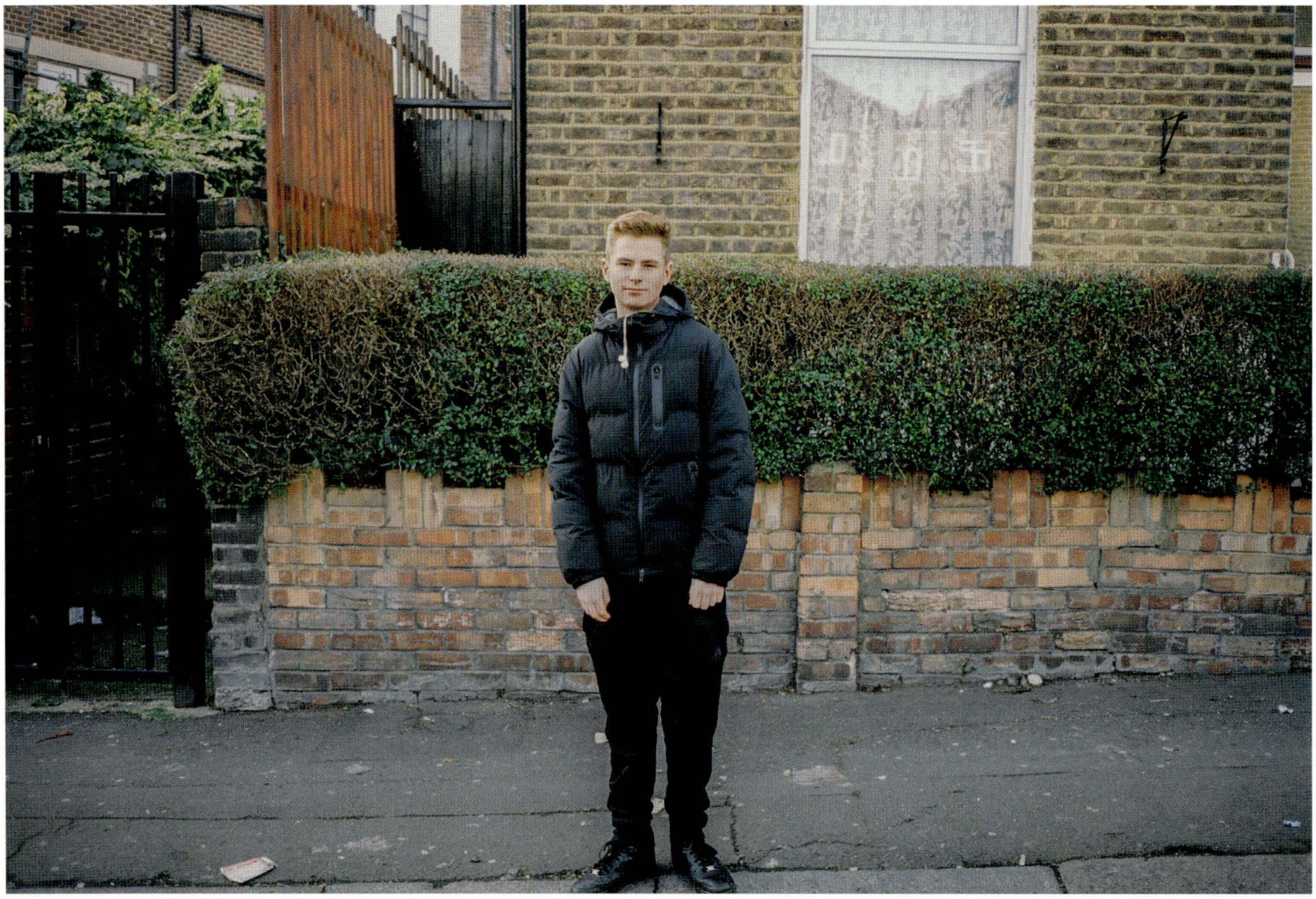

"Do you smoke?"

"Going to the shop
to buy some new trainers"

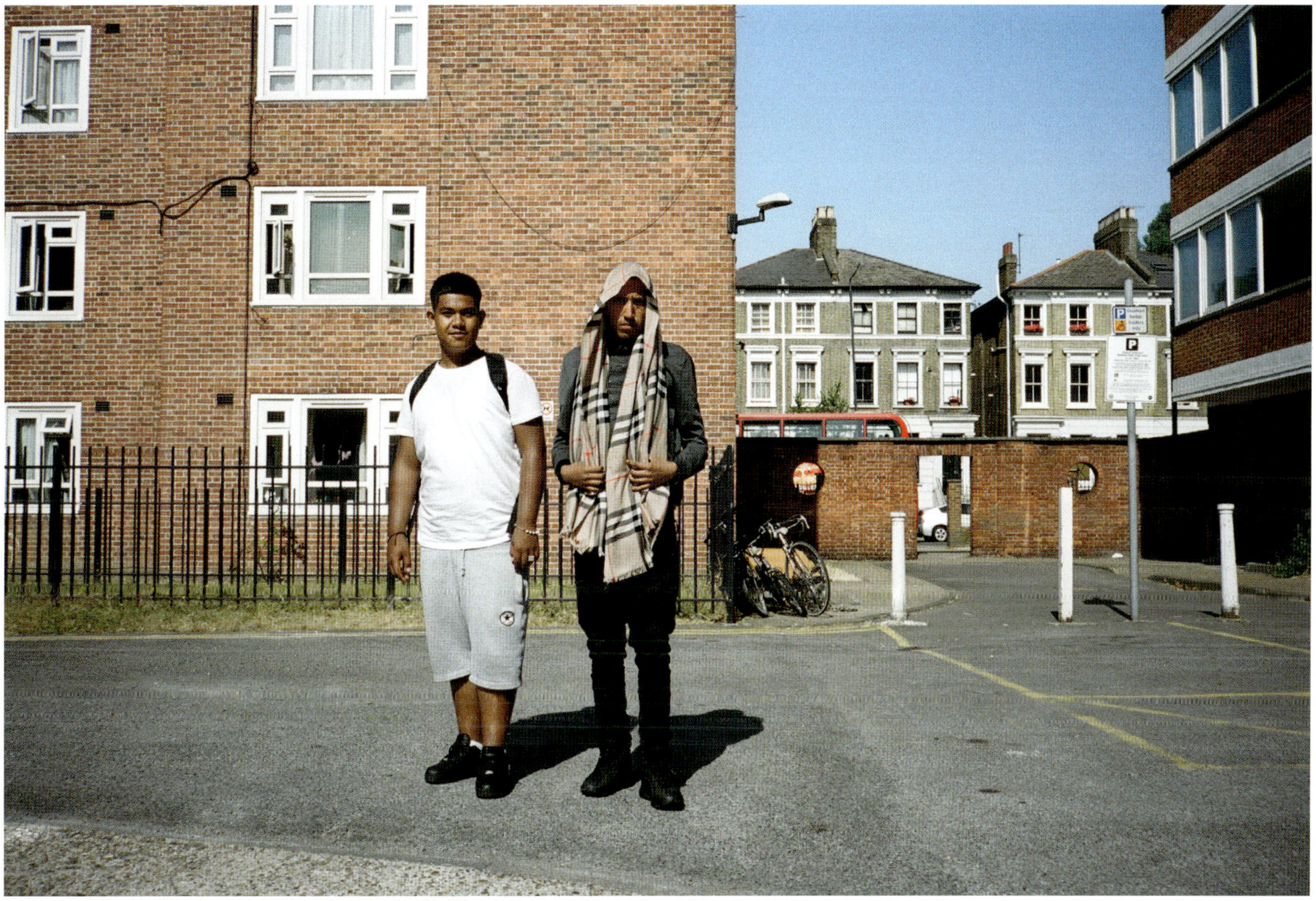

"Can't believe it,
just did my last exam,
no more revision.
Summer holidays,
then I start Psychology.
I'm actually bored,
don't even know
what to do"

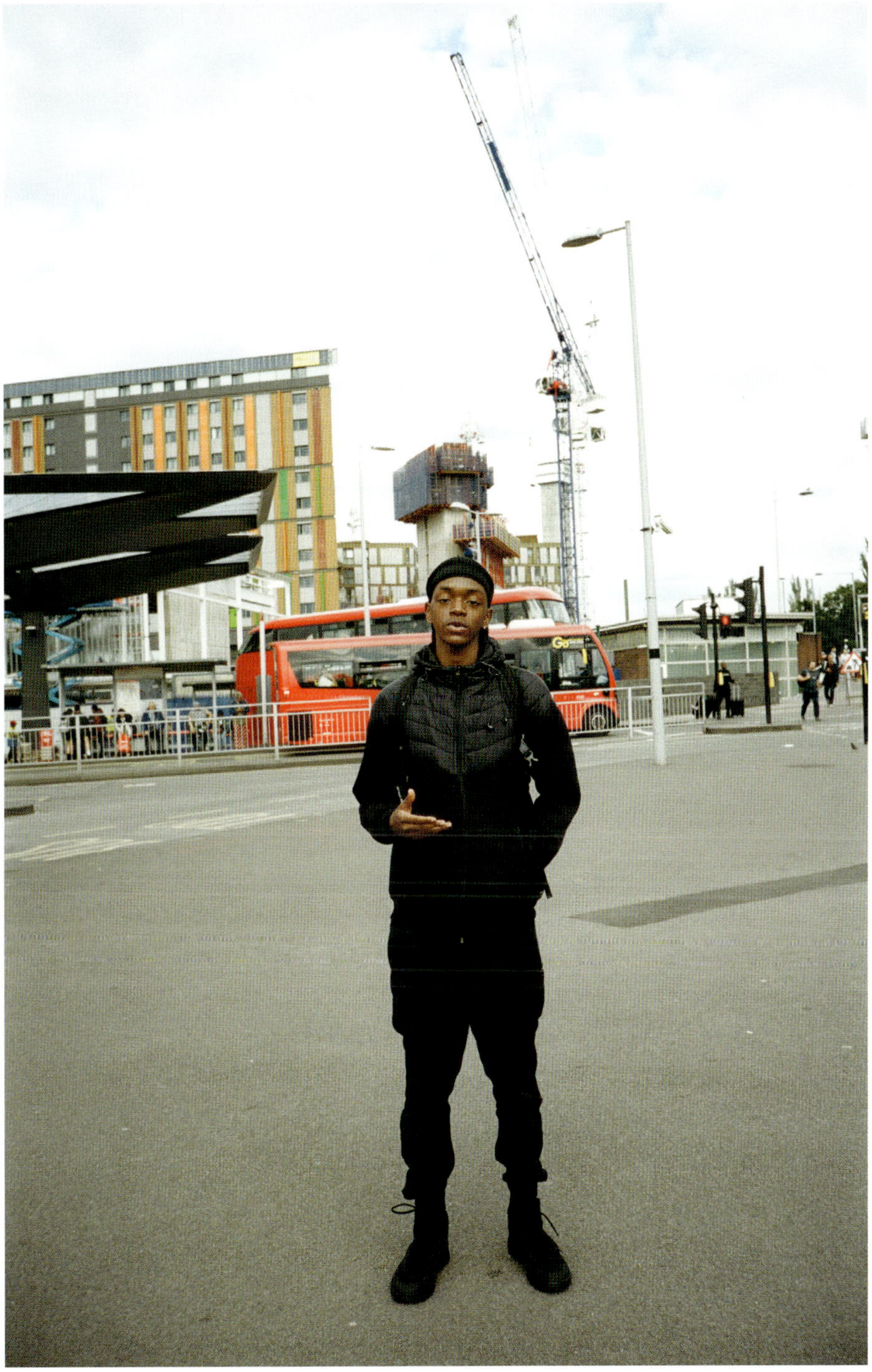

"We're on our way
to the mosque"

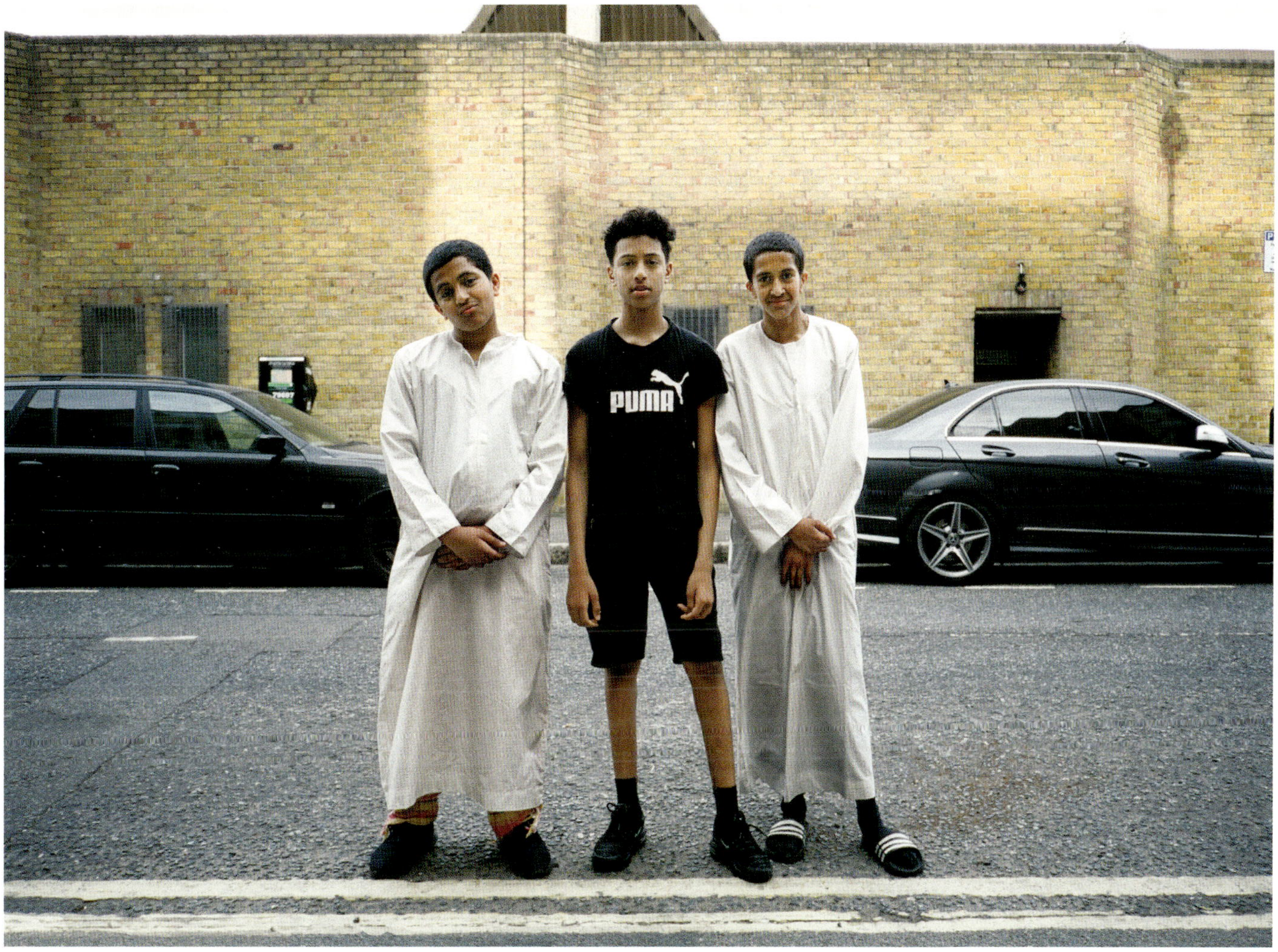
PUMA

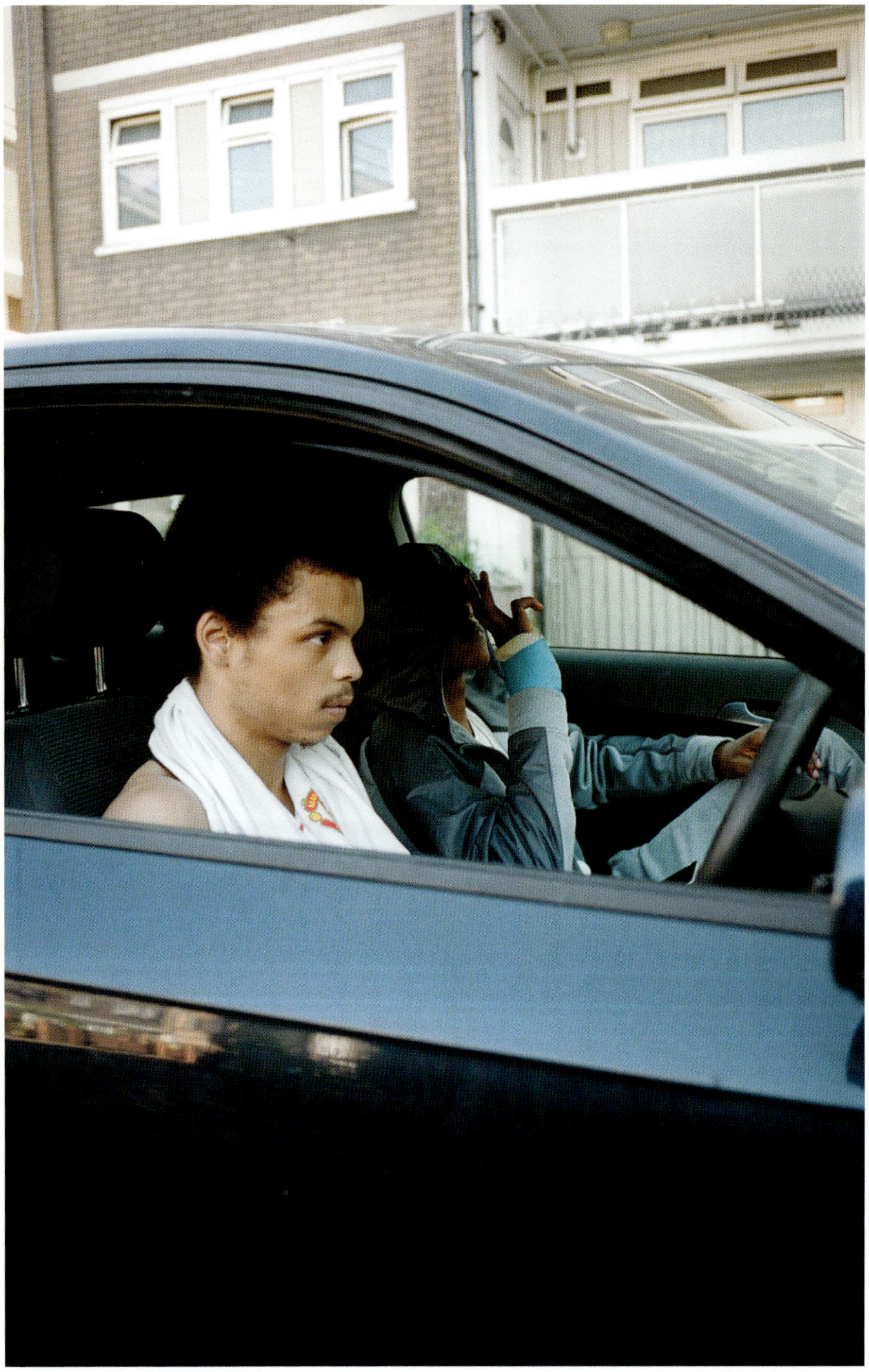

"I'm an artist,
Drill,
they trying
to kill it"

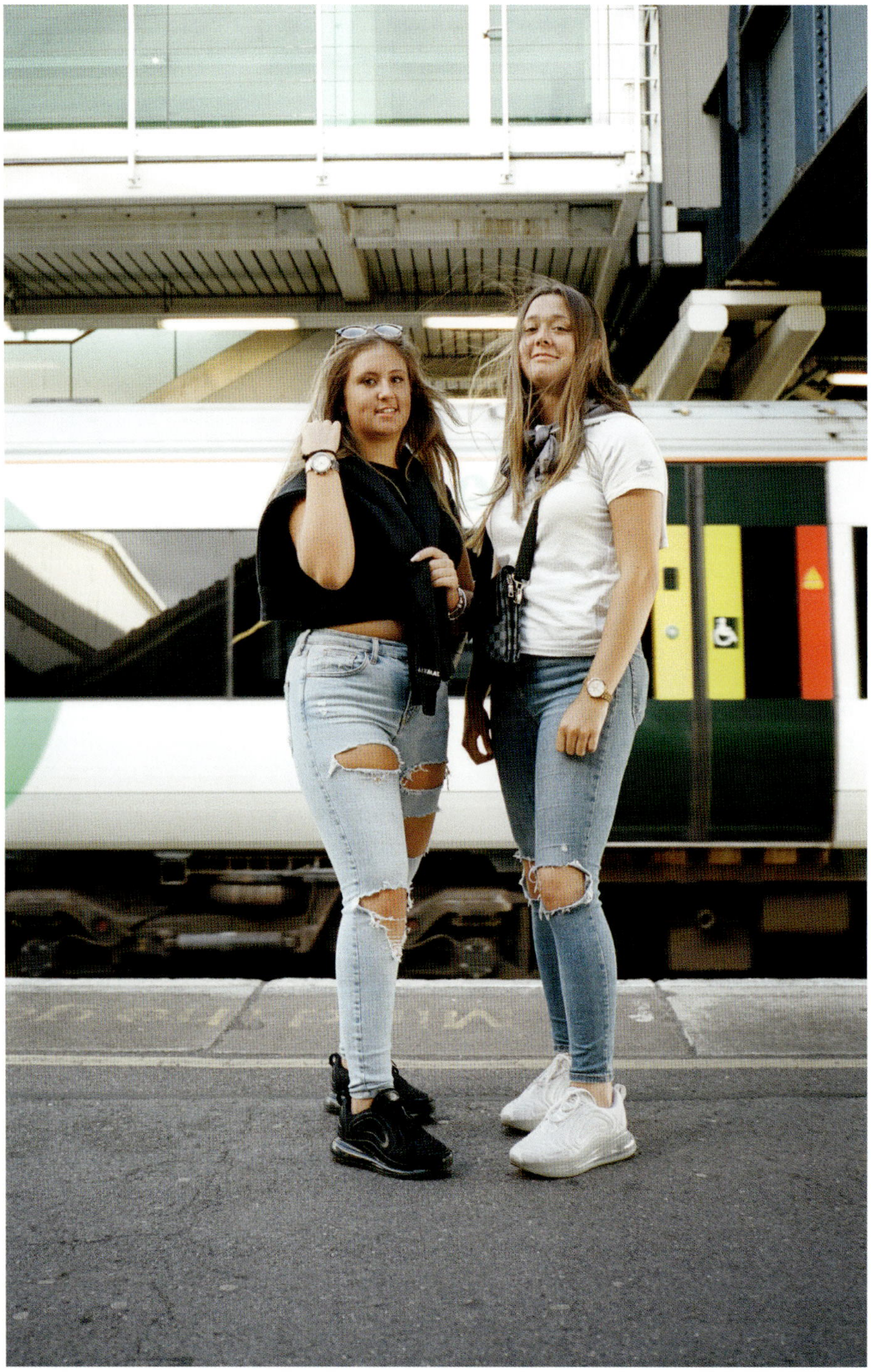

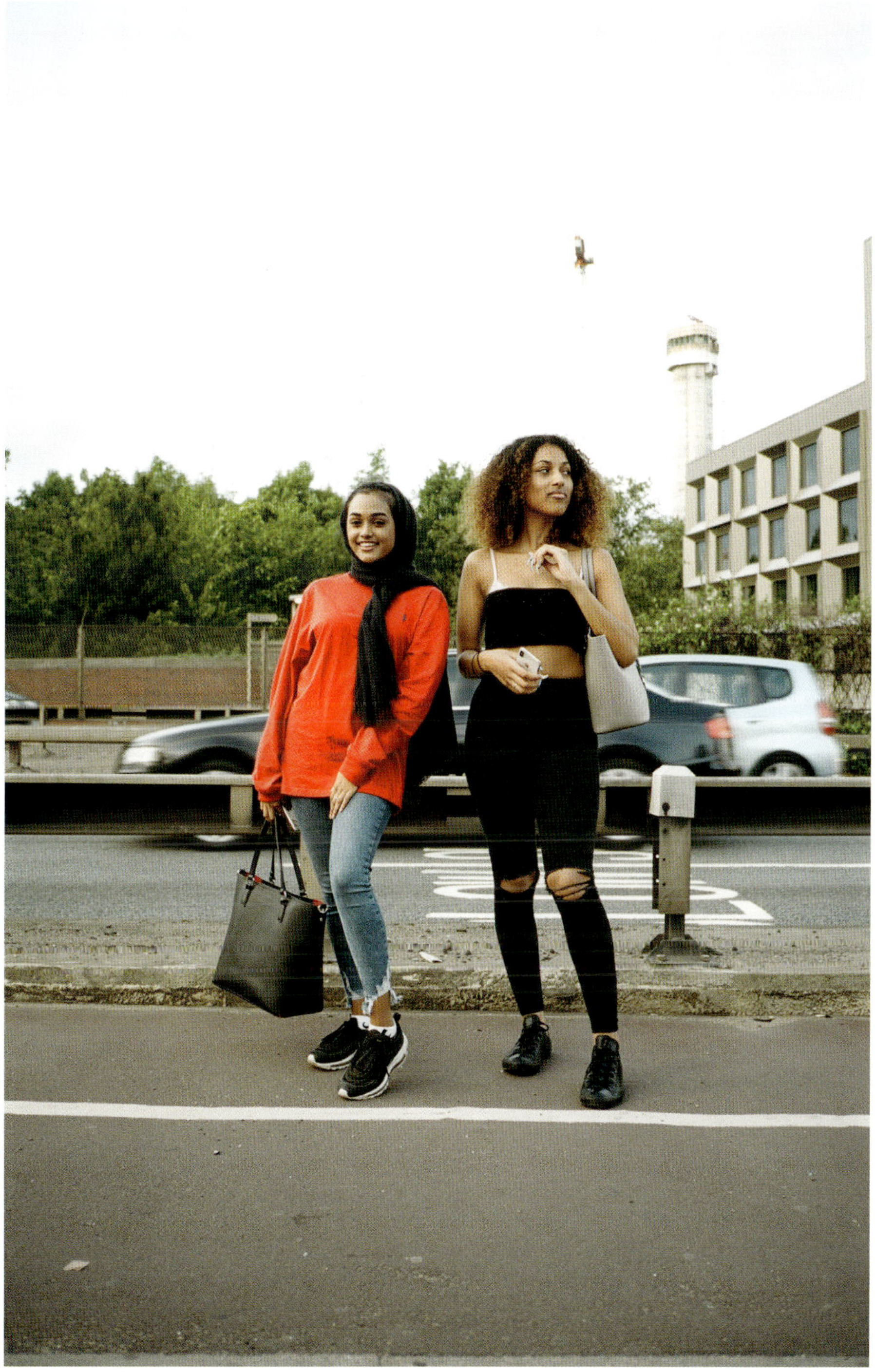

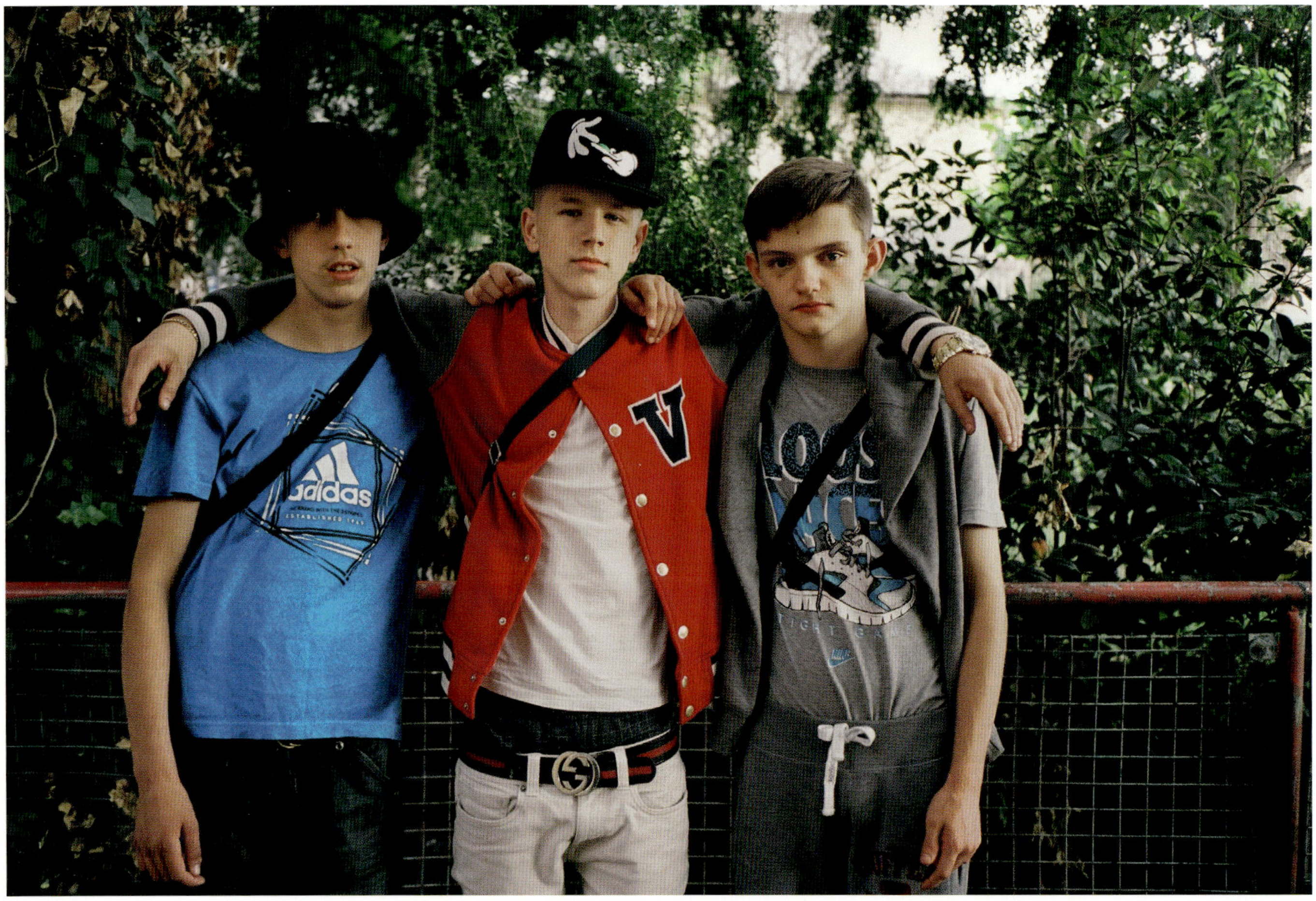
adidas

"I'm a

Gucci man"

"I'm out here on my
bike every day,
unless I'm at school"

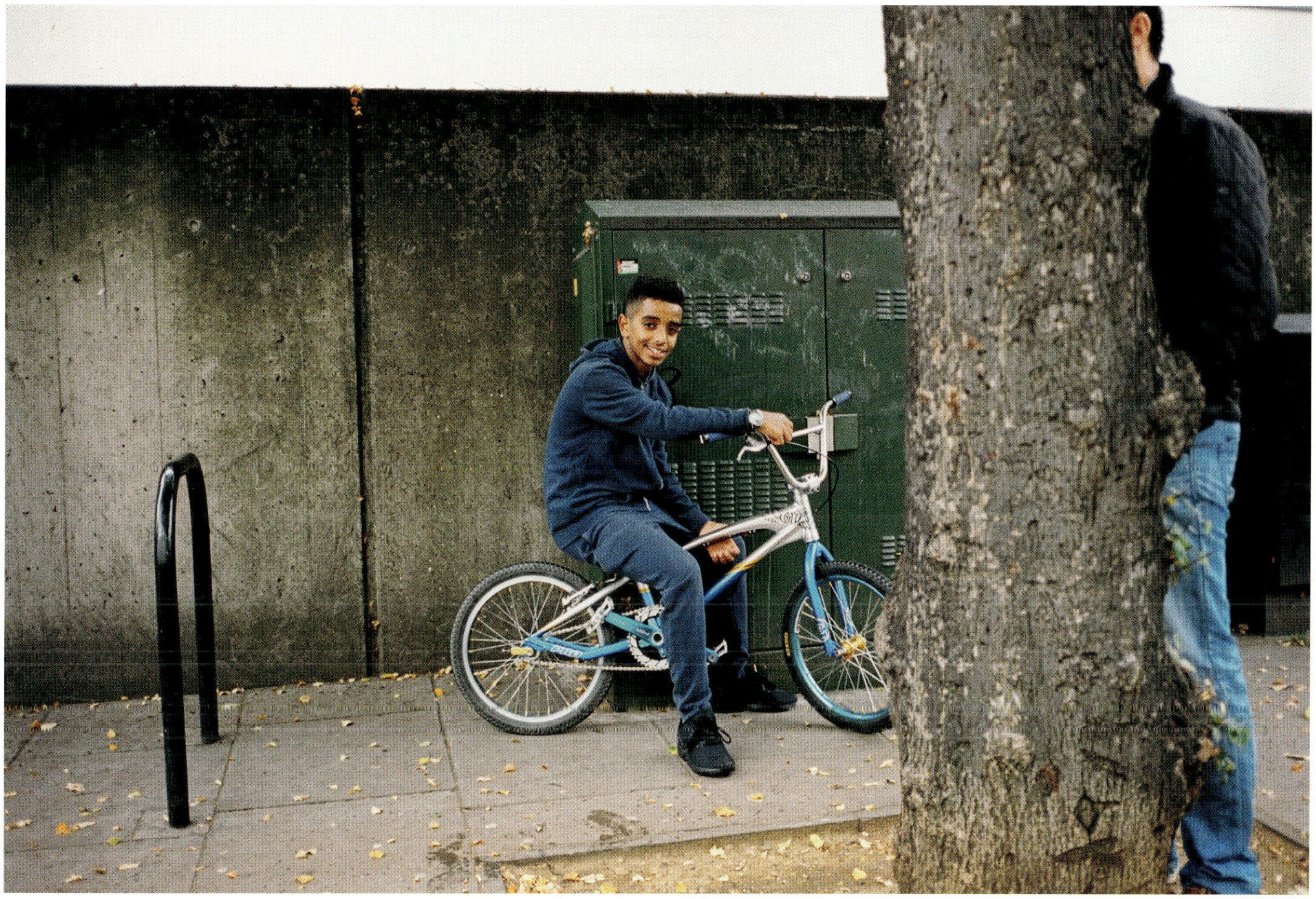

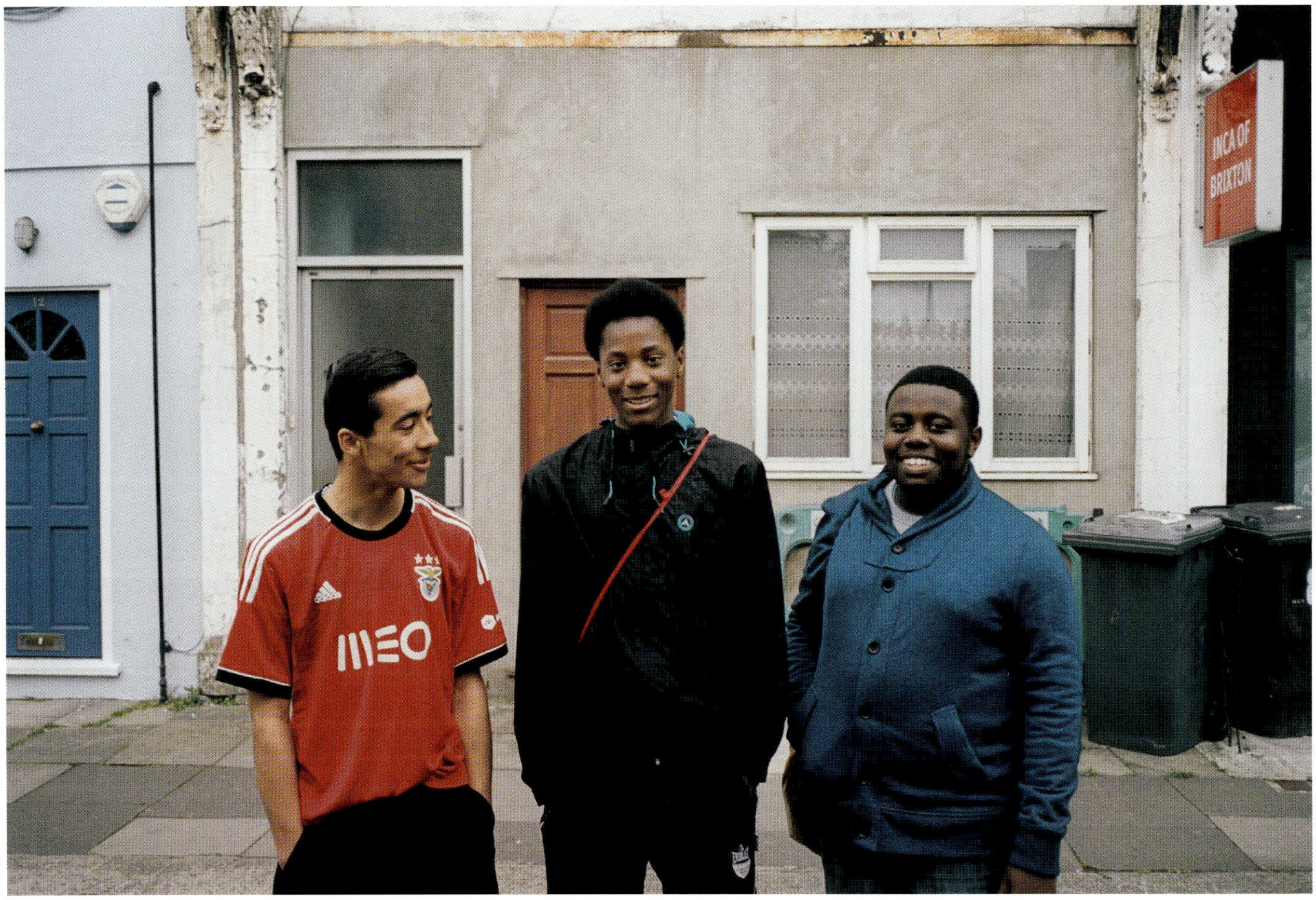
INCA OF
BRIXTON
MEO

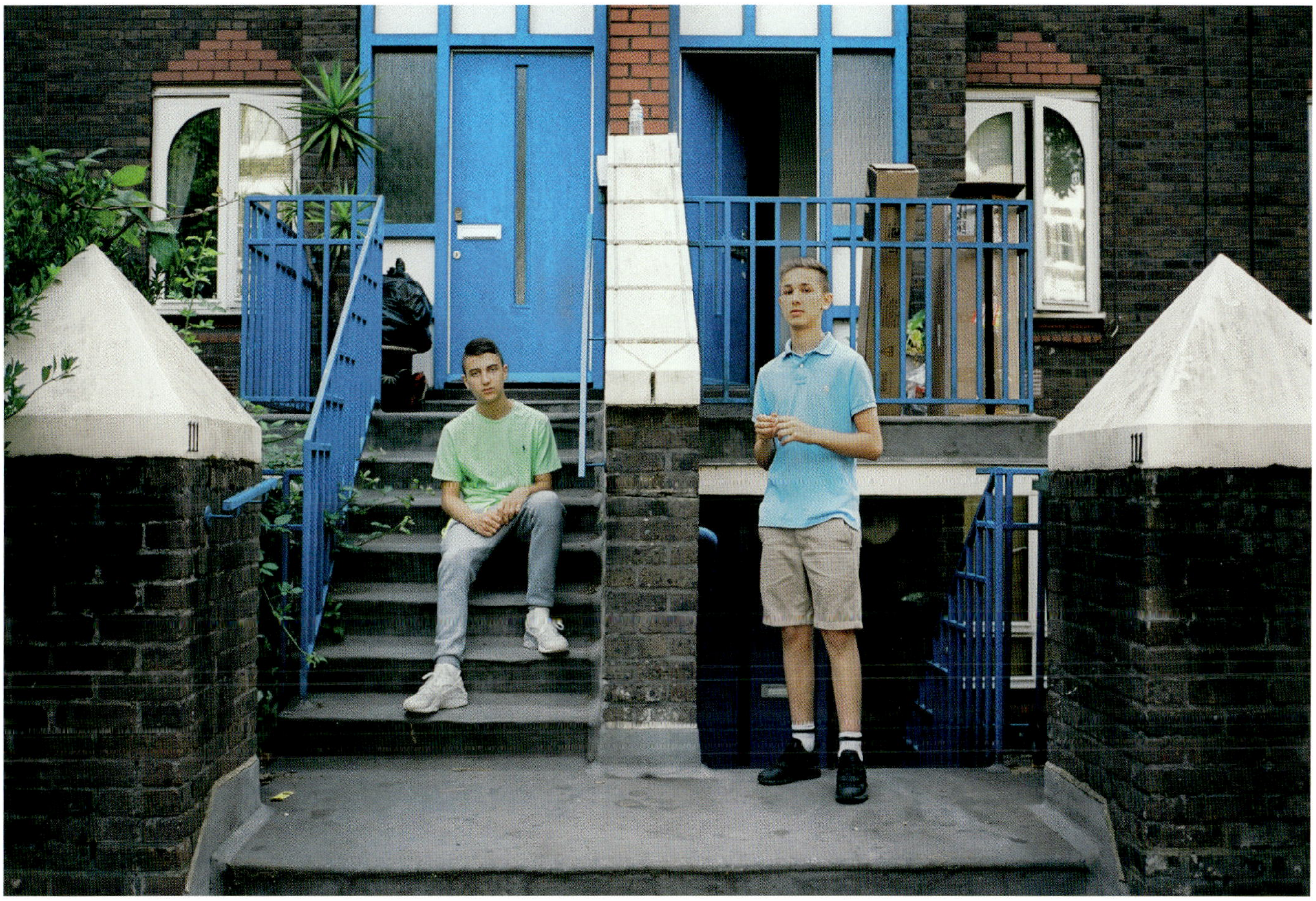
111
111

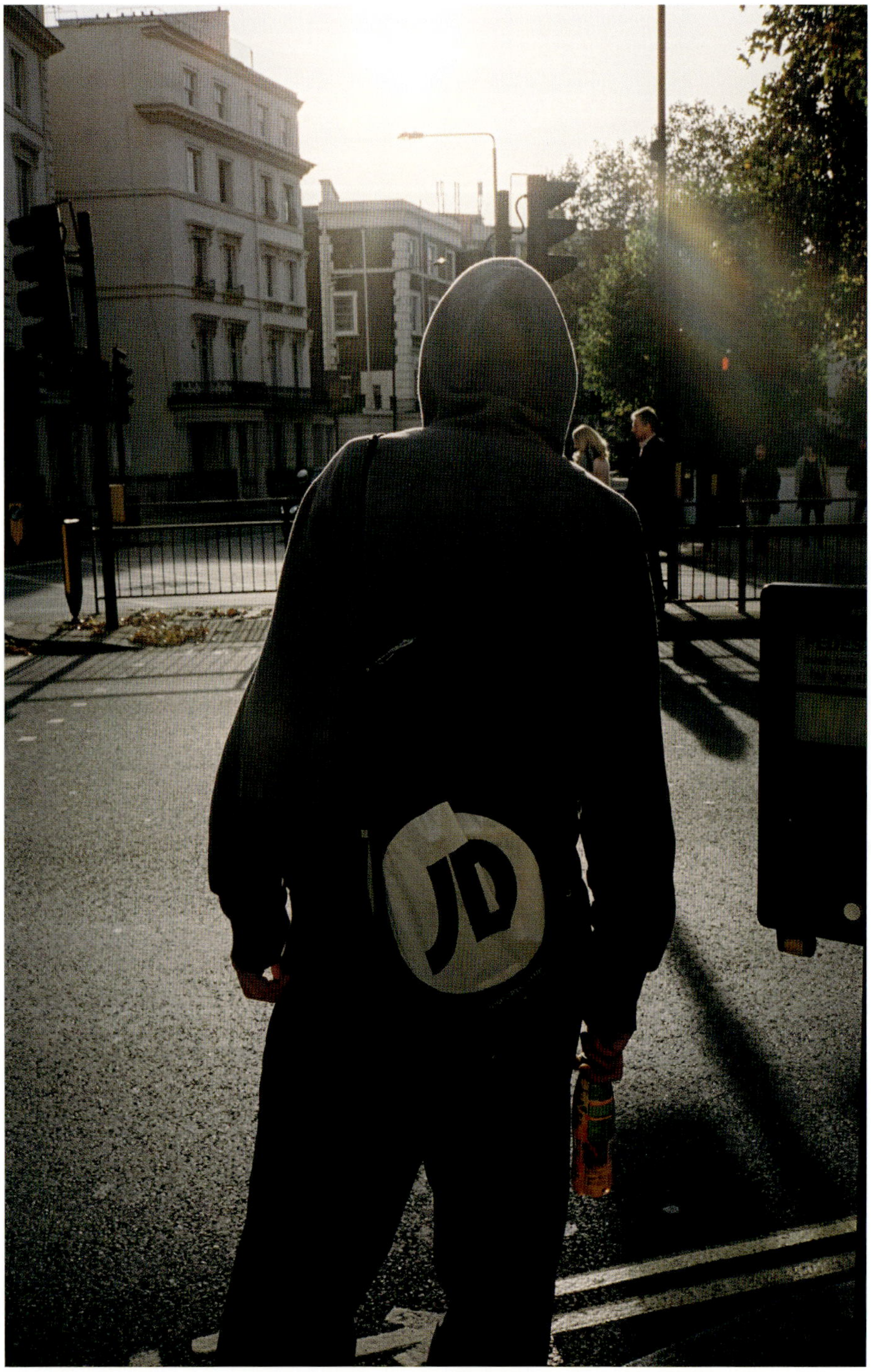
JD

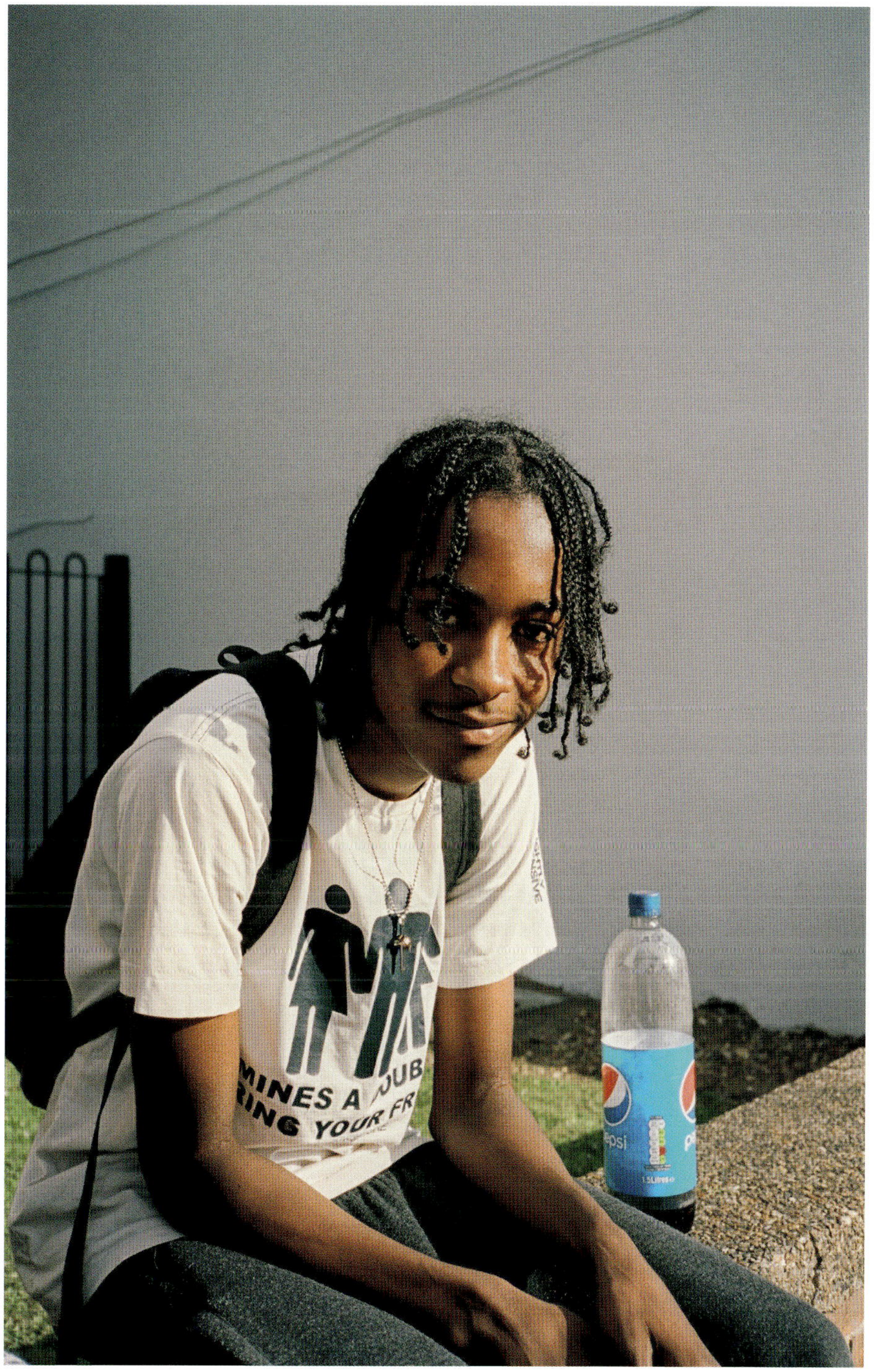
MINES A
YOUR

"He's Man City,
I'm Arsenal"

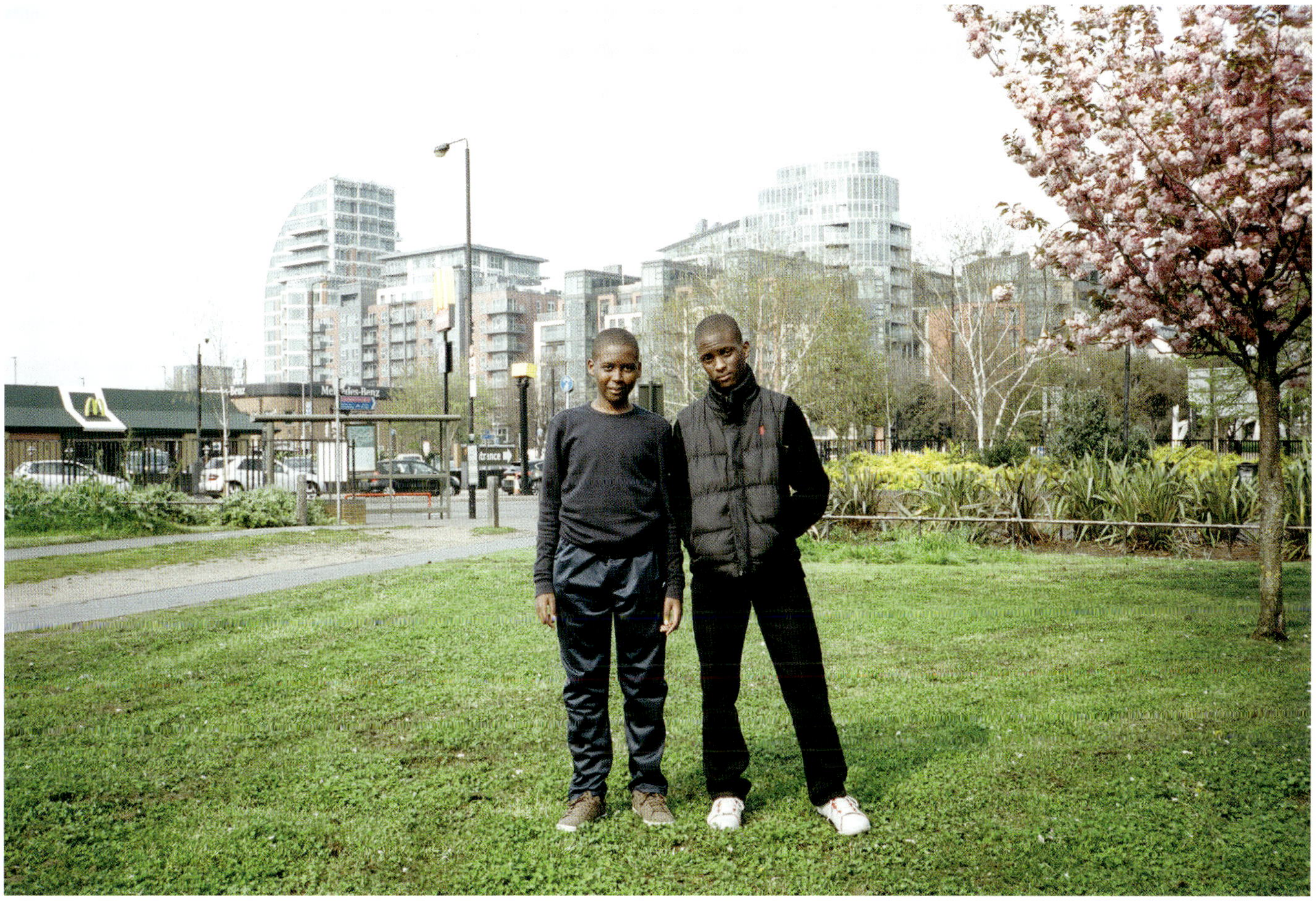

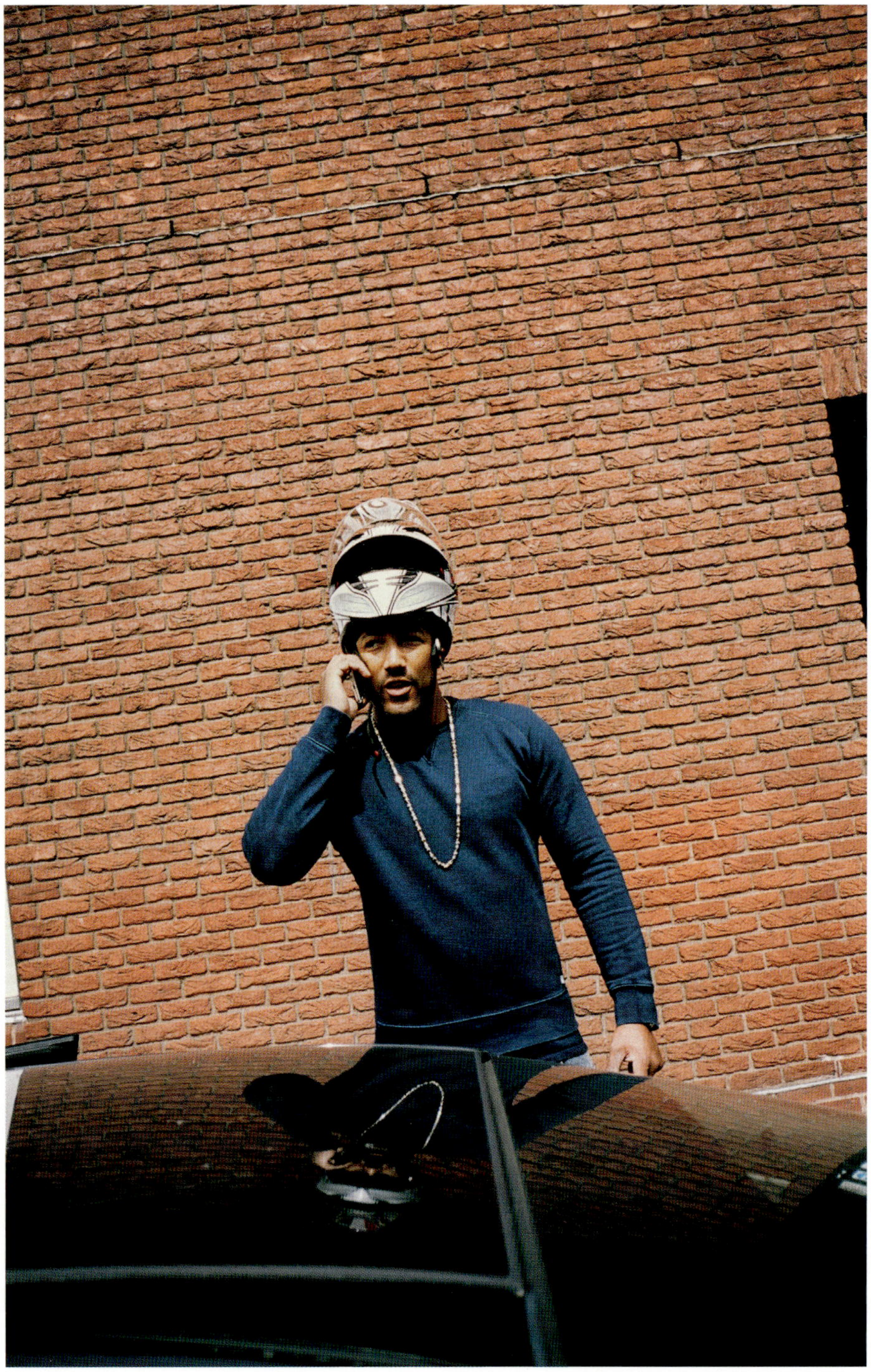

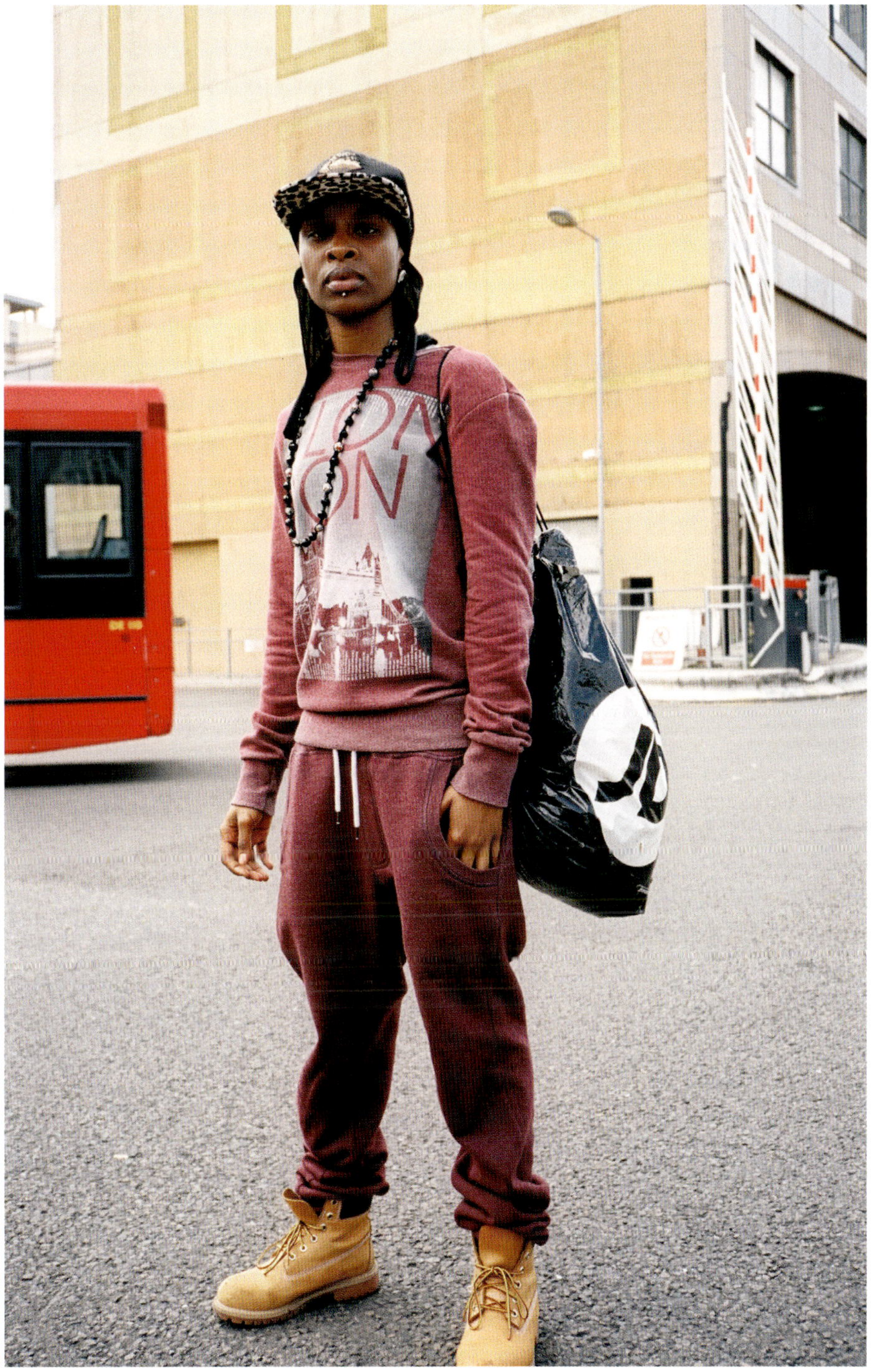

"Minorities get a lot of police attention
but it's just banter to us
you know.
Yeah,
I'm 18,
studying IT,
born in London,
this is home"

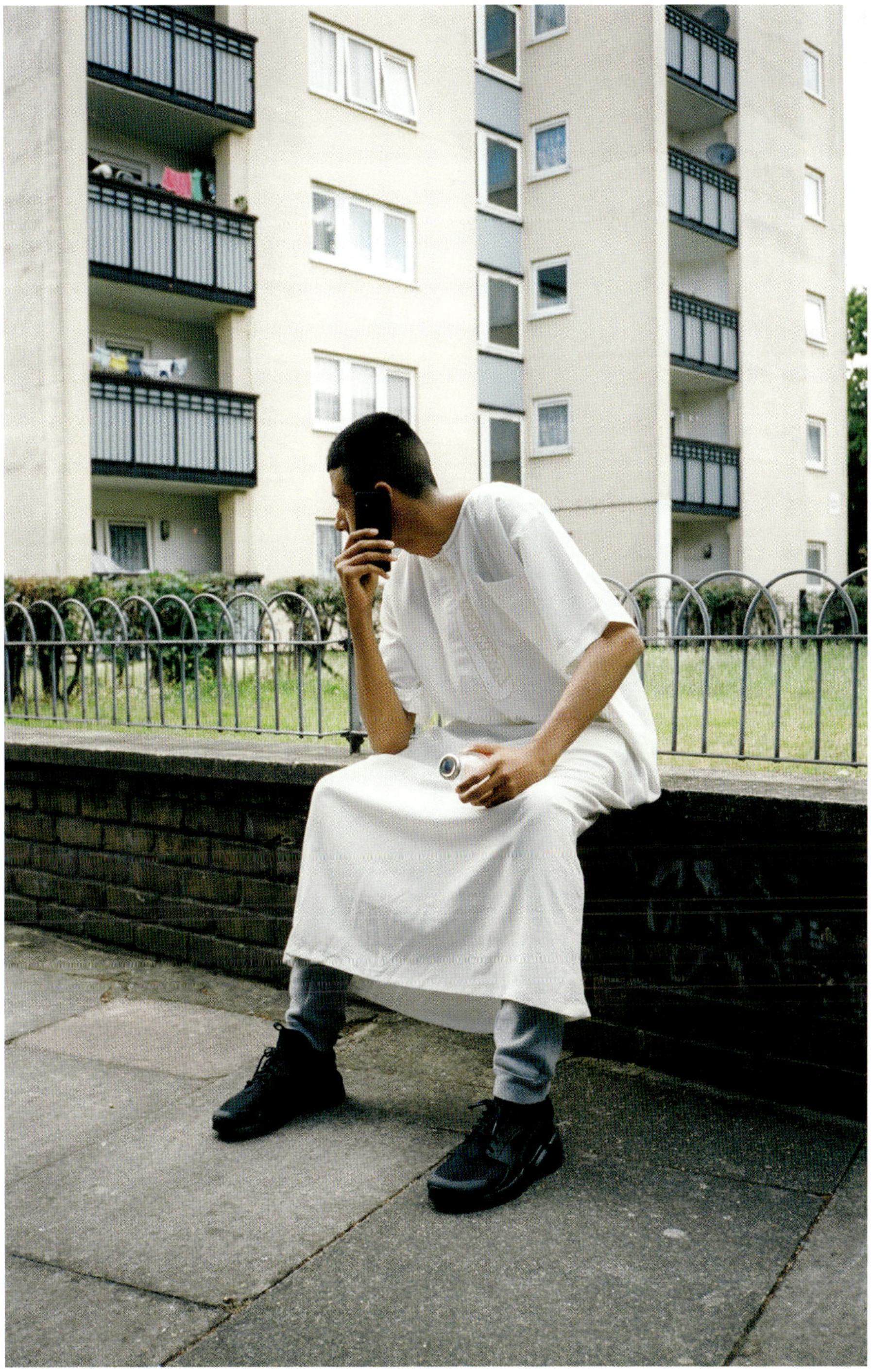

"I'm an Electrician"

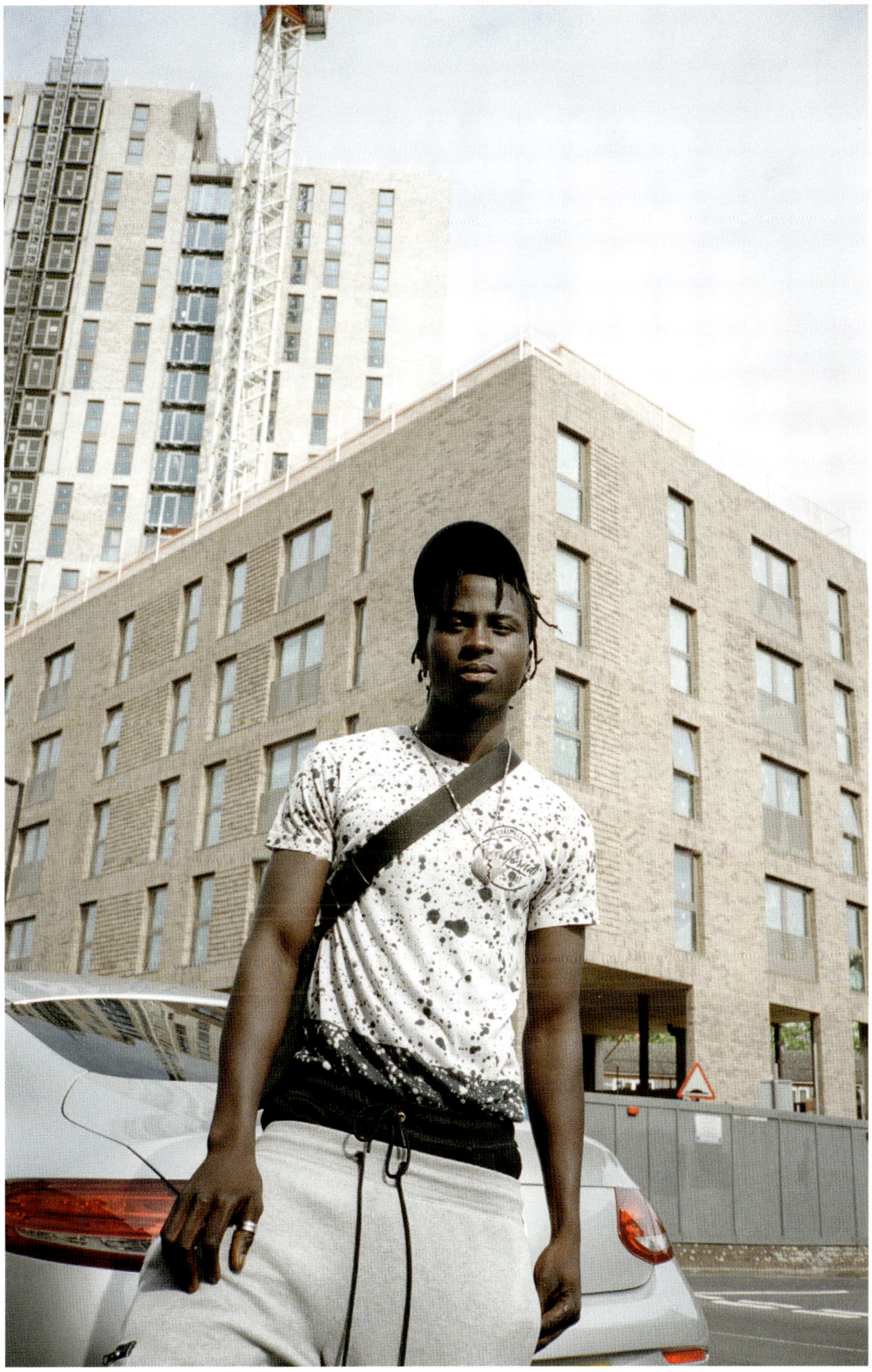

"We've known each other
for time"

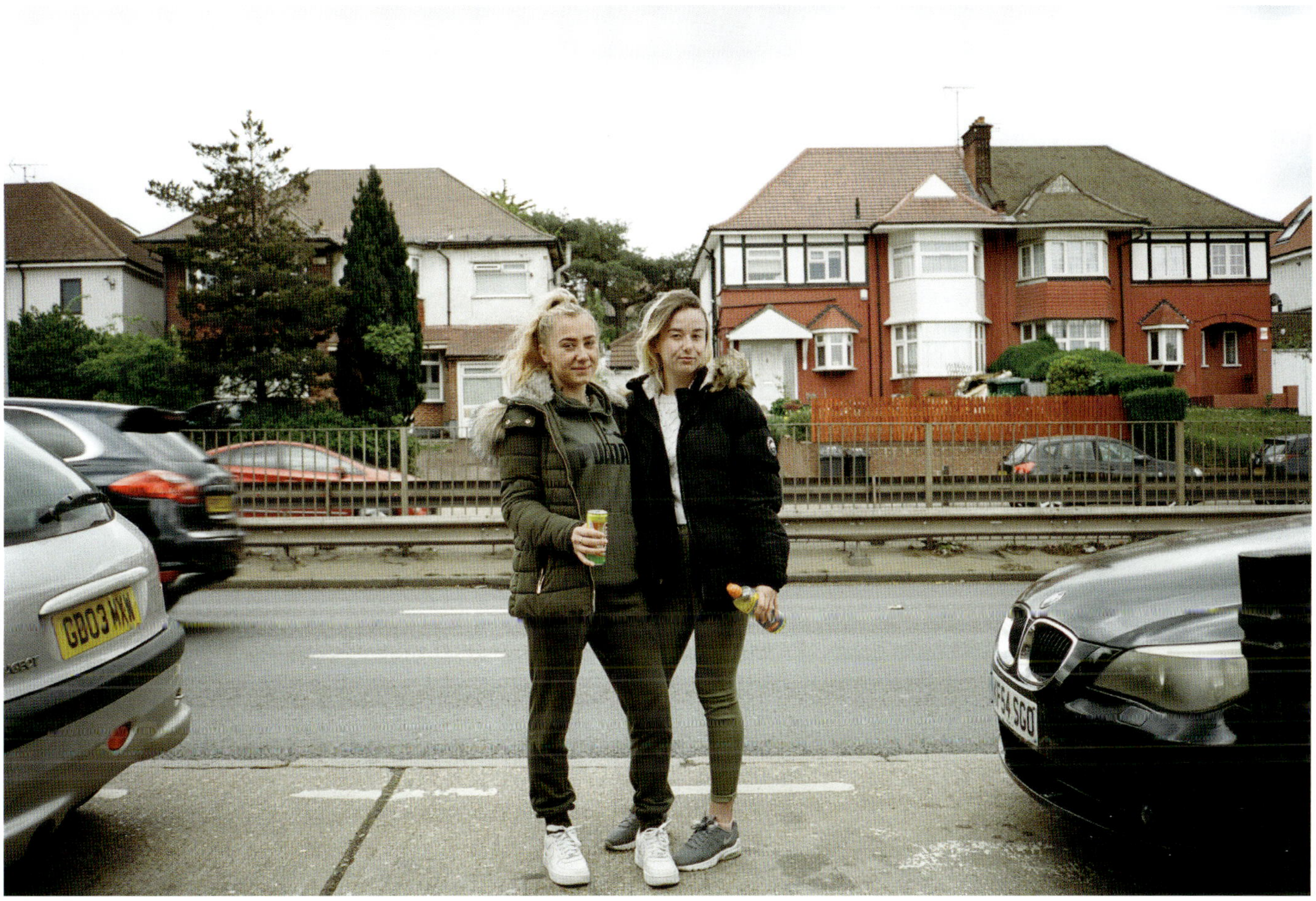
GB03 WKK

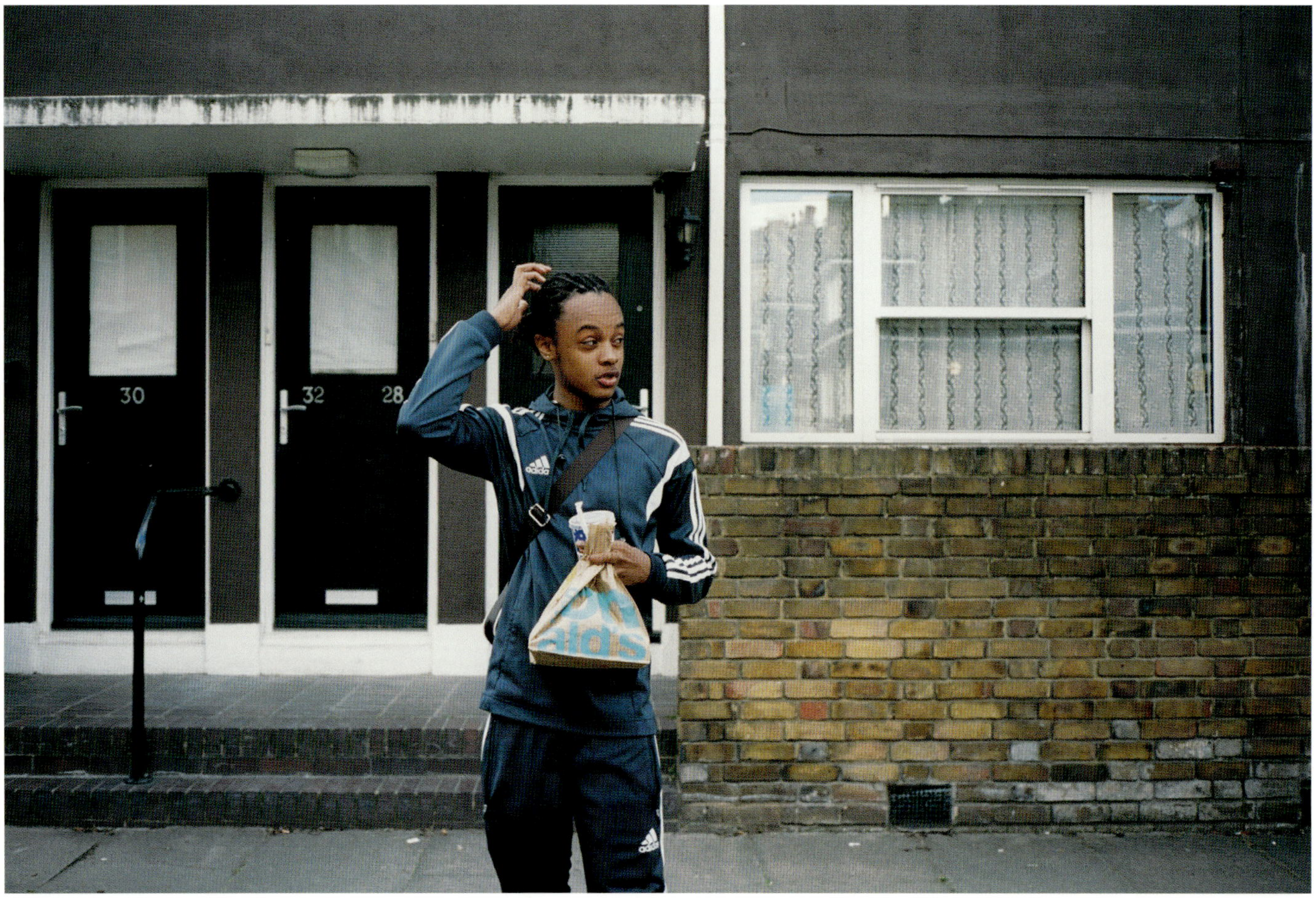
30
32
28

"I just got back from studying
for my baccalaureate in Dubai,
it's been good to be back in London.
My plans for the future?
I'm going to do
charity work in Jamaica"

"I'm just on my lunch break from Nike,
I'm also at uni
doing Physics"

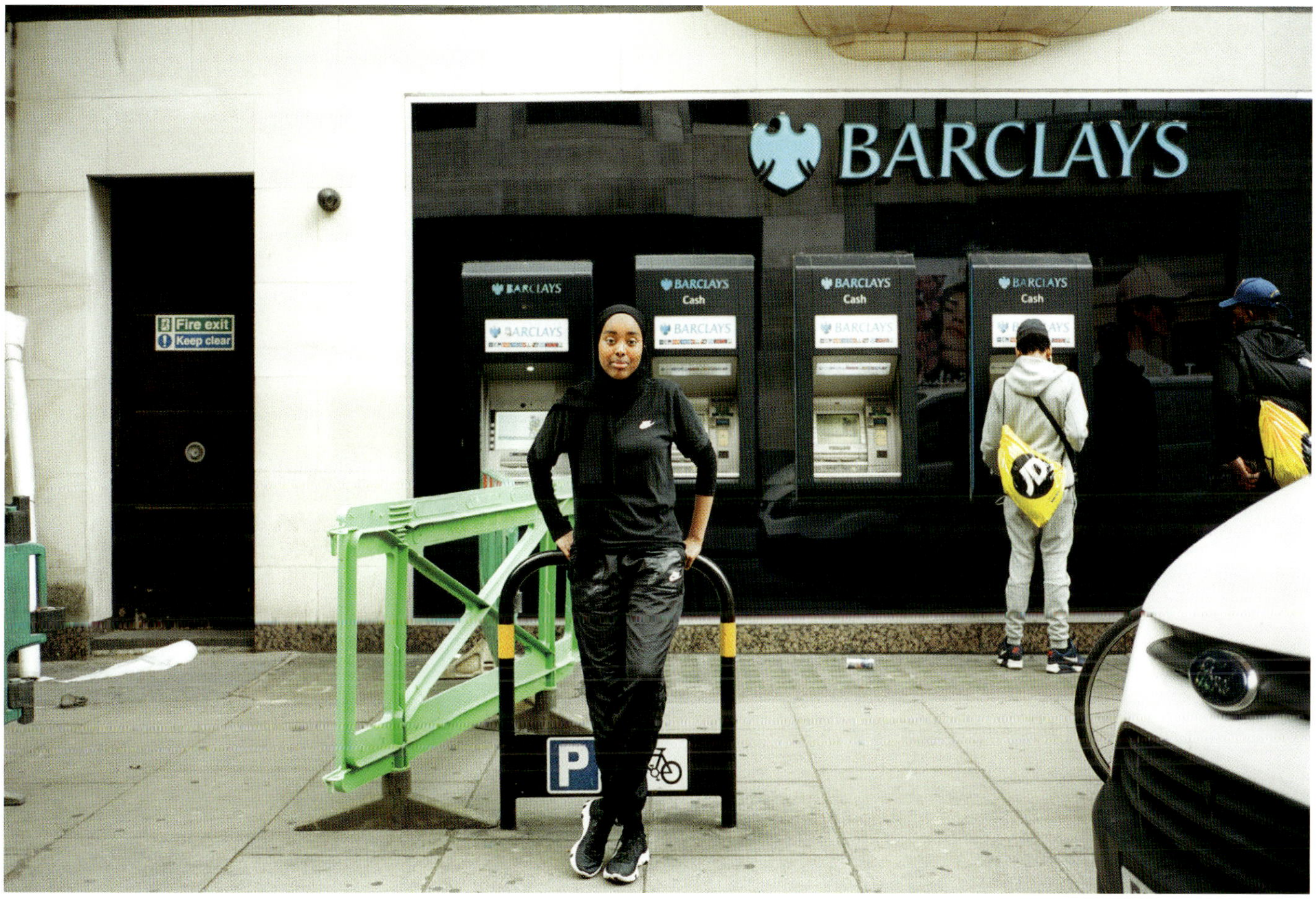
BARCLAYS
Fire exit
Keep clear
BARCLAYS
BARCLAYS
Cash
BARCLAYS
Cash
BARCLAYS
Cash

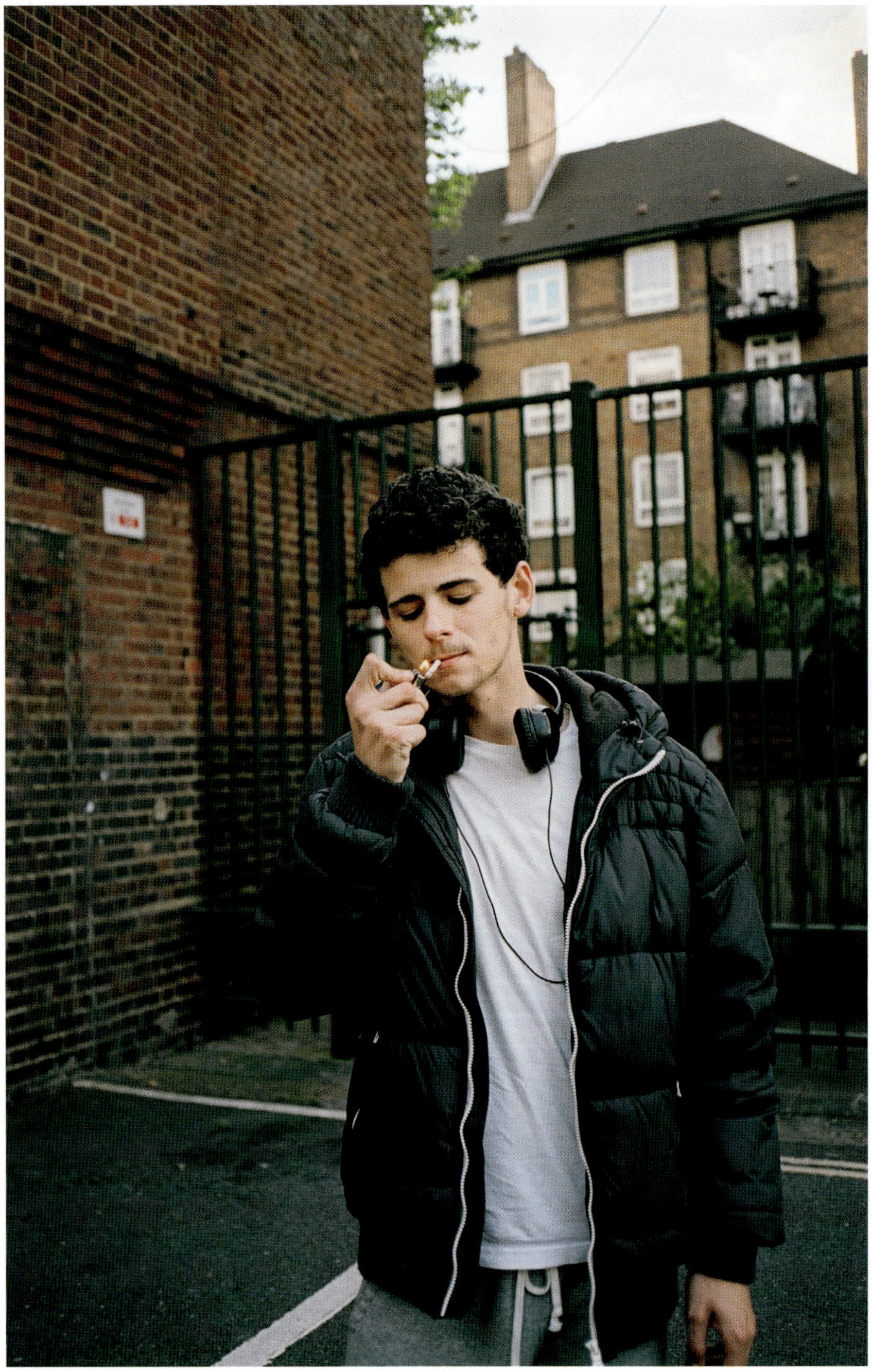

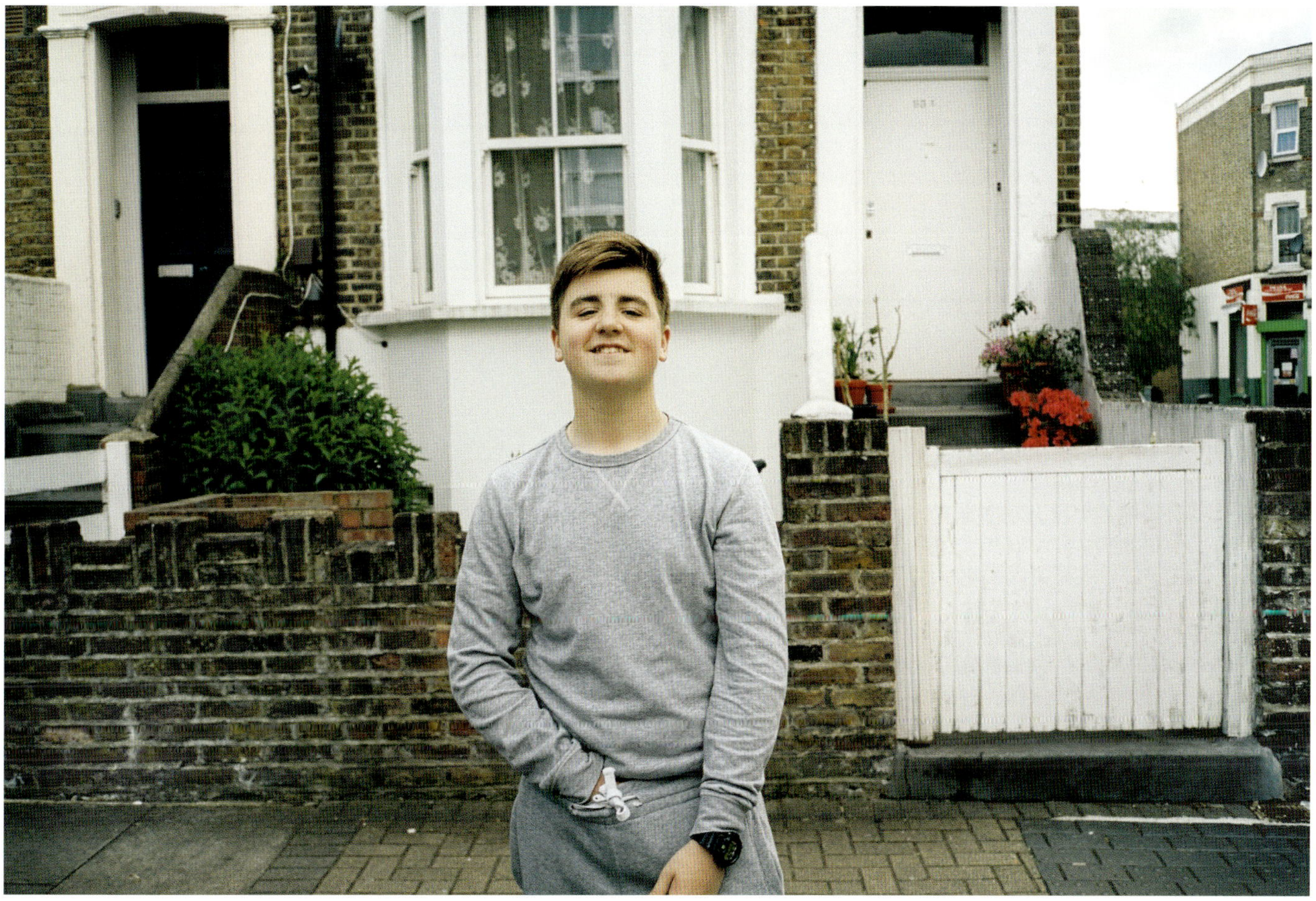

"Wait,
we gotta push the car
off this road"

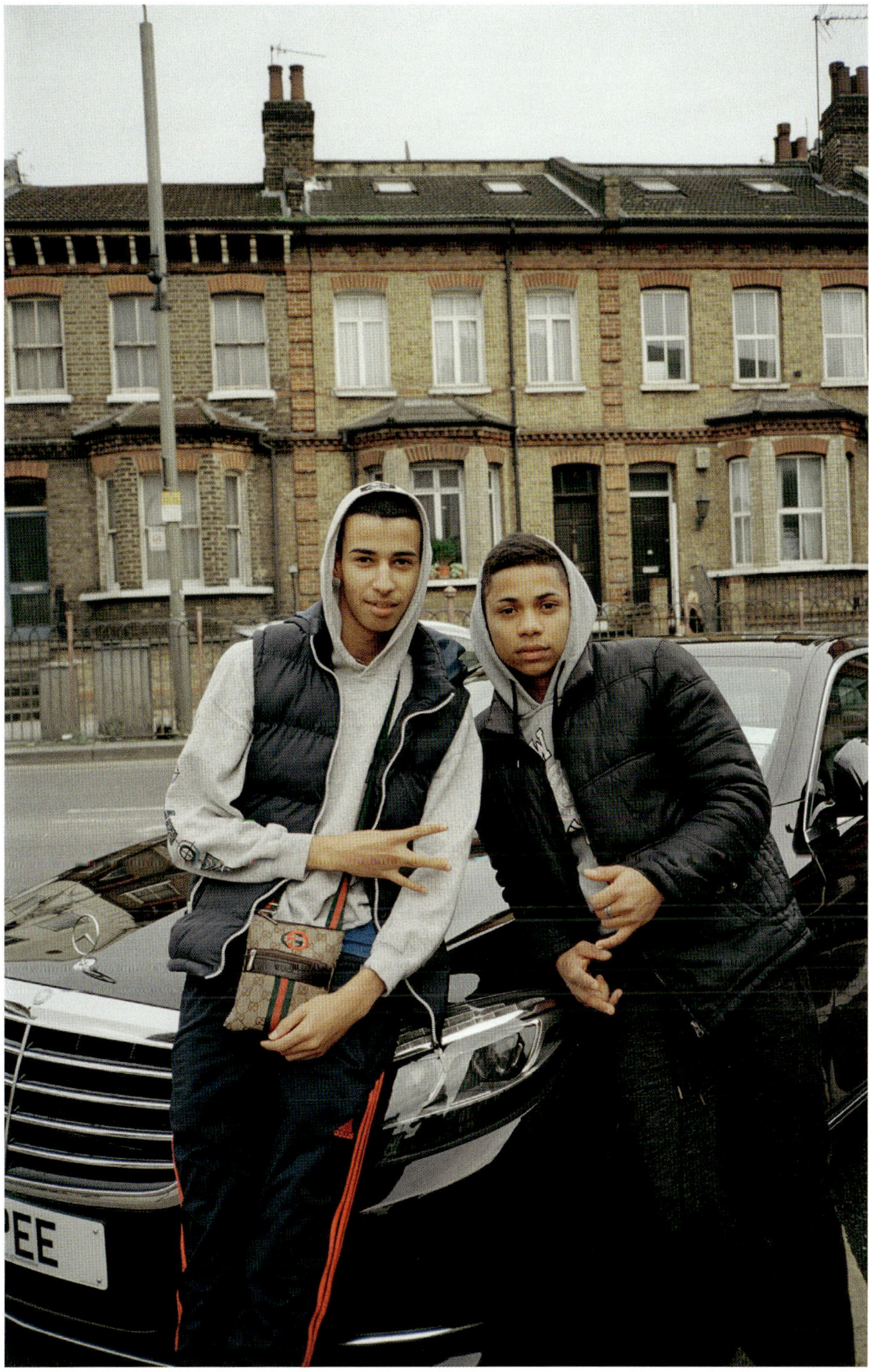
PEE

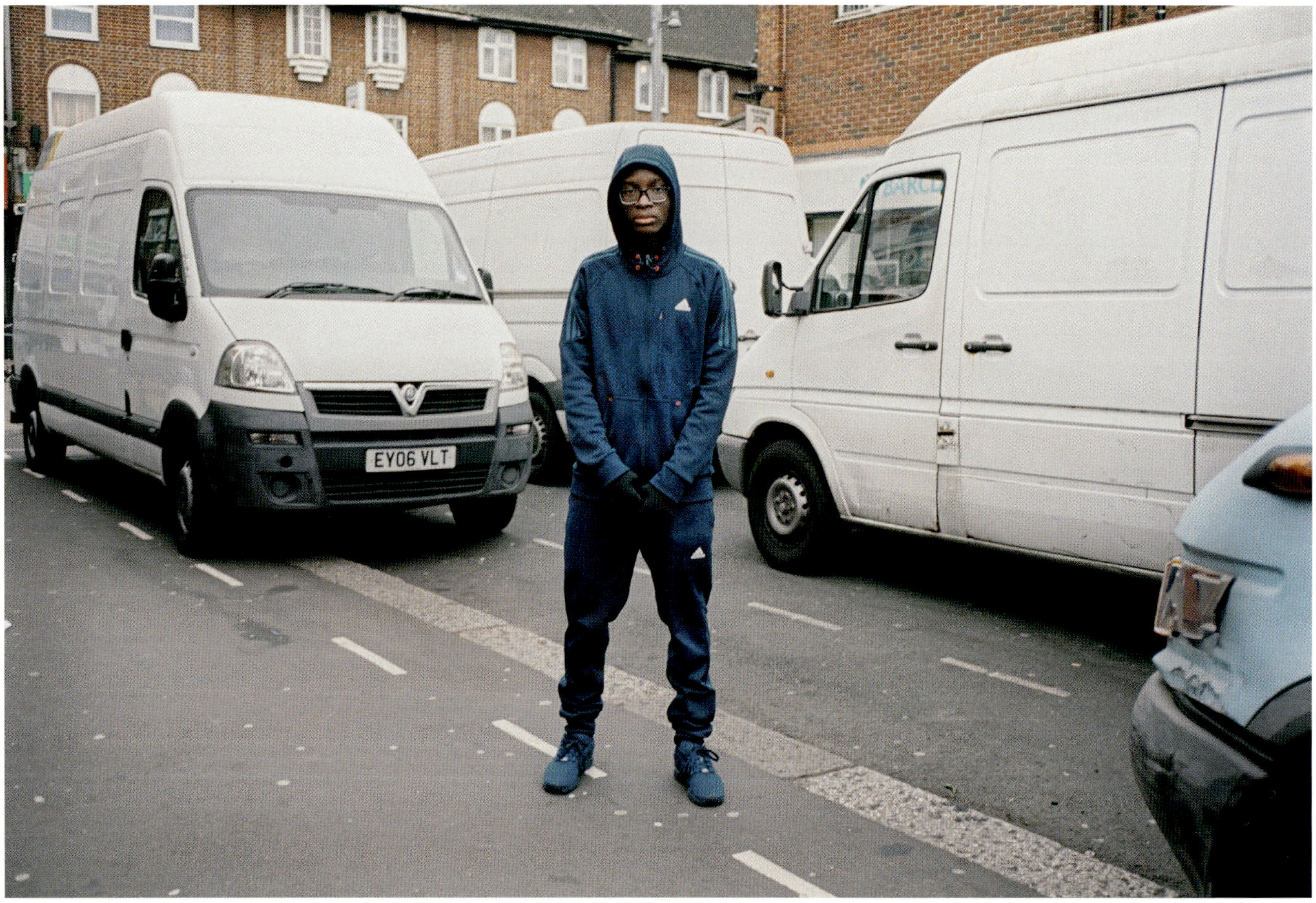
EY06 VLT

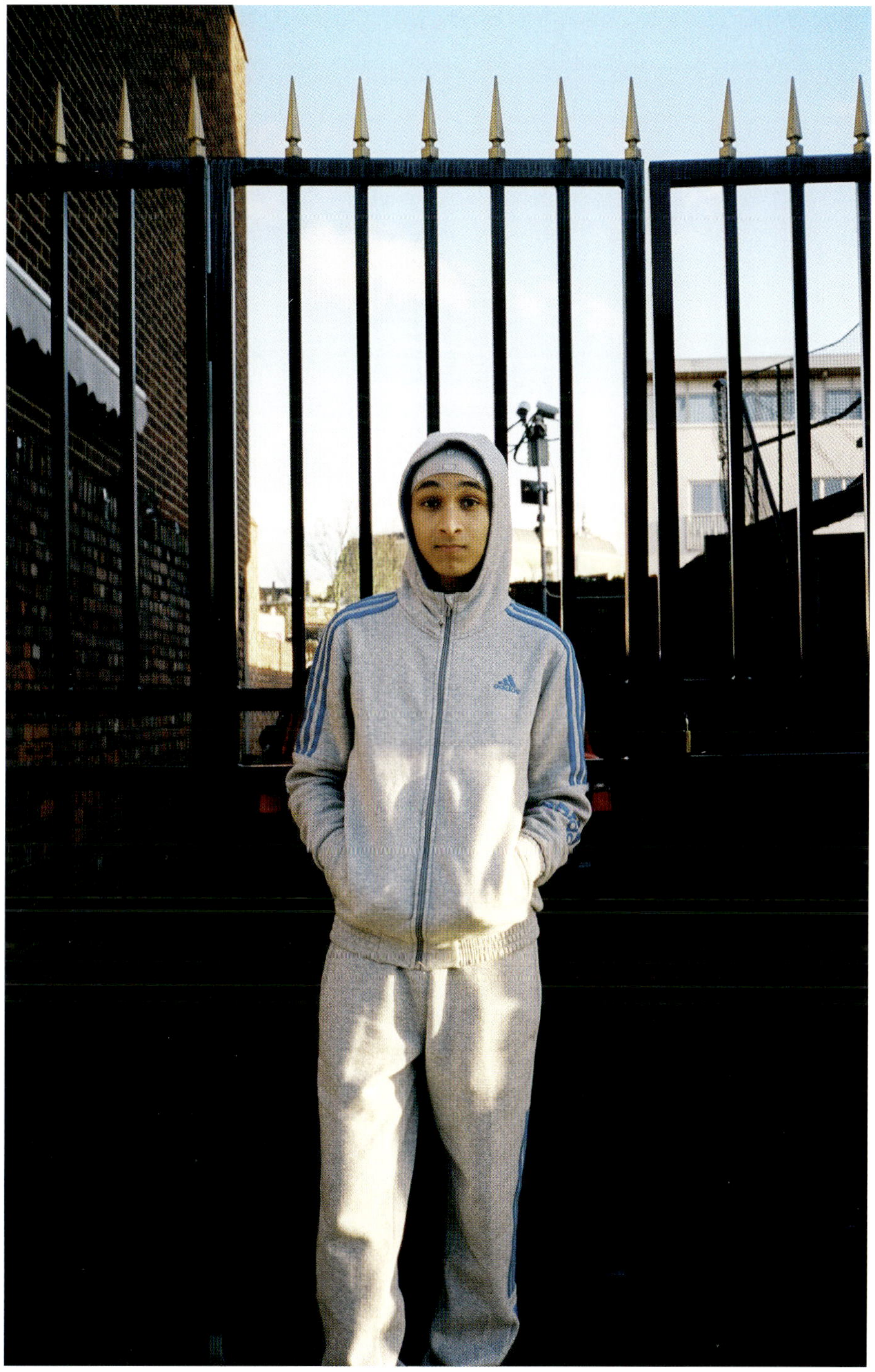

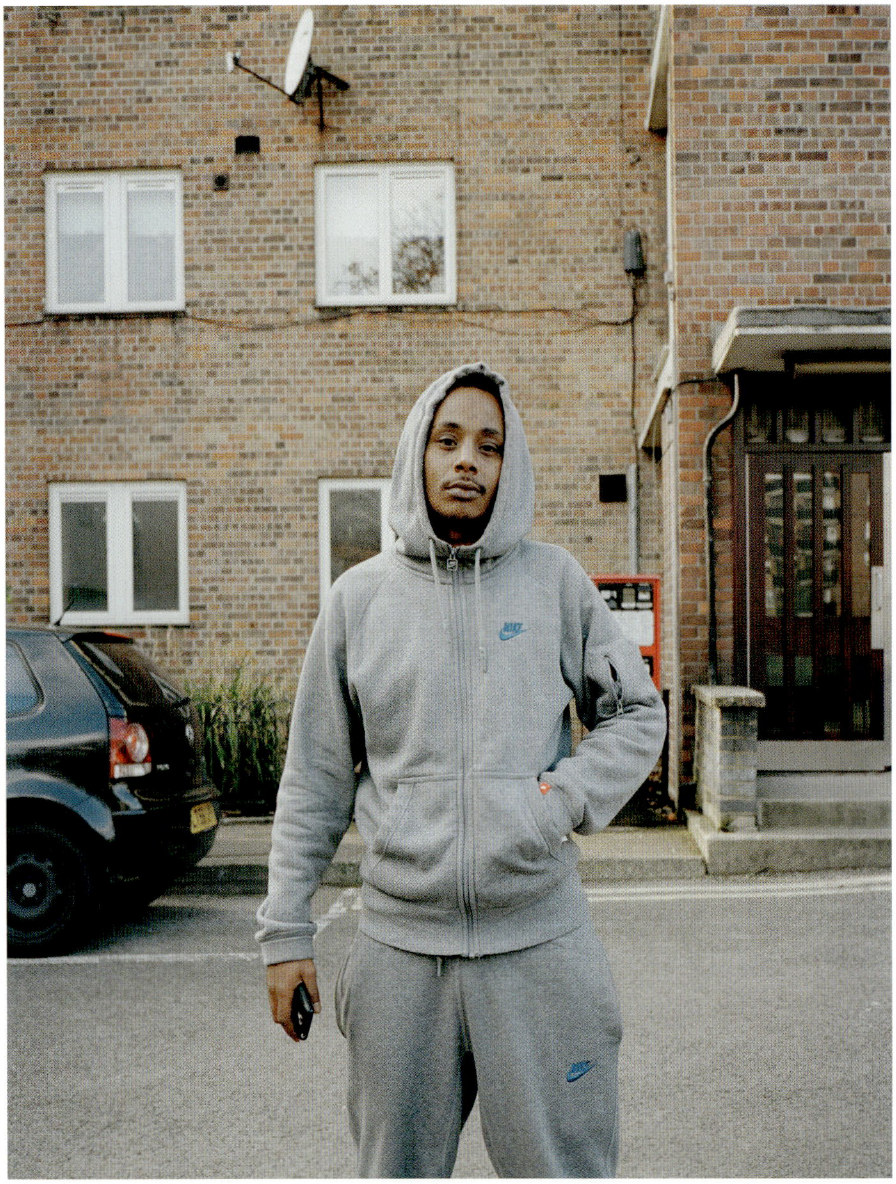

"I got you

one hundred per cent,

you should know this"

"No face,
no case,
it's a Drill video"

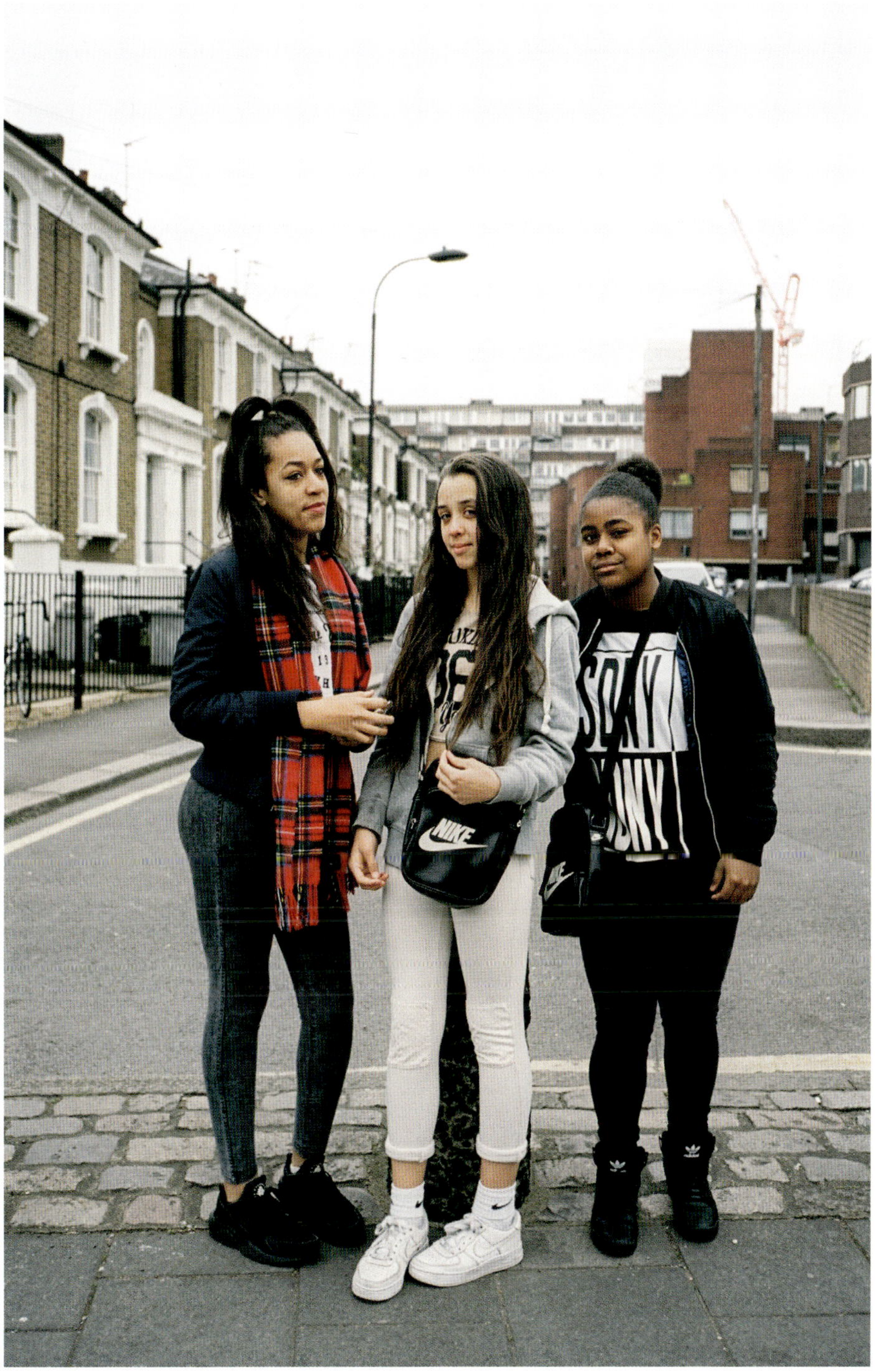
NIKE

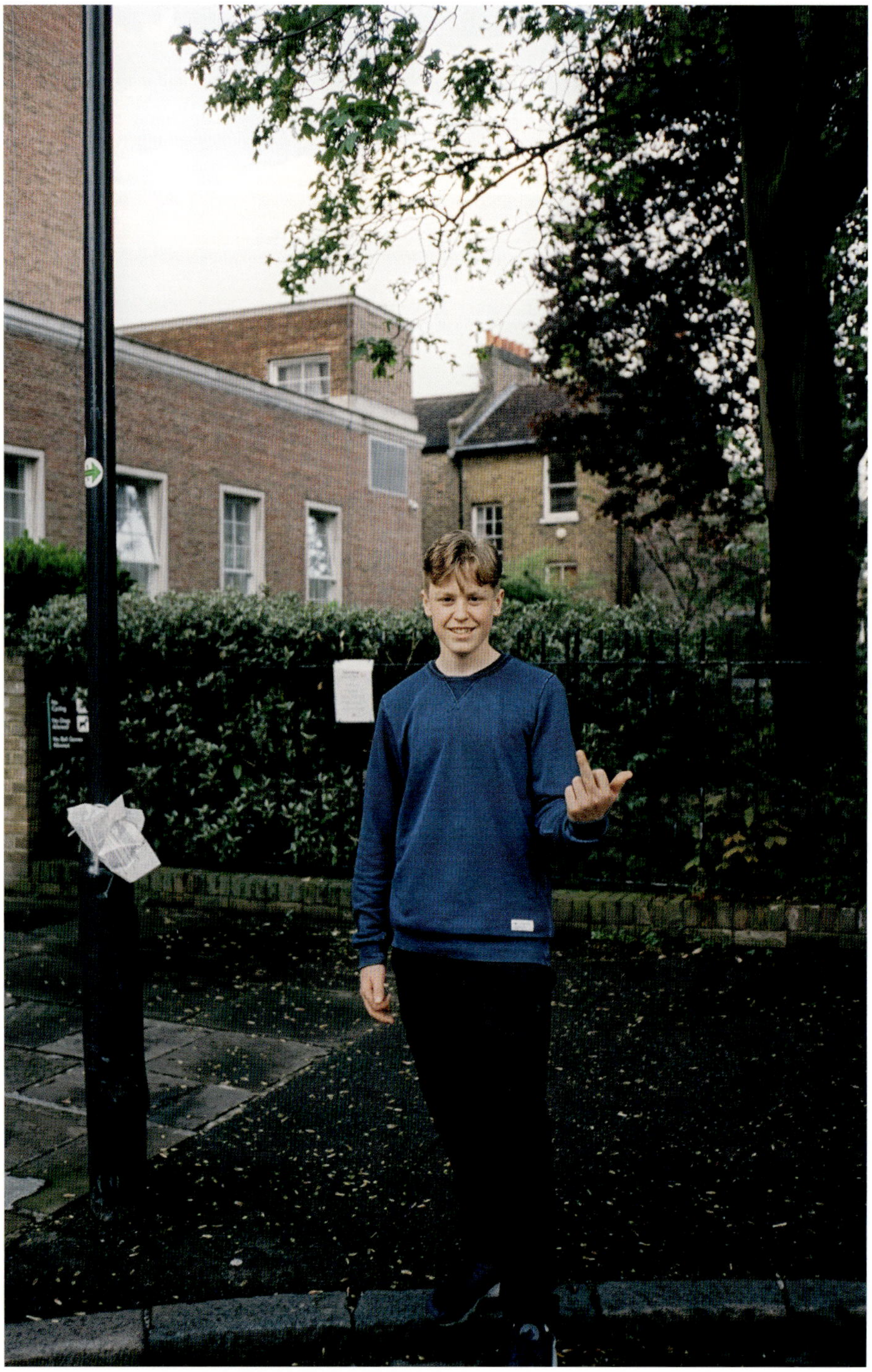

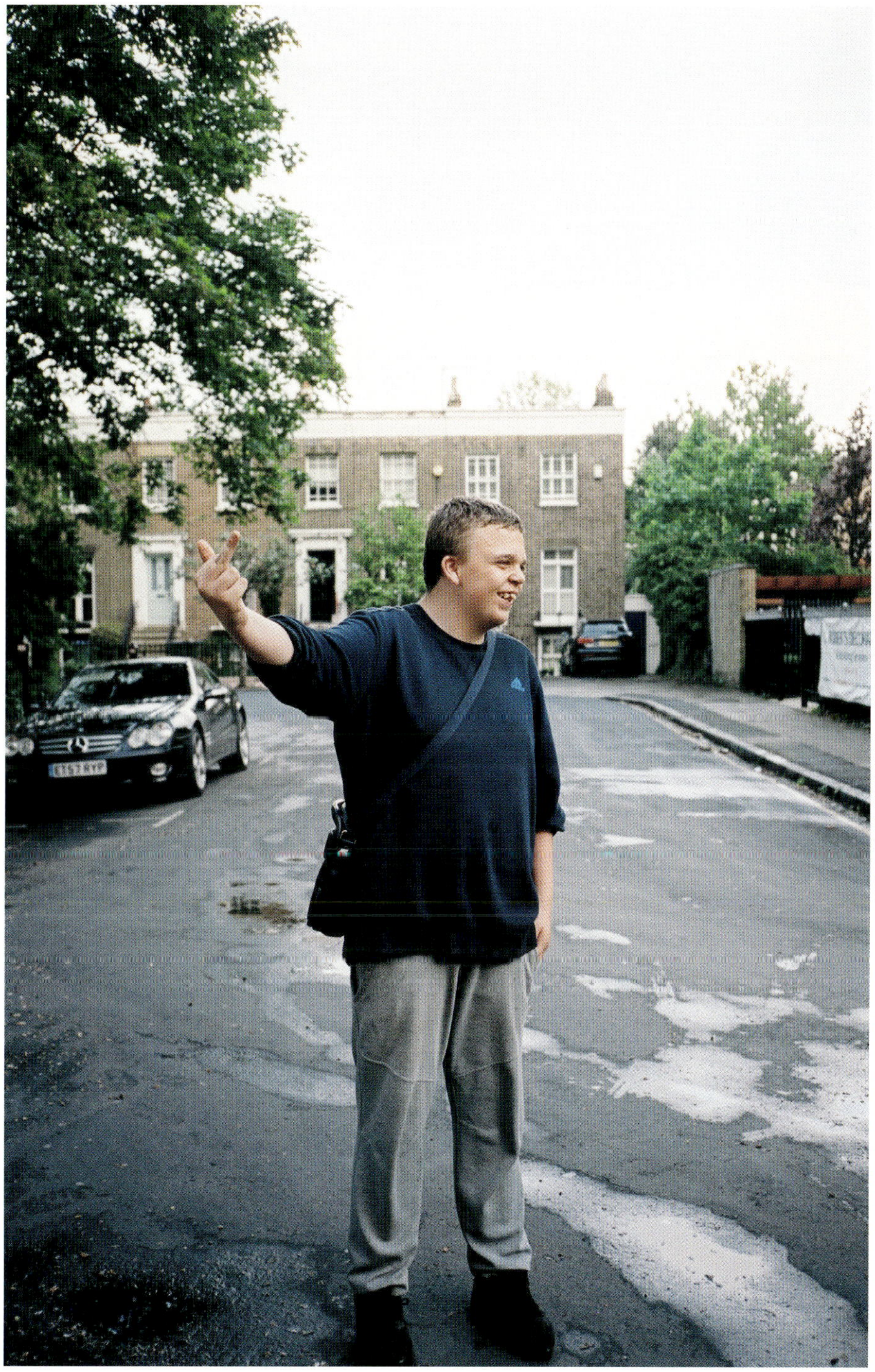

"It's a struggle
with Khan and Diamond,
they're strong,
my dad will help us out"

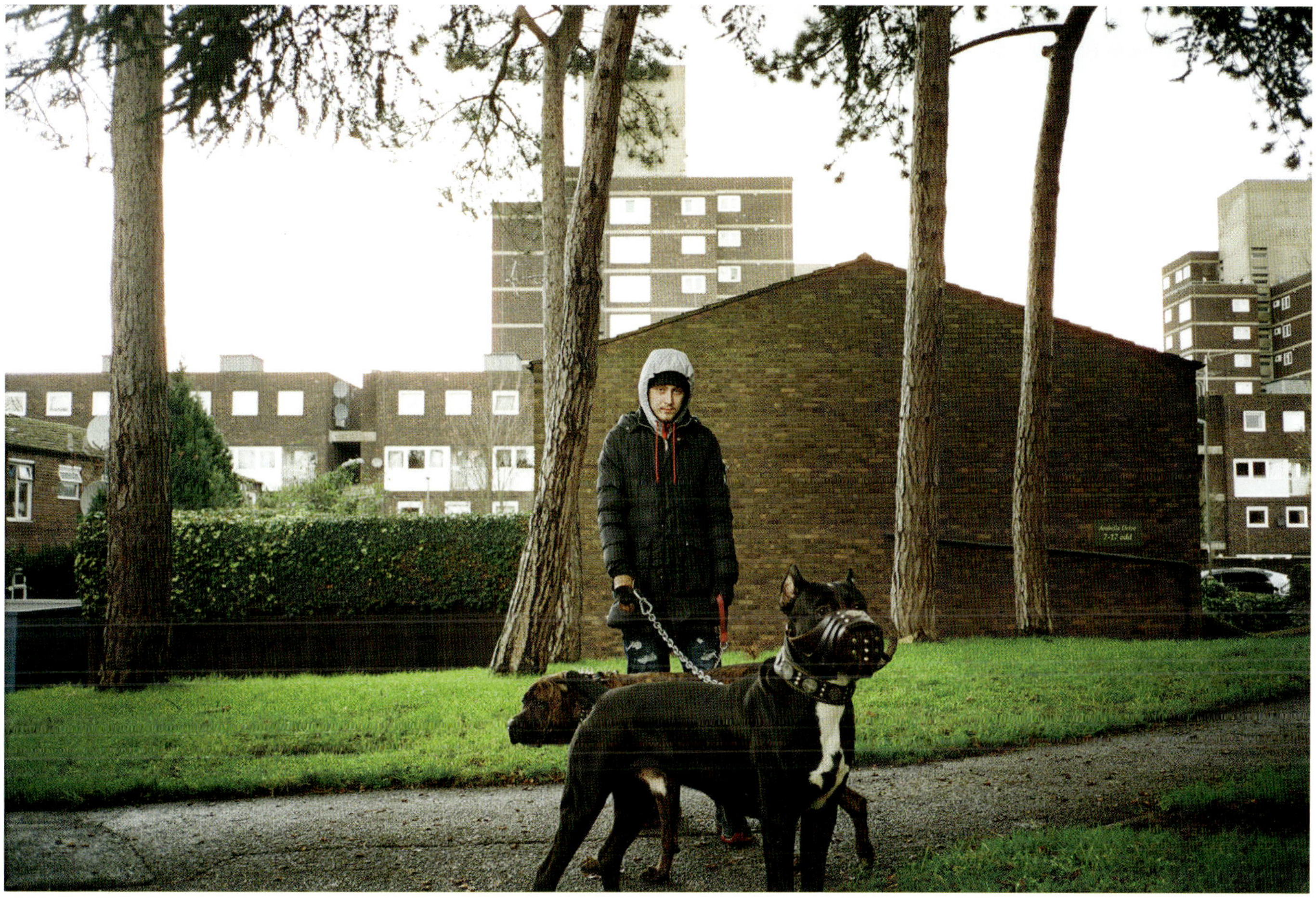

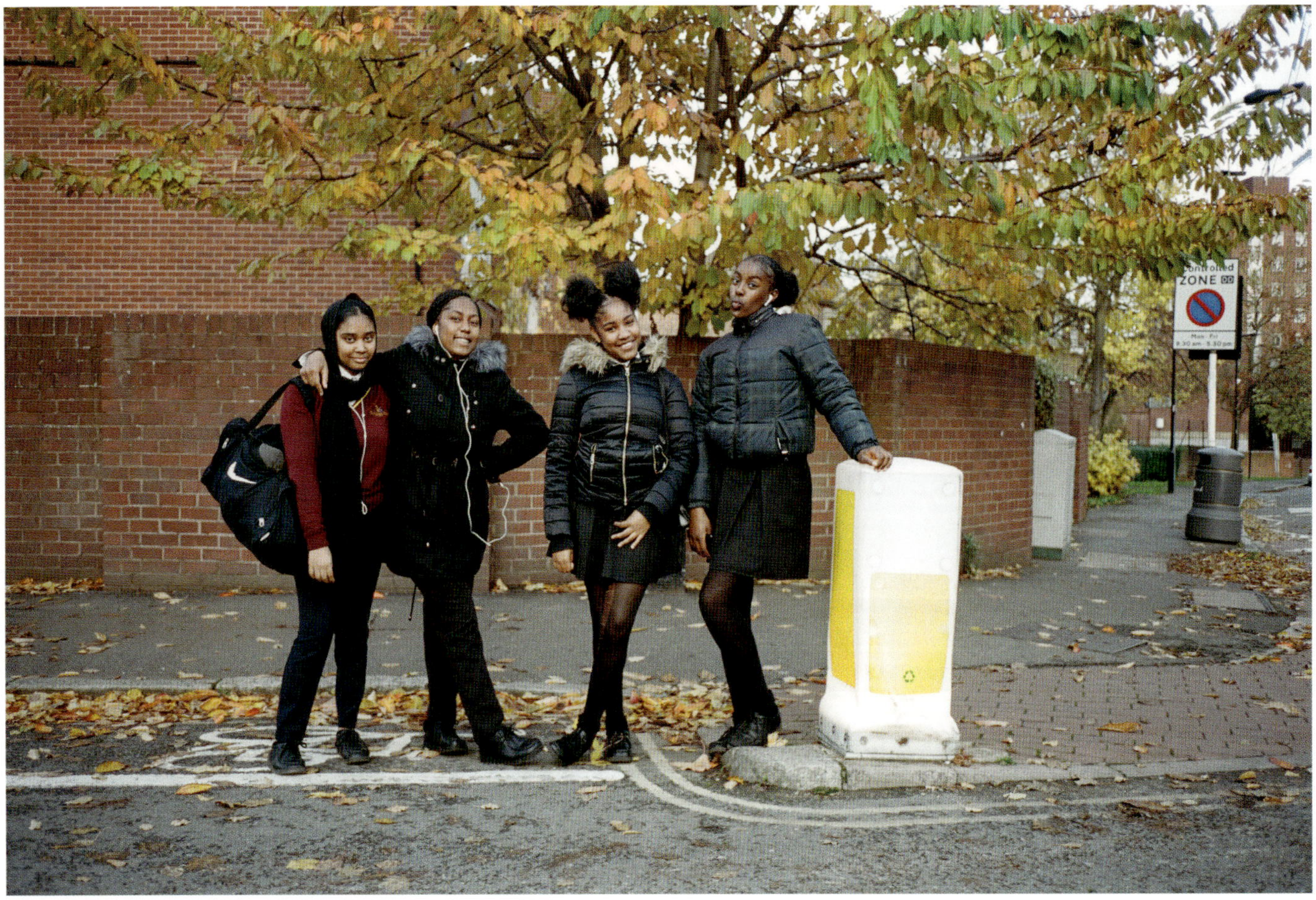
ZONE

"You only live once, bruv"

"I'm waiting
for the 72,
are you training tonight?"

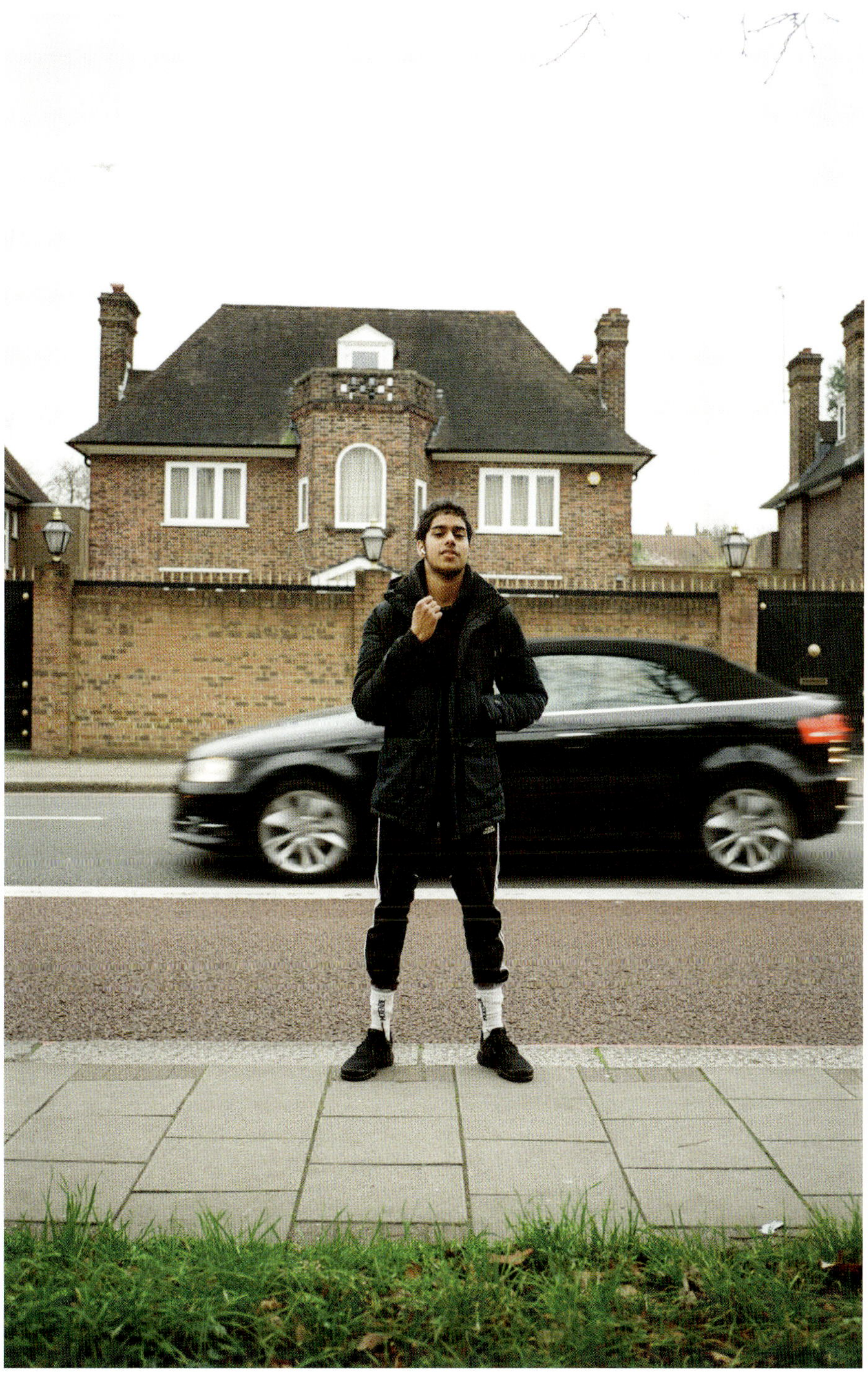

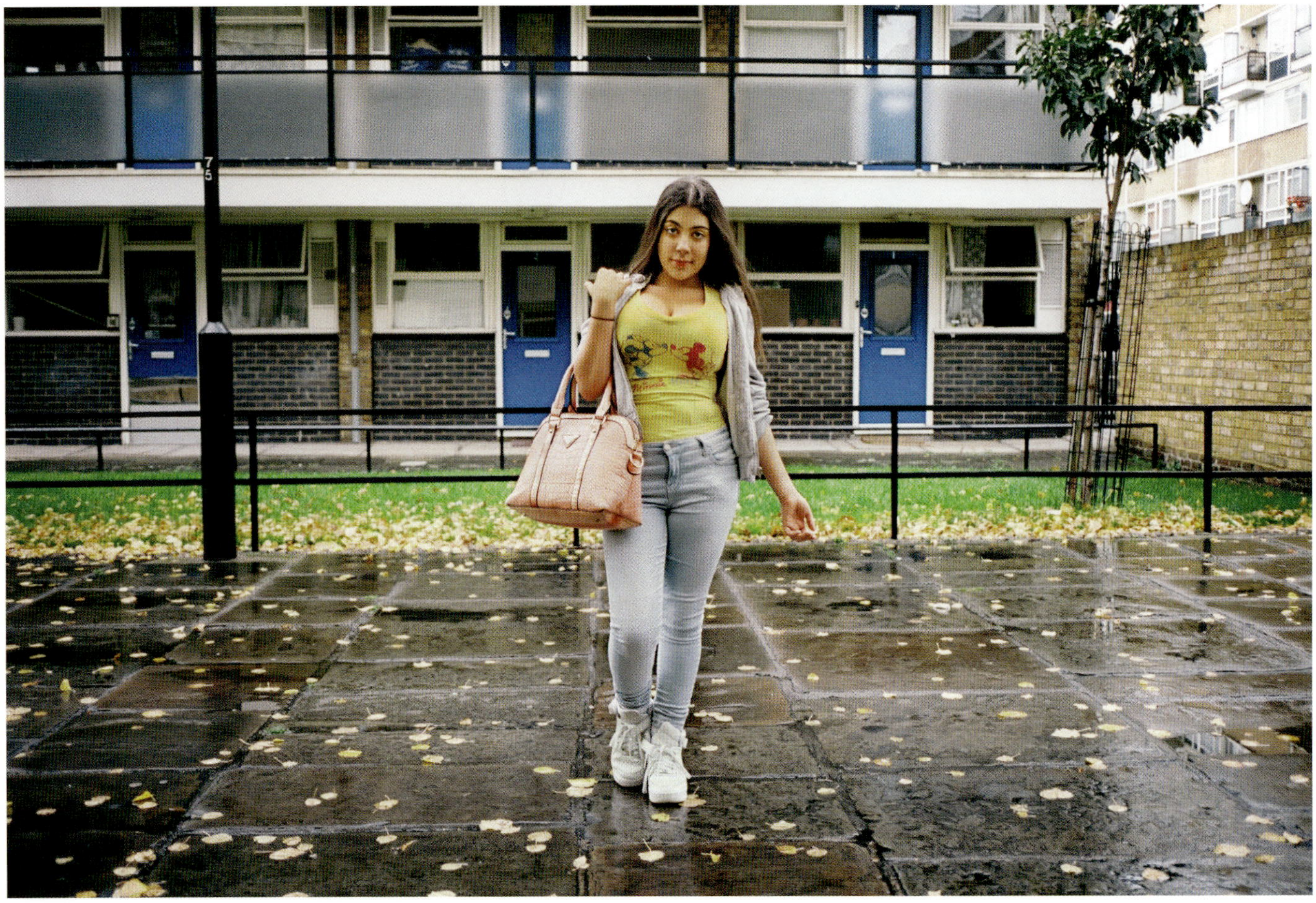

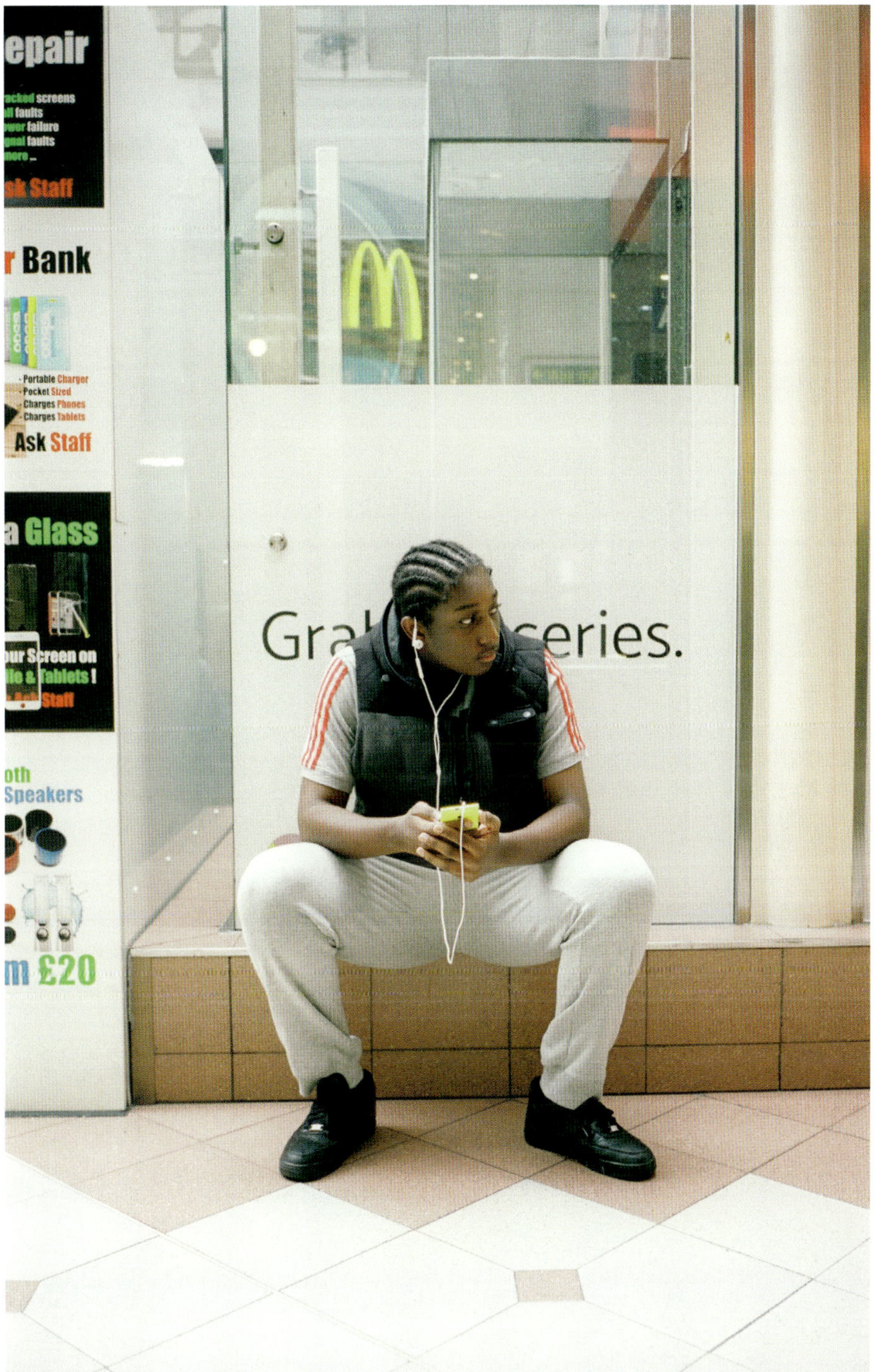
Portable Charger
Pocket Sized
Charges Phones
Charges Tablets
Ask Staff
£20

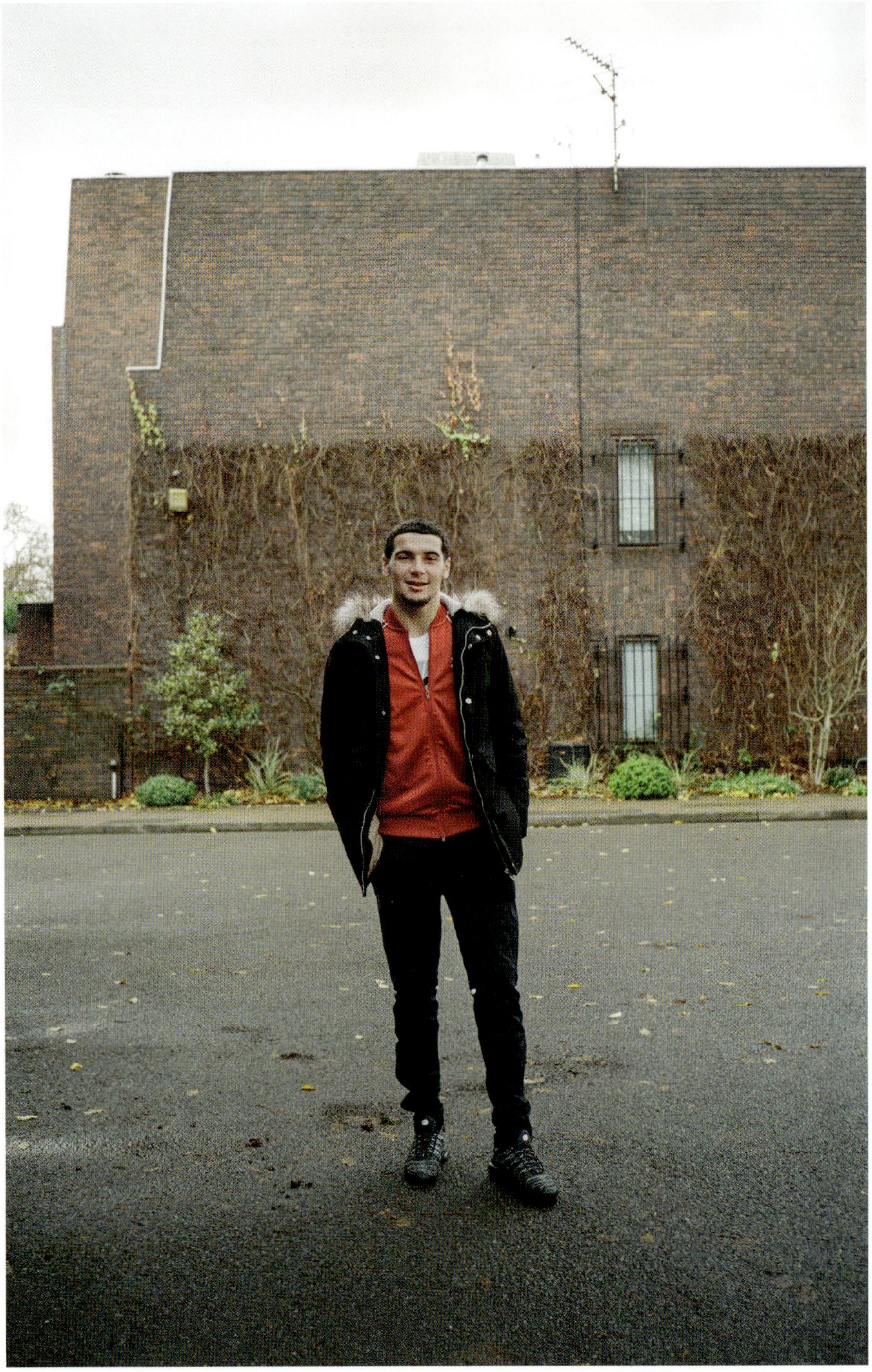

"I set my alarm for 4am
to watch the
Tyson Fury fight in Vegas
and had me
a bowl of Cheerios"

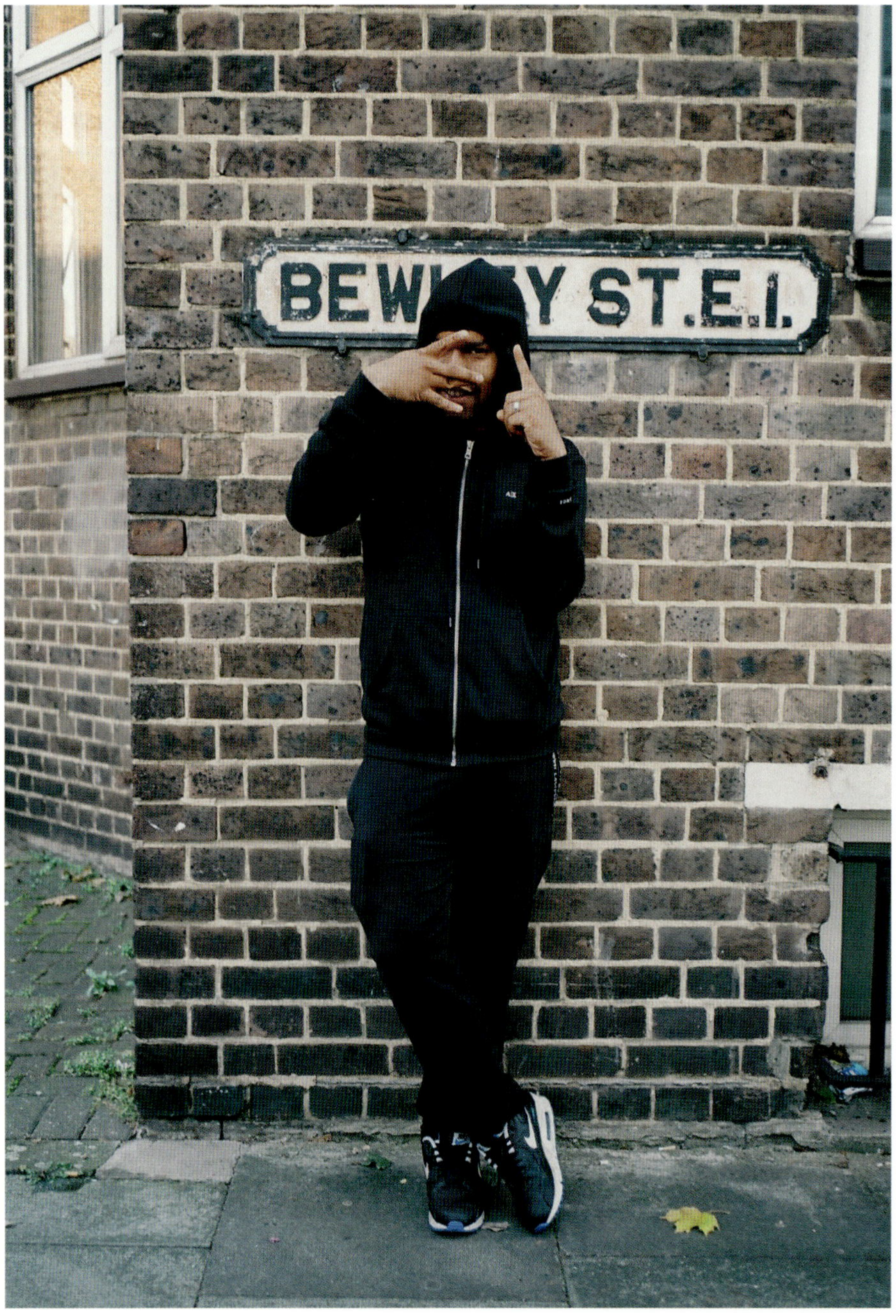

*"We got rockets
and bangers"*

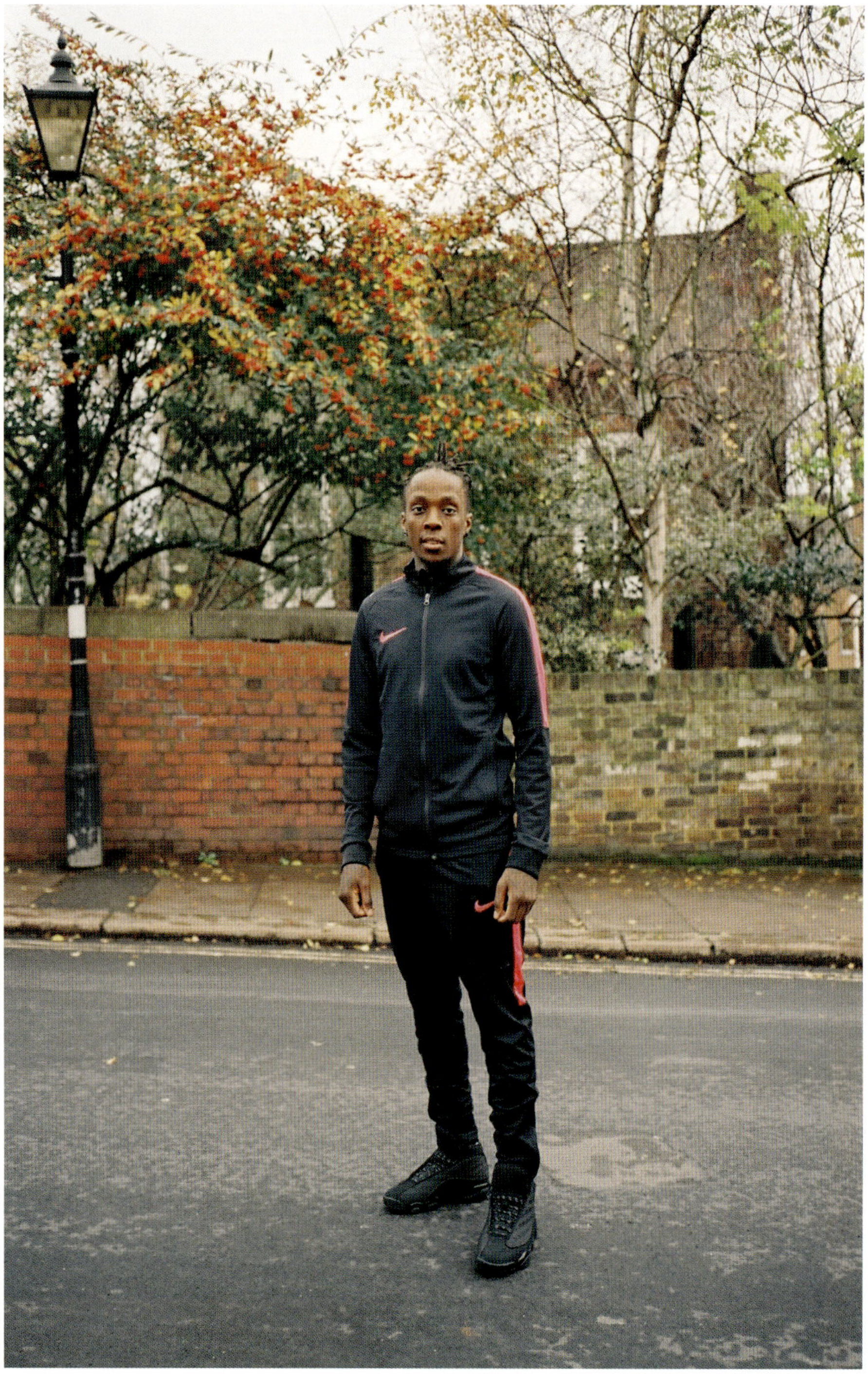

"Boxing has a funny way
of bringing
different people together"

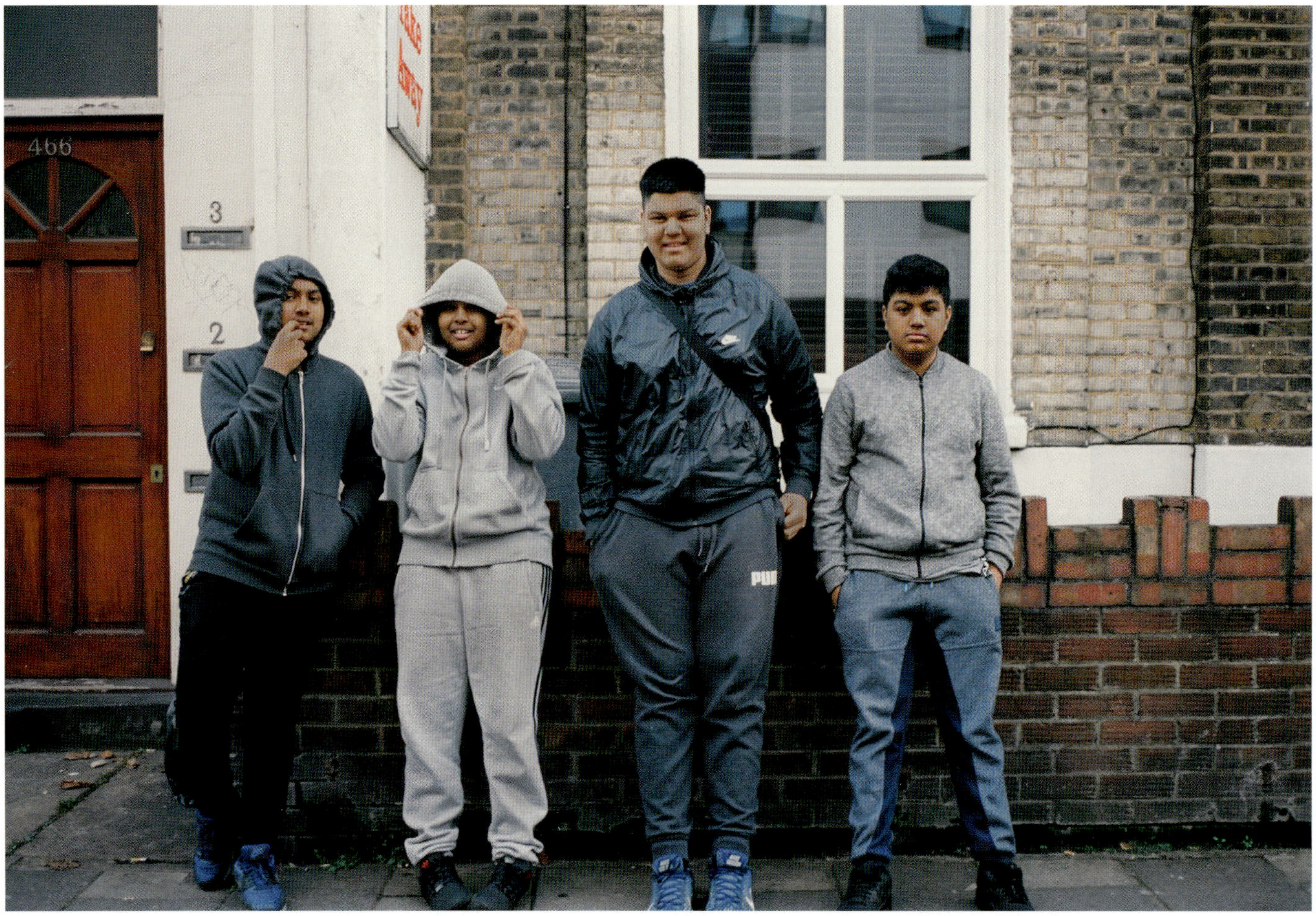
466
3
2

"I got

2k followers"

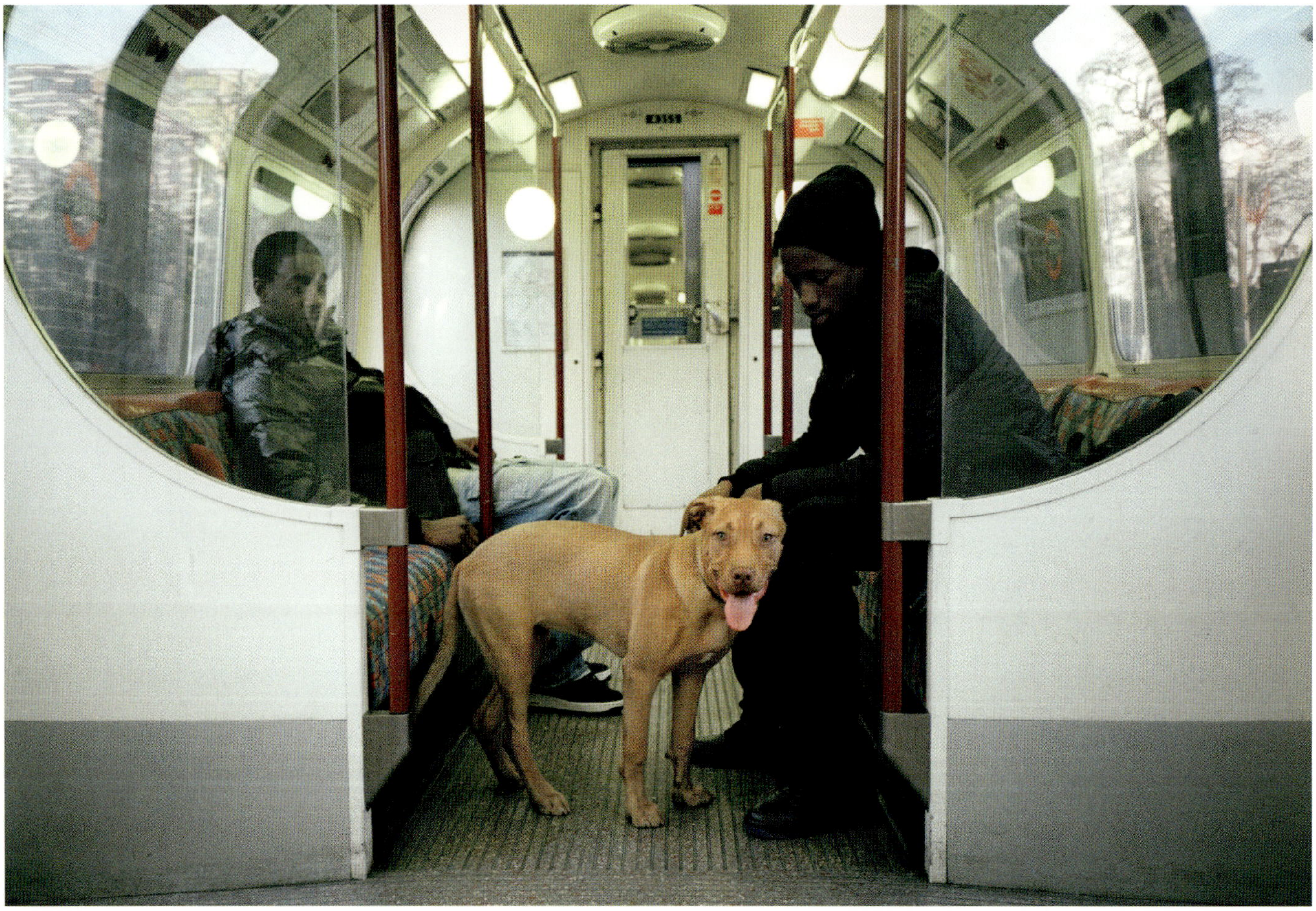

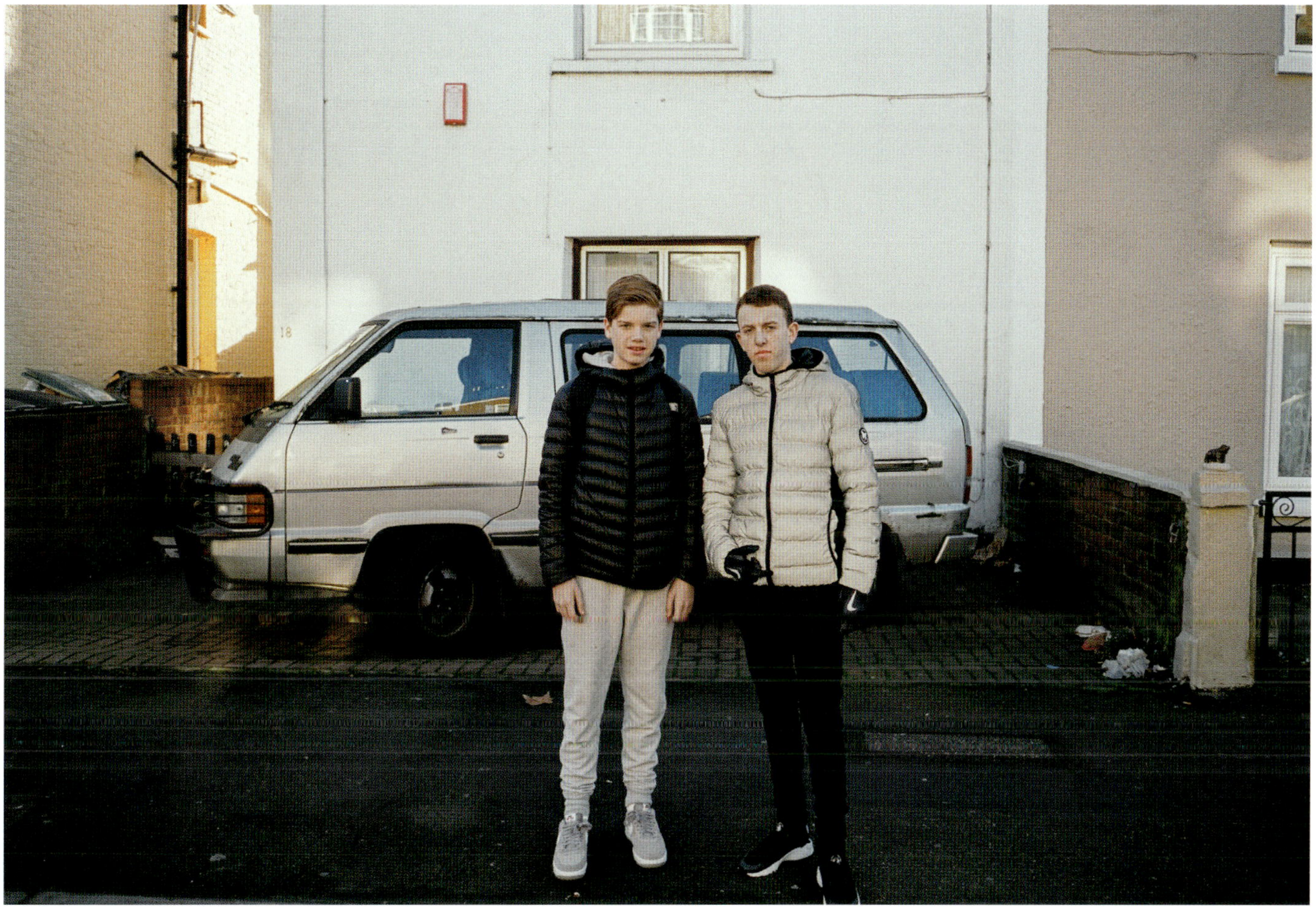

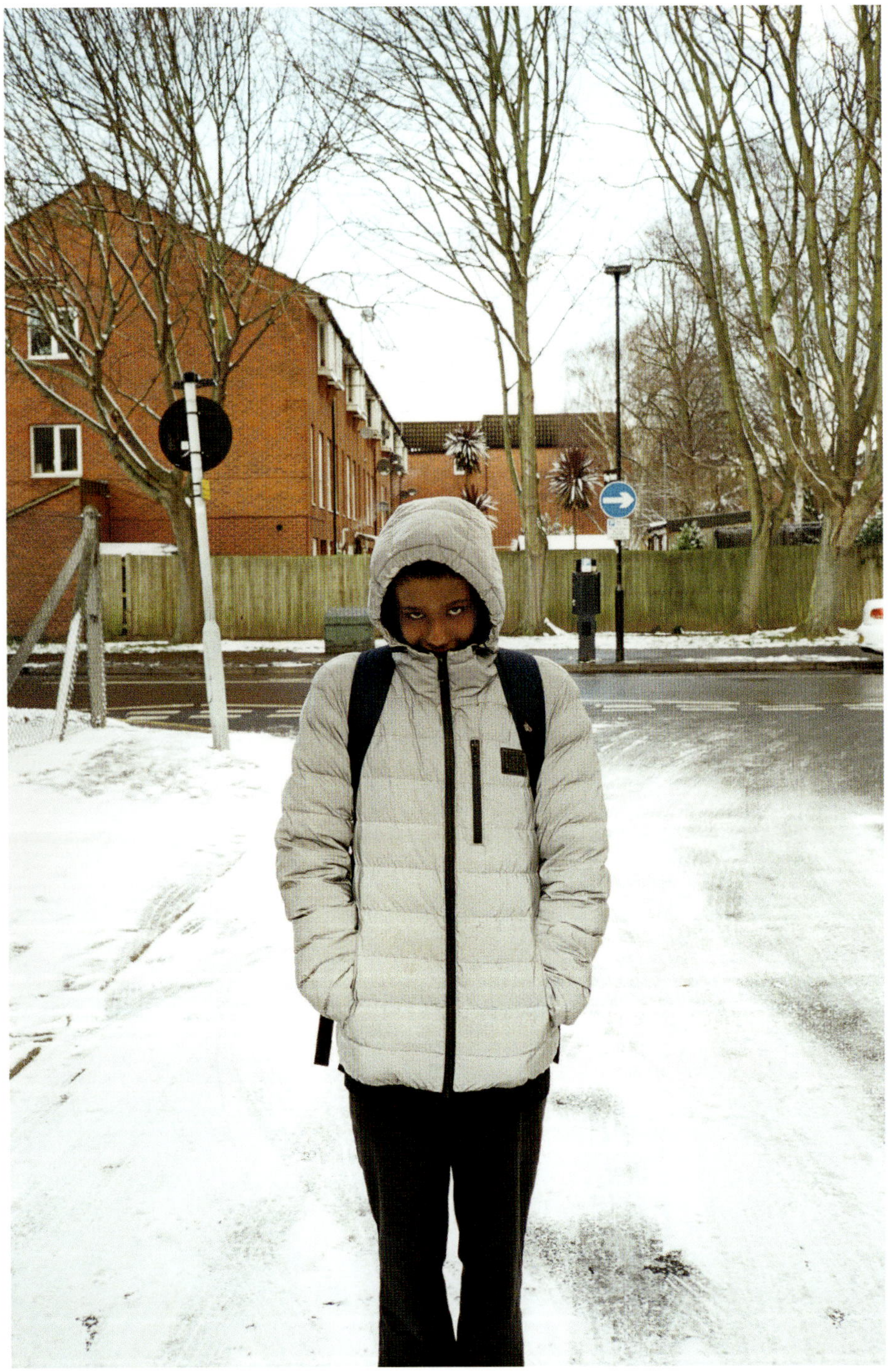

"Gonna have a snowball fight"

"School's shut because of the snow"

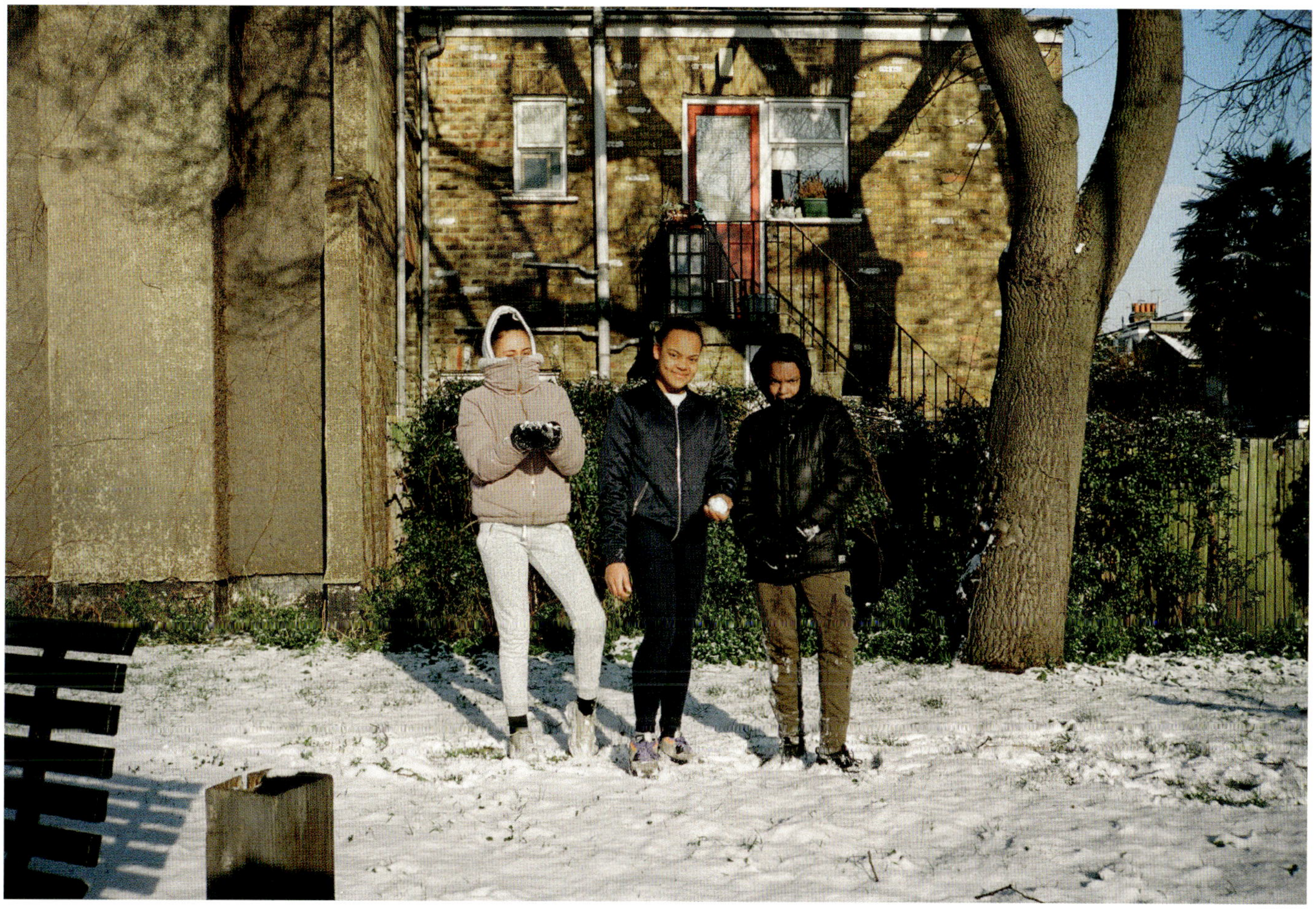

"Meeting my brother,
I've got the lunch money"

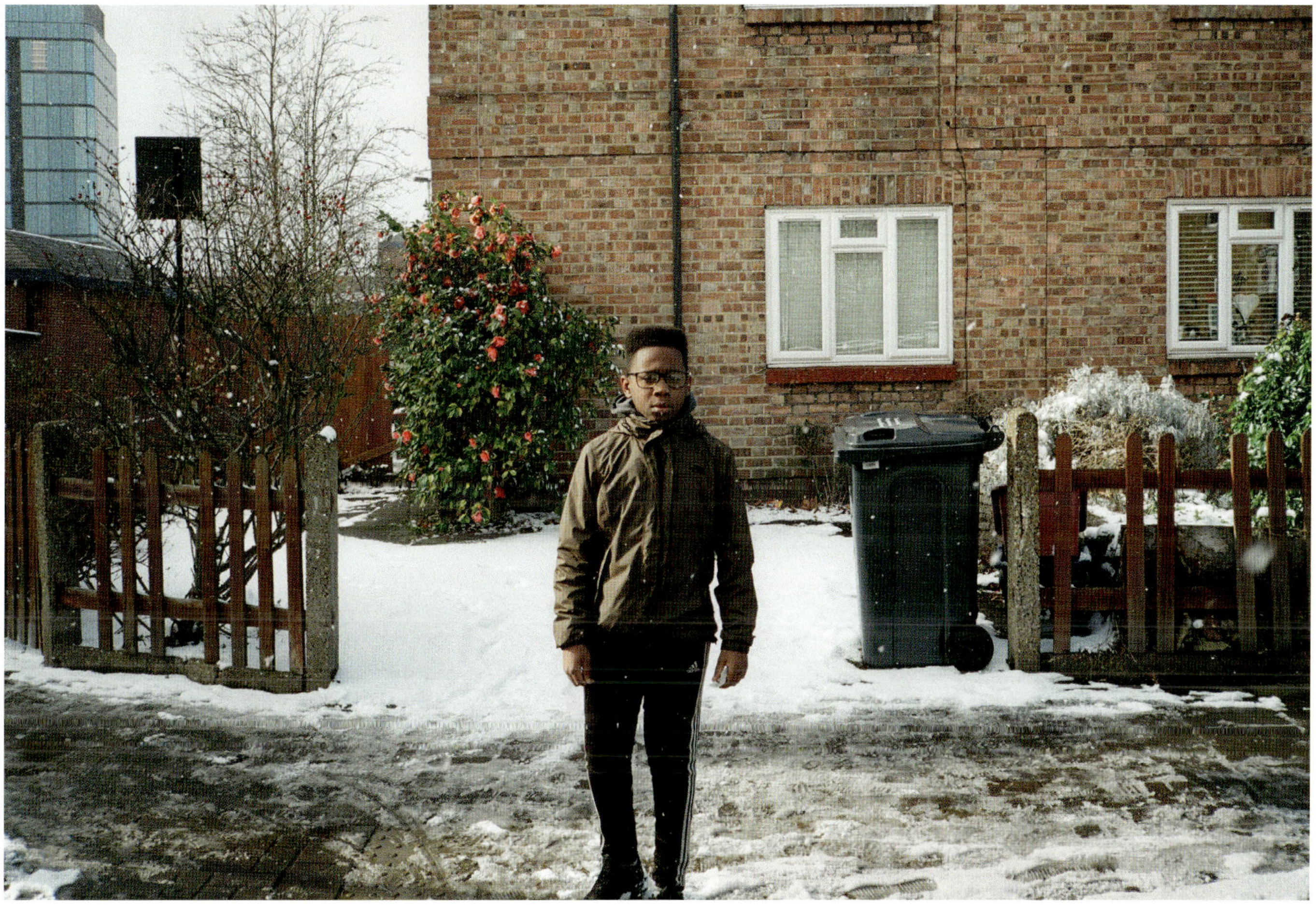

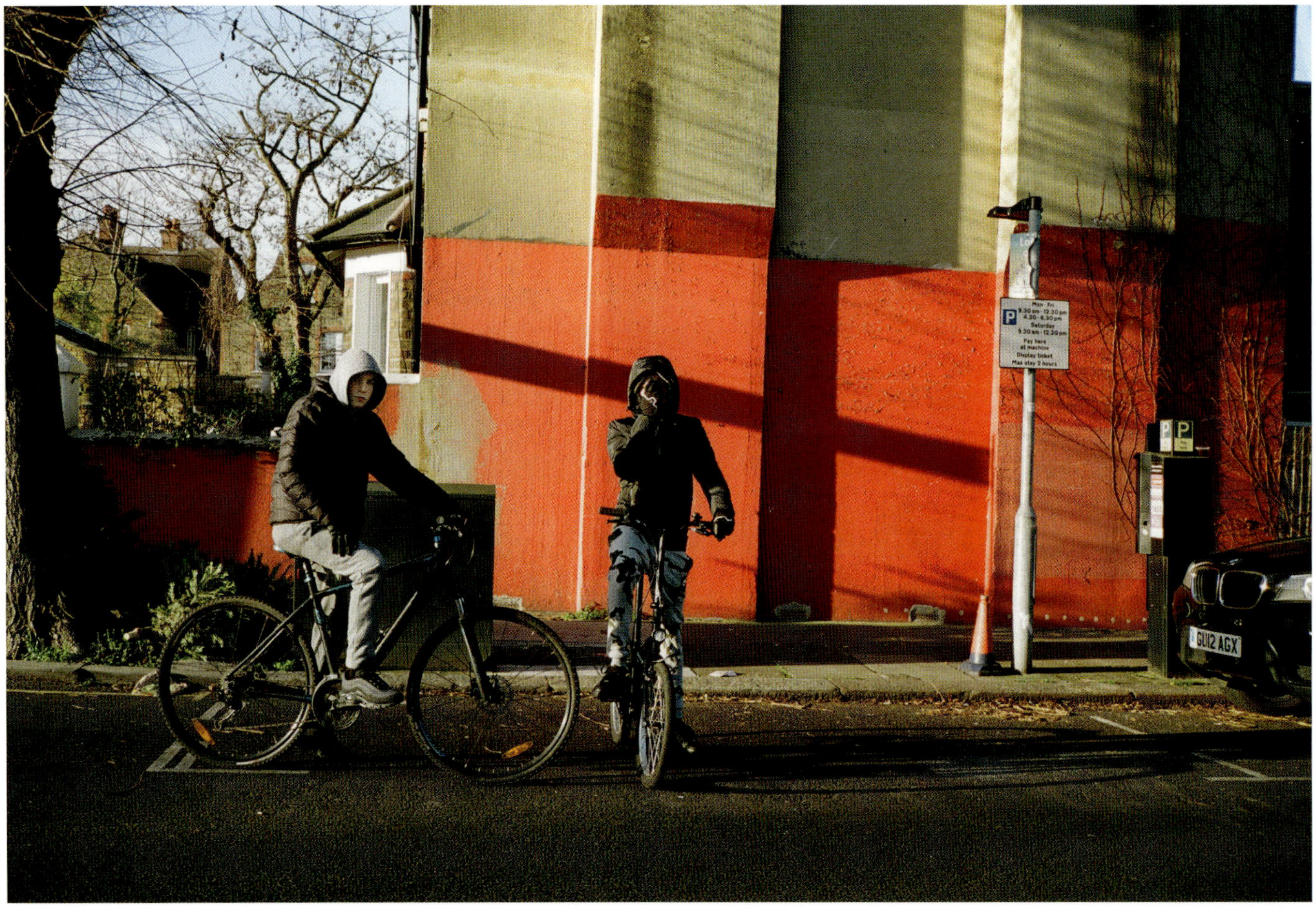
P
Mon - Fri
9.30 am - 12.30 pm
4.30 - 6.30 pm
Saturday
9.30 am - 12.30 pm
Pay here
at machine
Display ticket
Max stay 2 hours
GU12 AGX

"Want me to do a wheelie?"

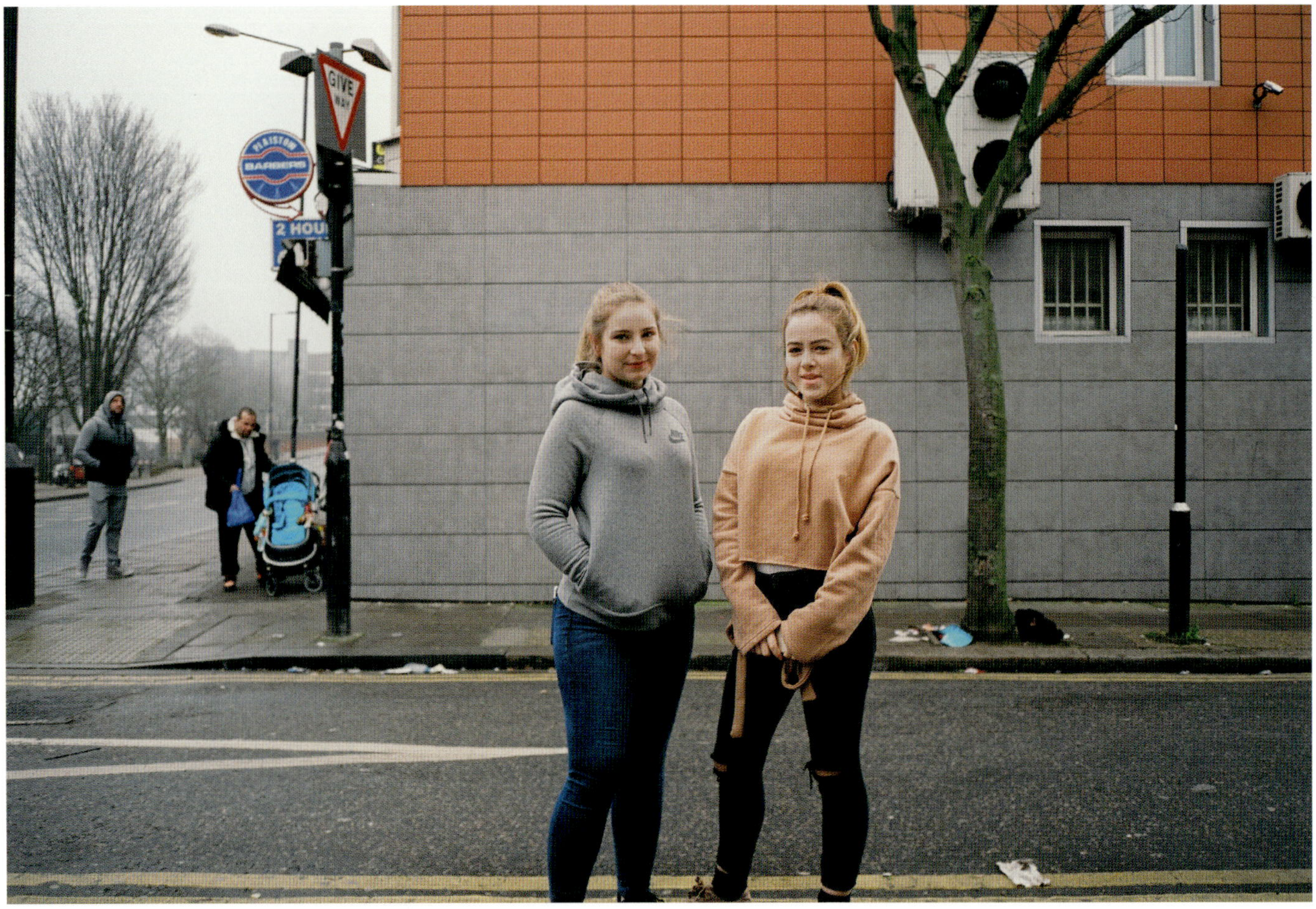
GIVE
WAY
PLAISTOW
BARBERS

"A lot of pressure
to have the right phone,
the right brands.
School?
It's more like a fashion show"

"Haven't even done my make up yet,
you know"

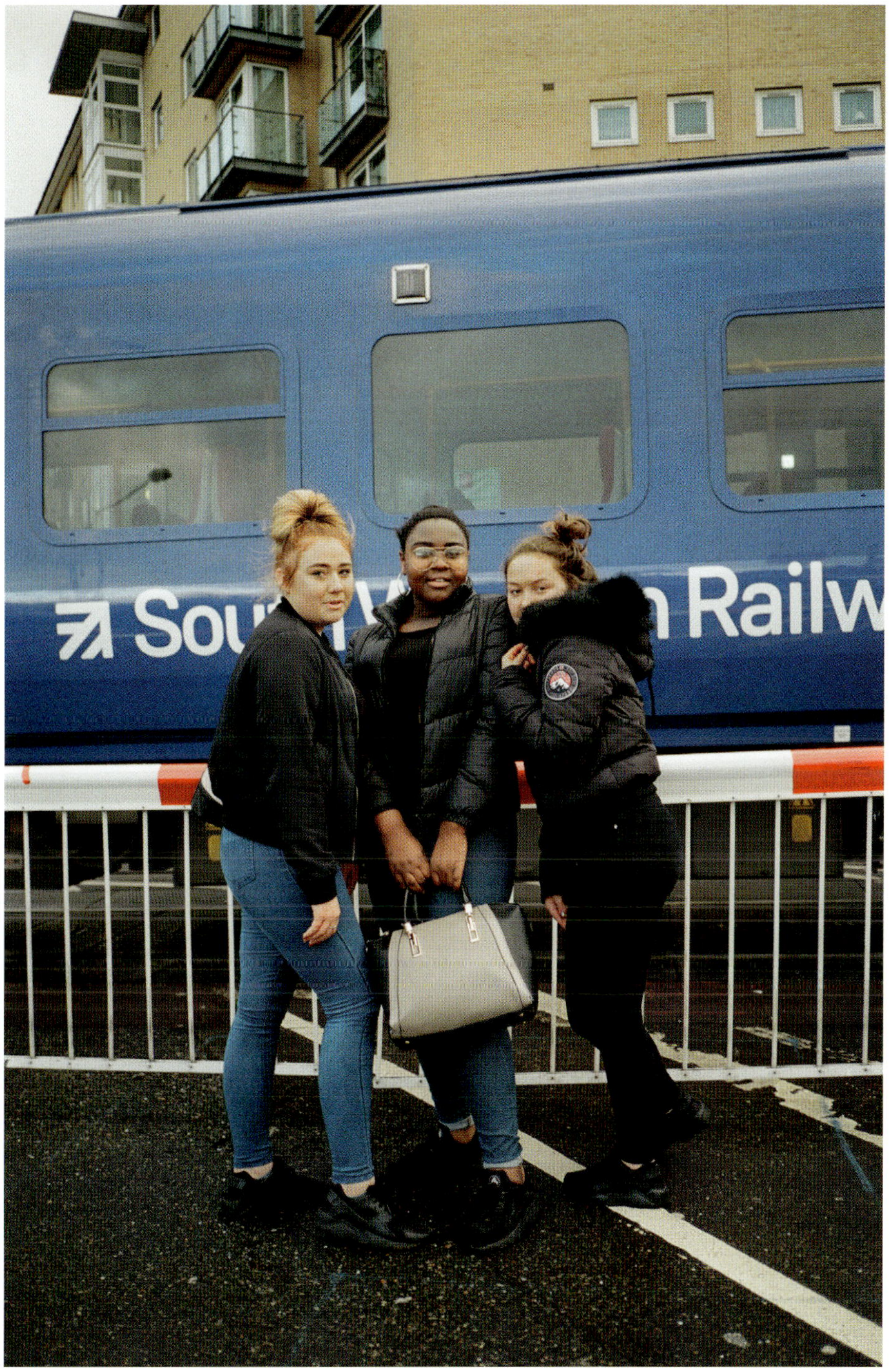

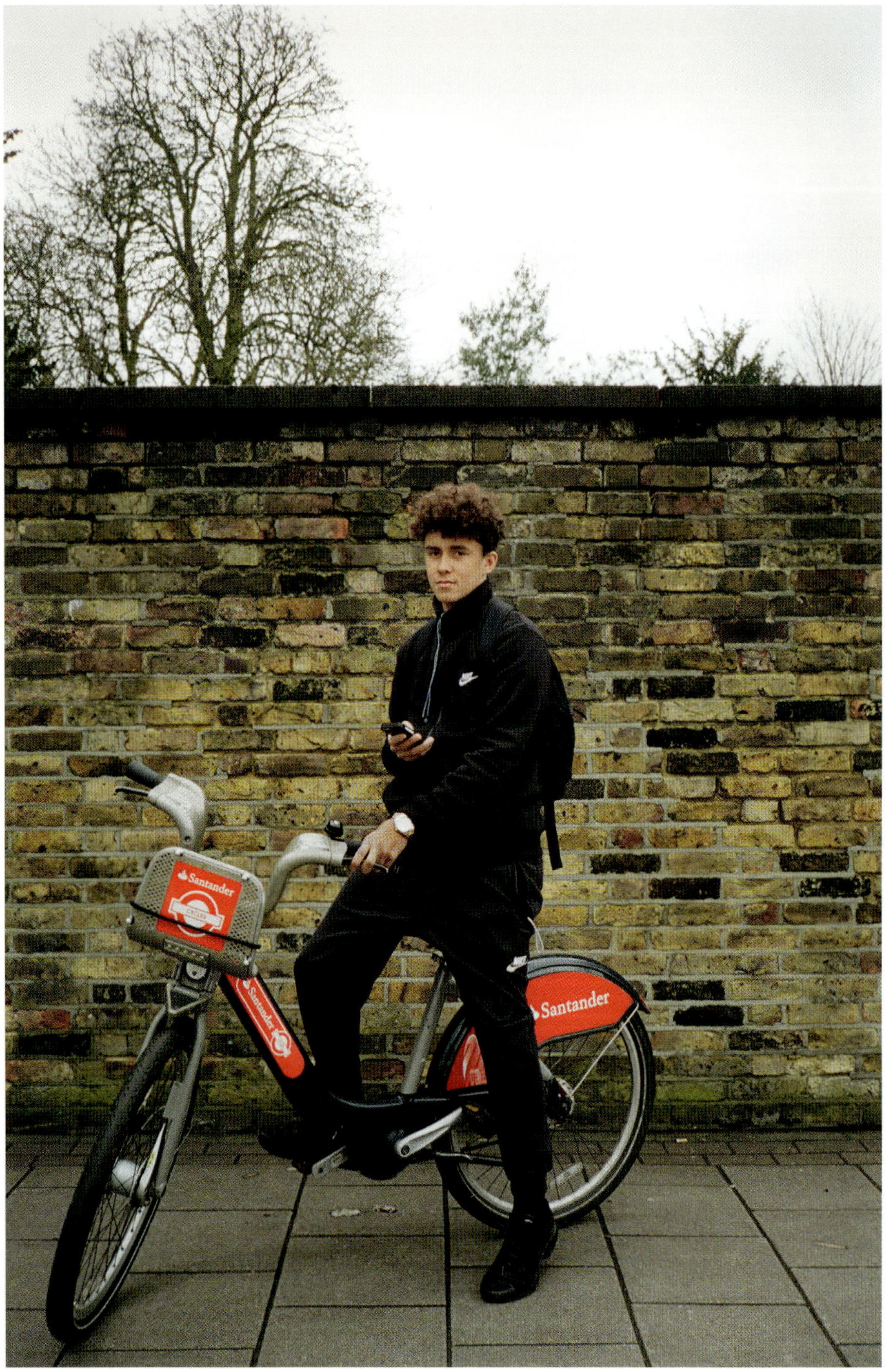
Santander
Santander
Santander

"I want to be an Aircraft Engineer"

"I'm doing Business at Cambridge,
just got back to London
visiting my mum"

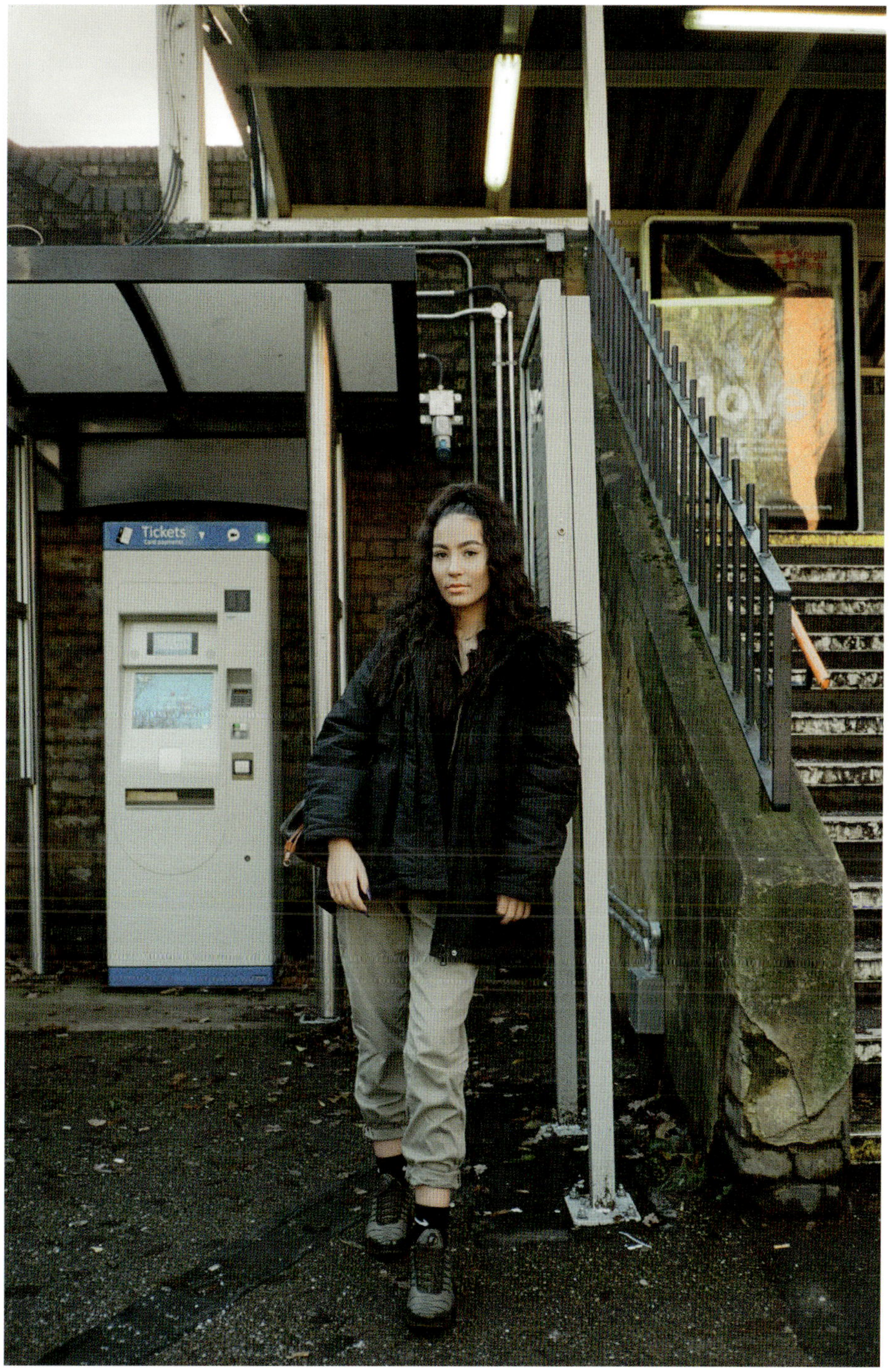
Tickets

"It's almost like it's cool
to be Black at the moment"

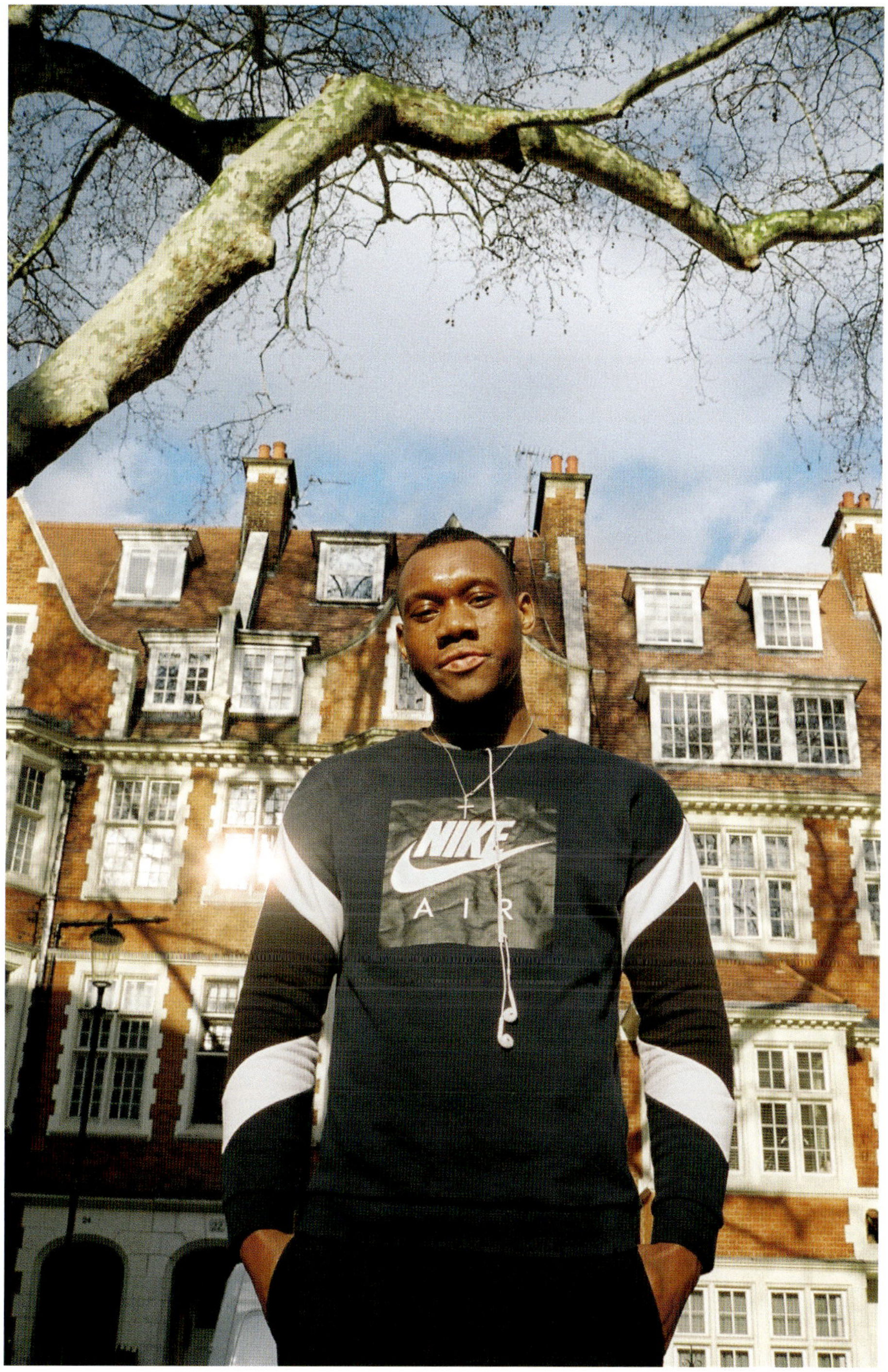
NIKE
AIR

"I'm doing ICT at college"

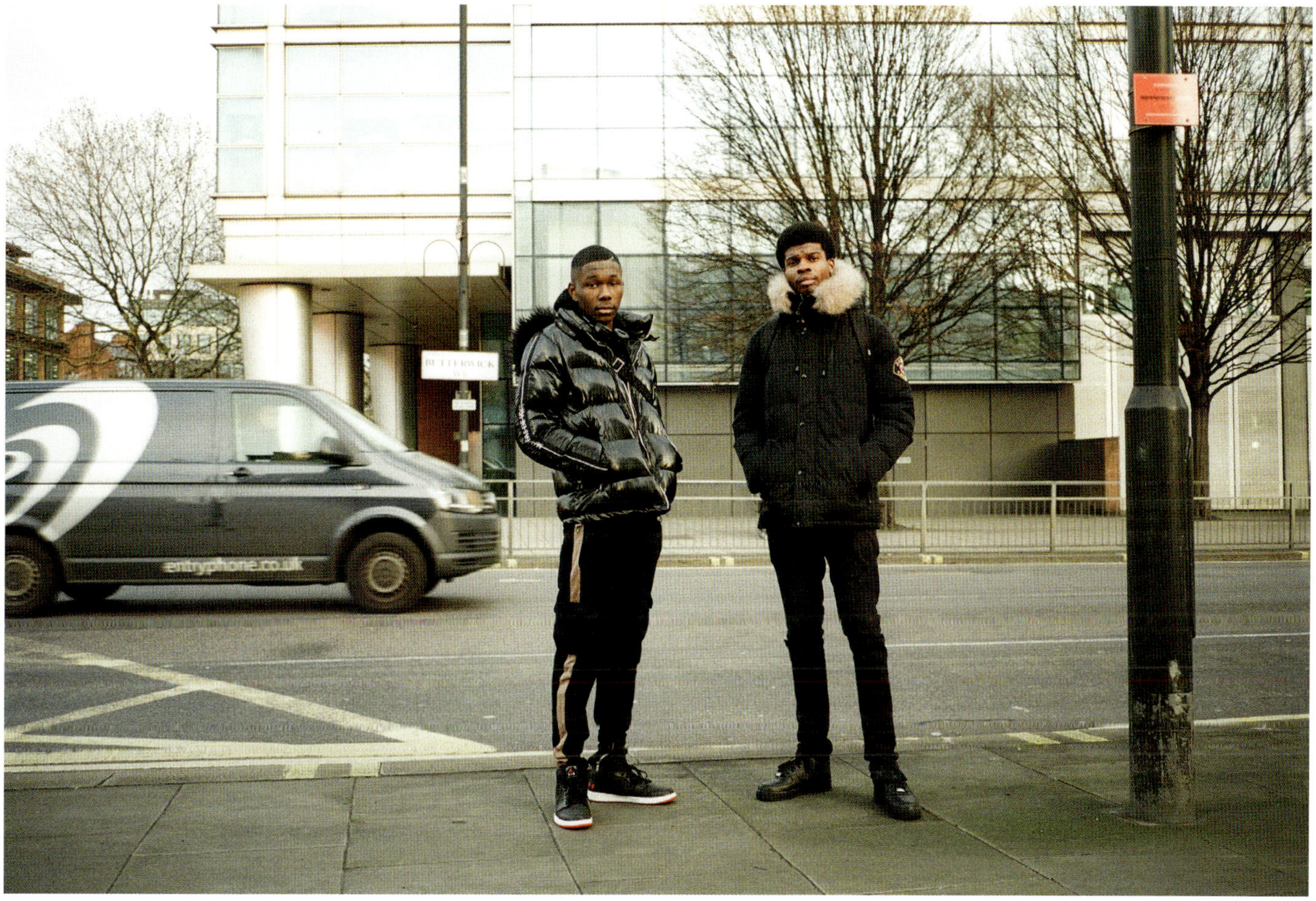
entryphone.co.uk

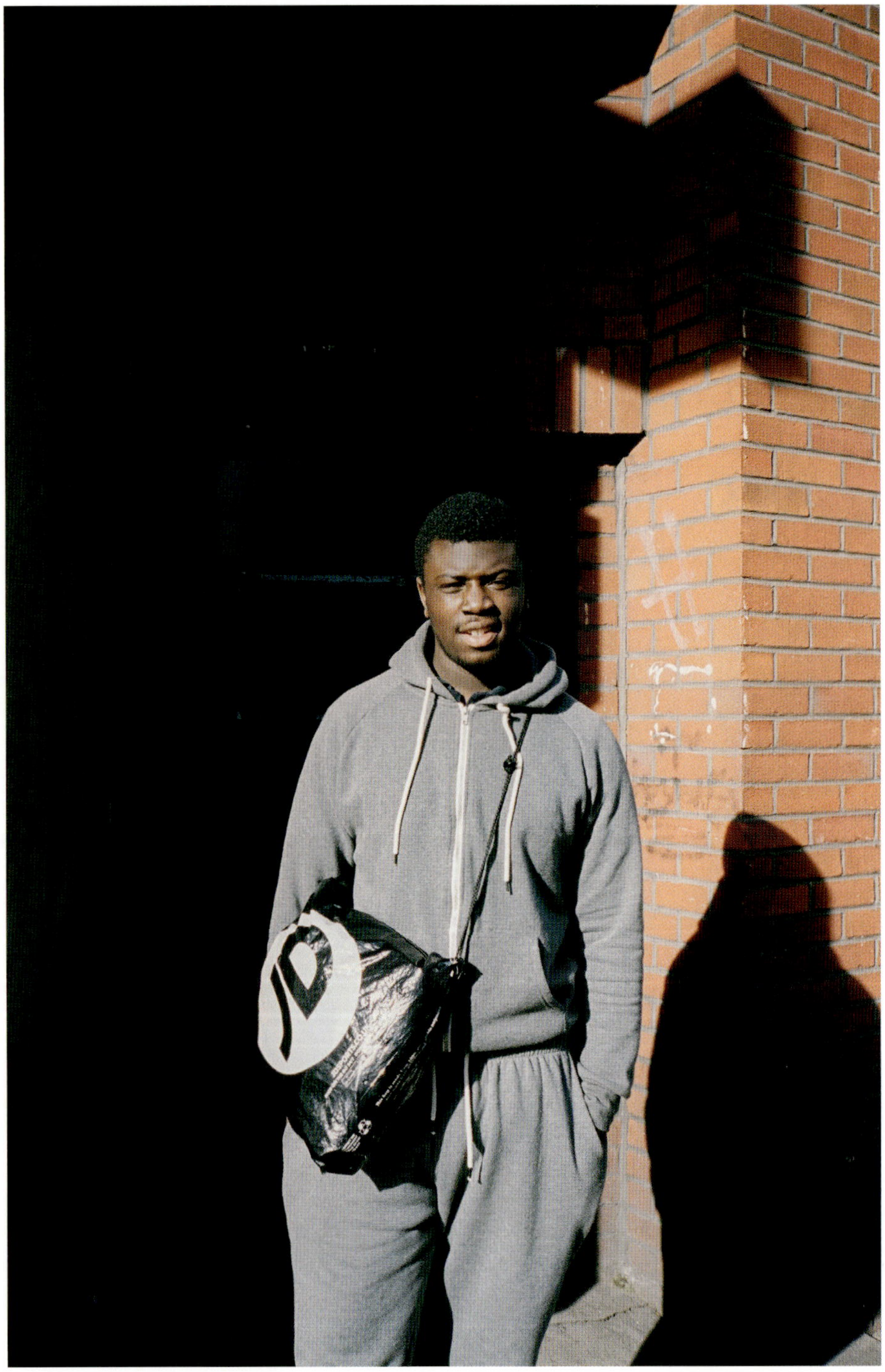

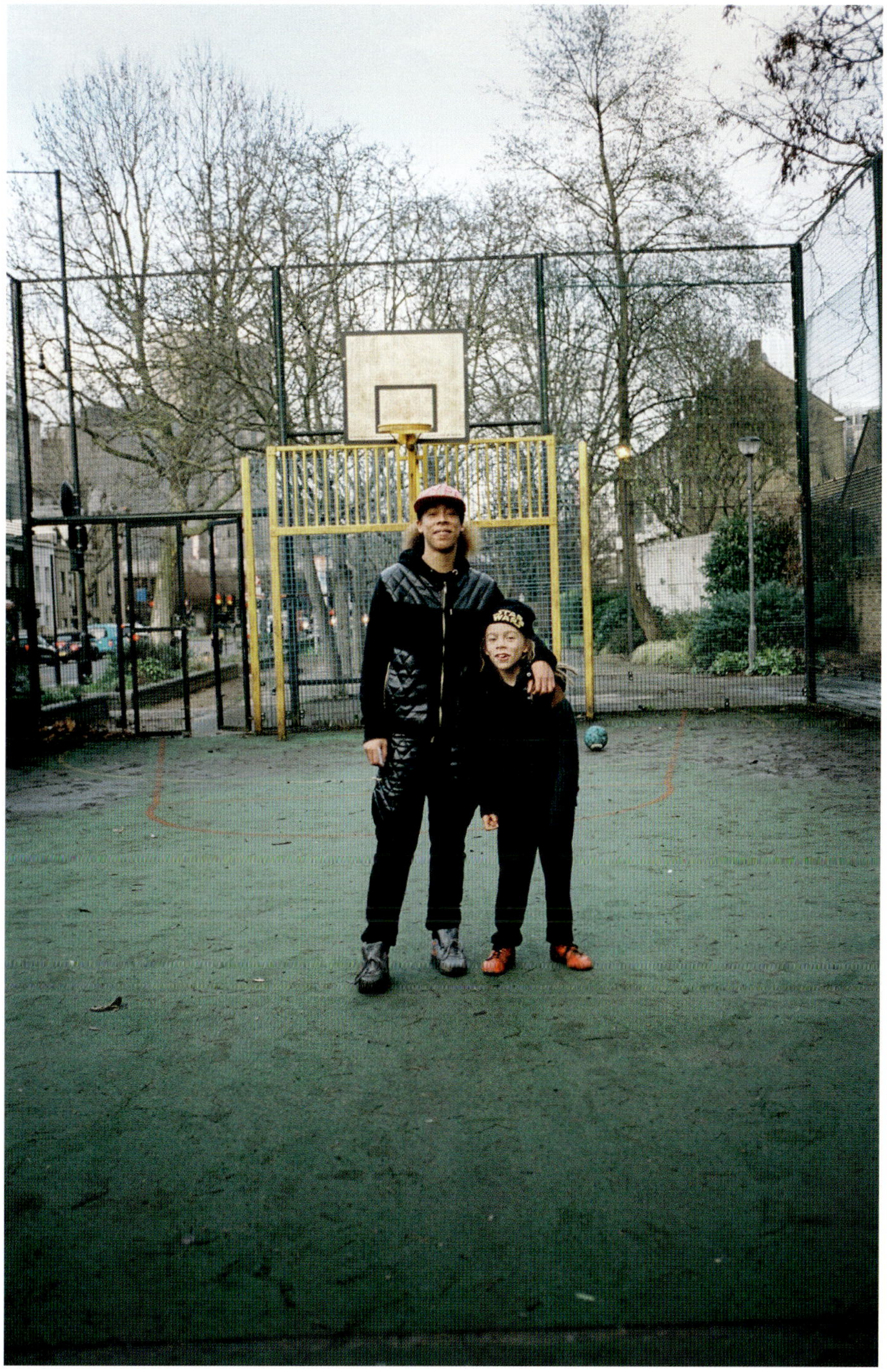

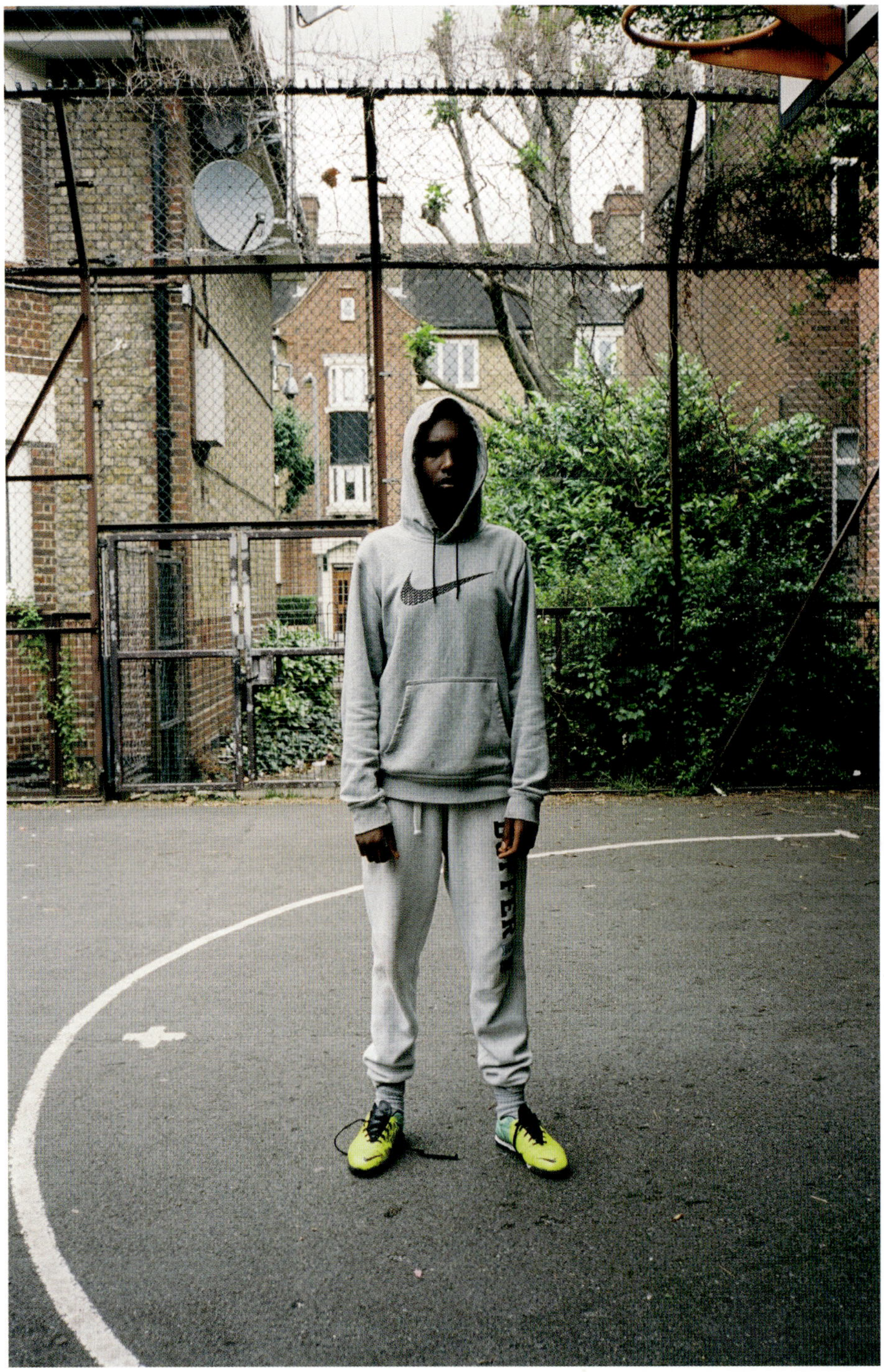

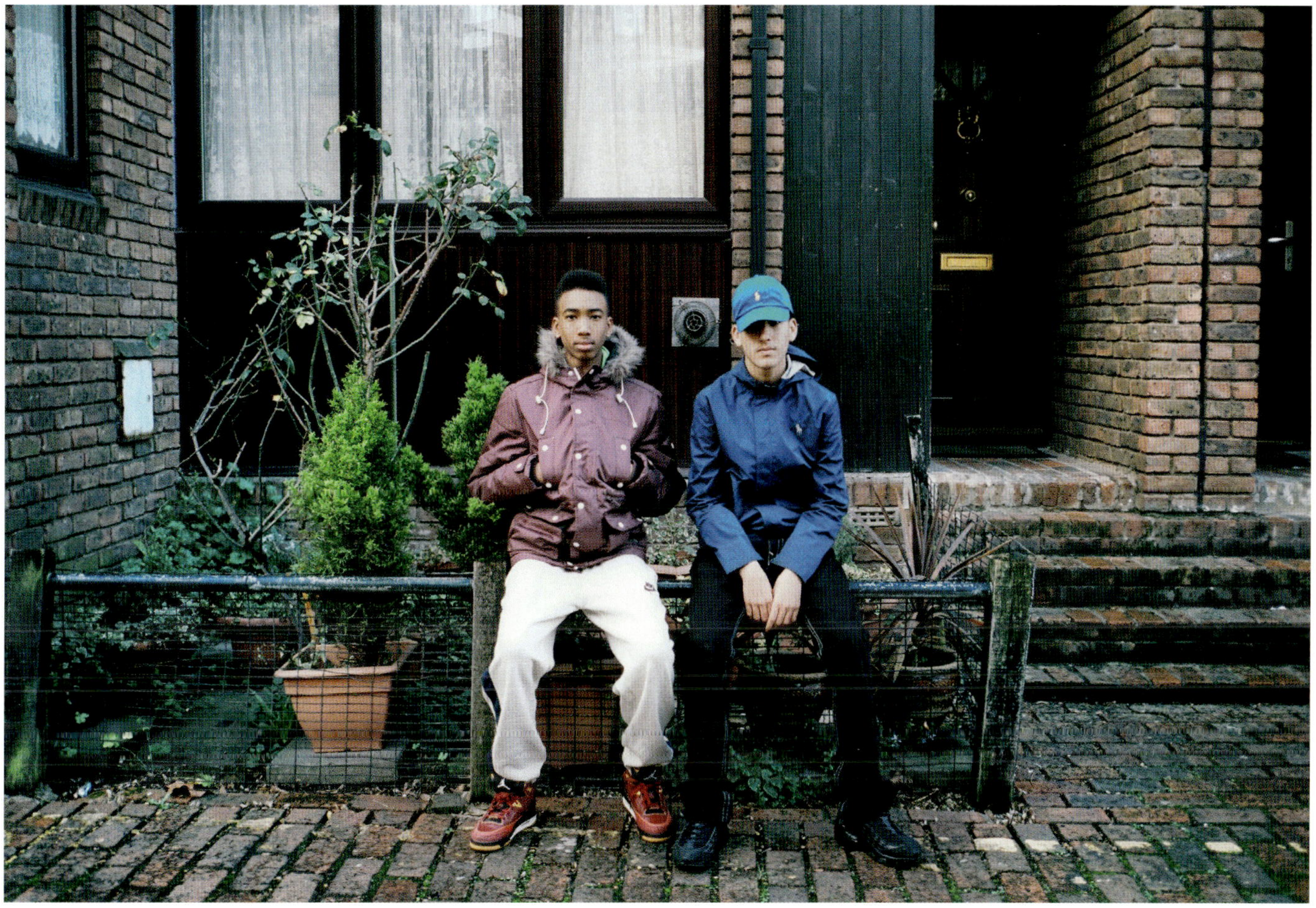

"I get out of London,
I go see mates in Birmingham,
Essex,
Manchester"

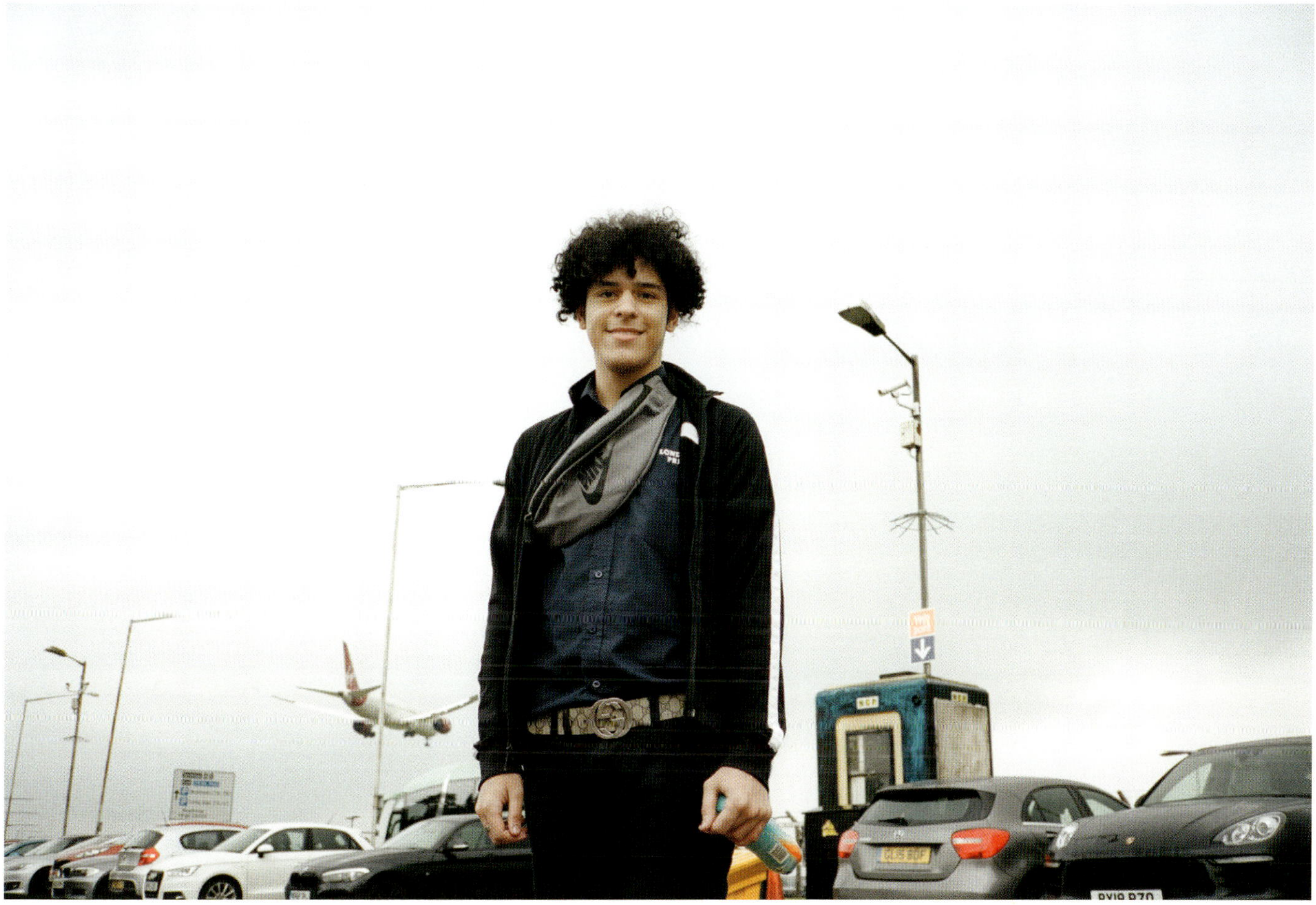

"I got these trainers for Christmas"

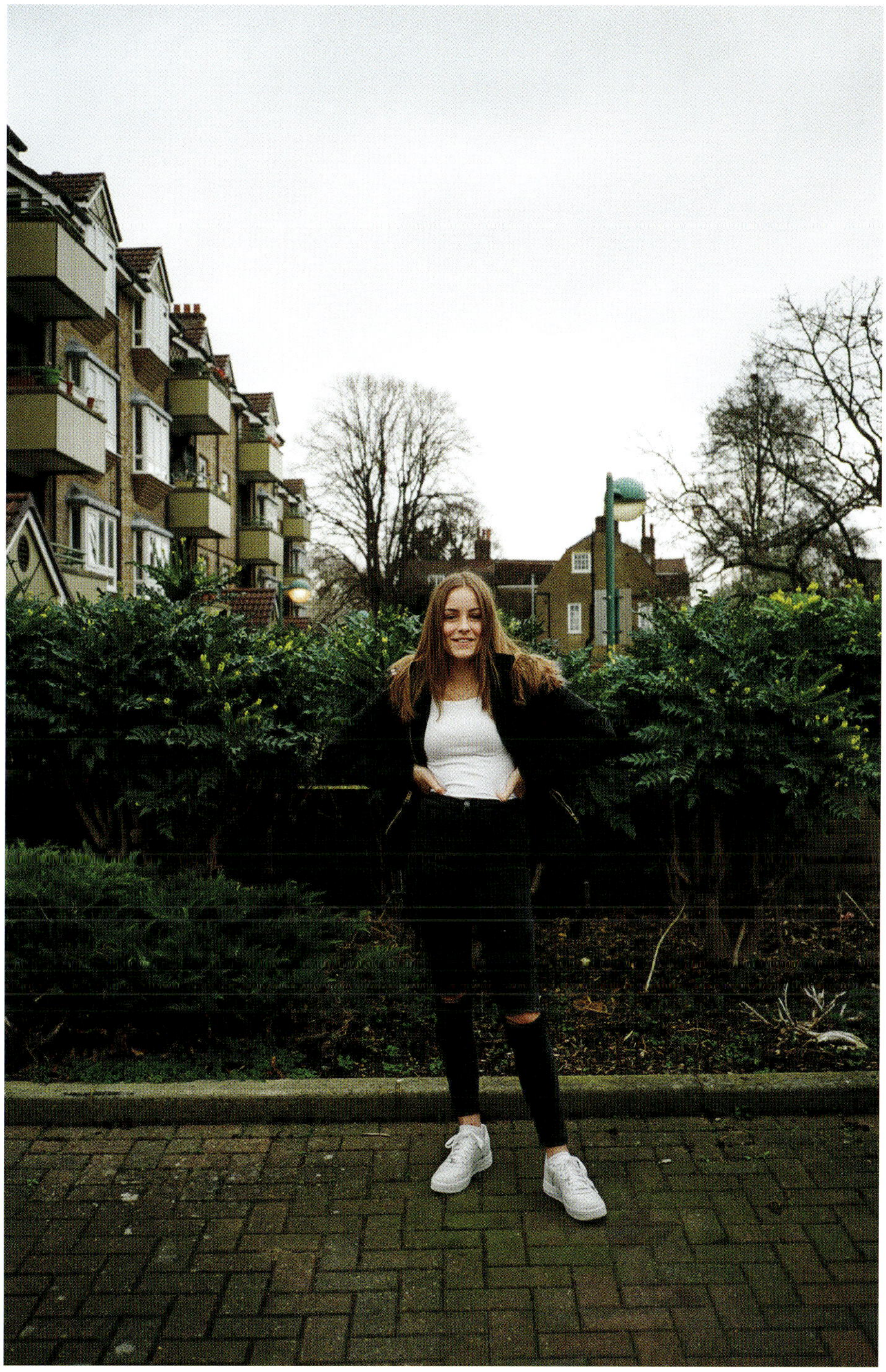

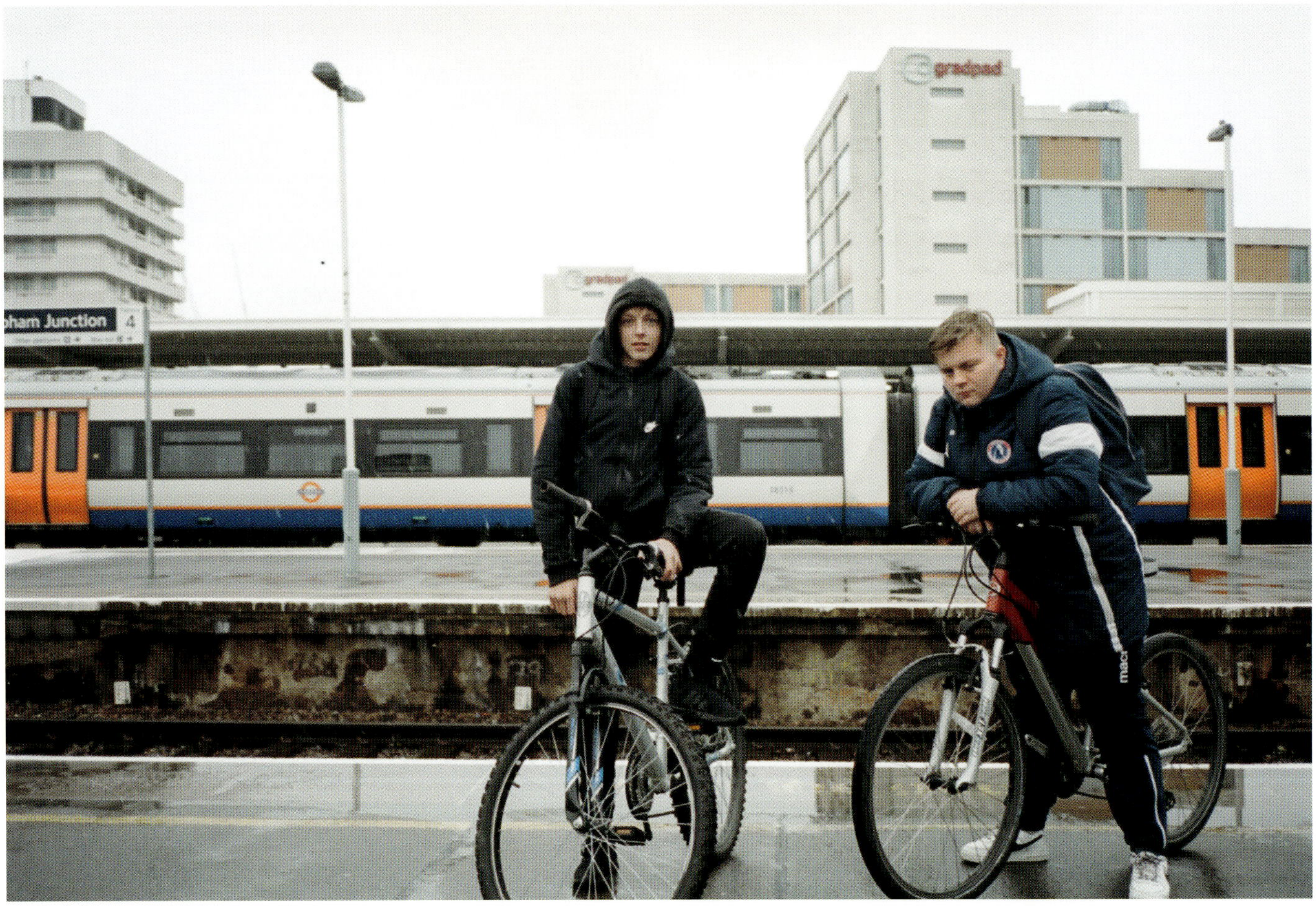
gradpad
pham Junction
4

"We're going Hounslow"

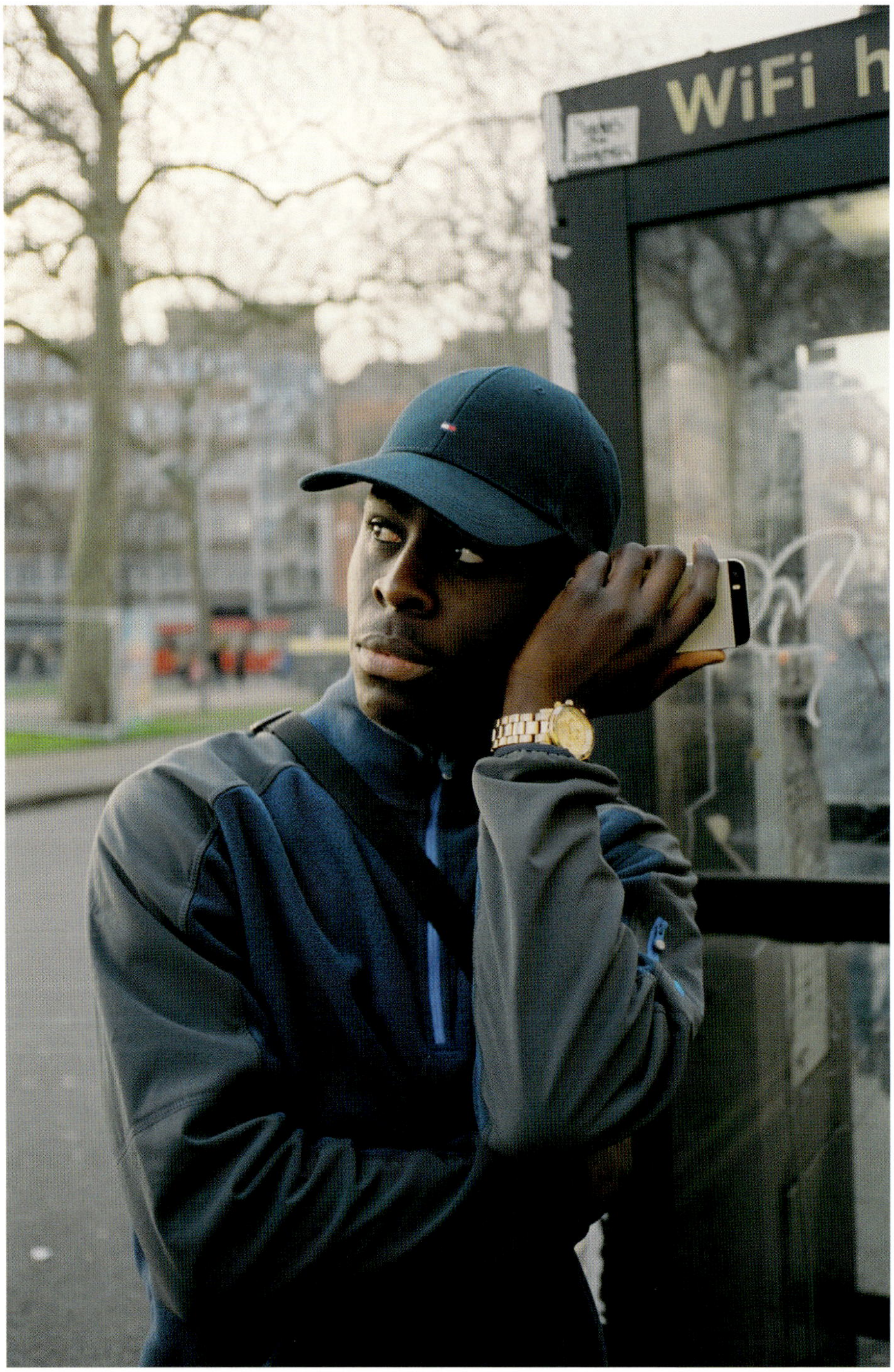
WiFi h

"Just meeting a mate"

*"It was good up until
a few years ago,
boys started getting stupid
and thinking they were brave
with stupid postcode wars"*

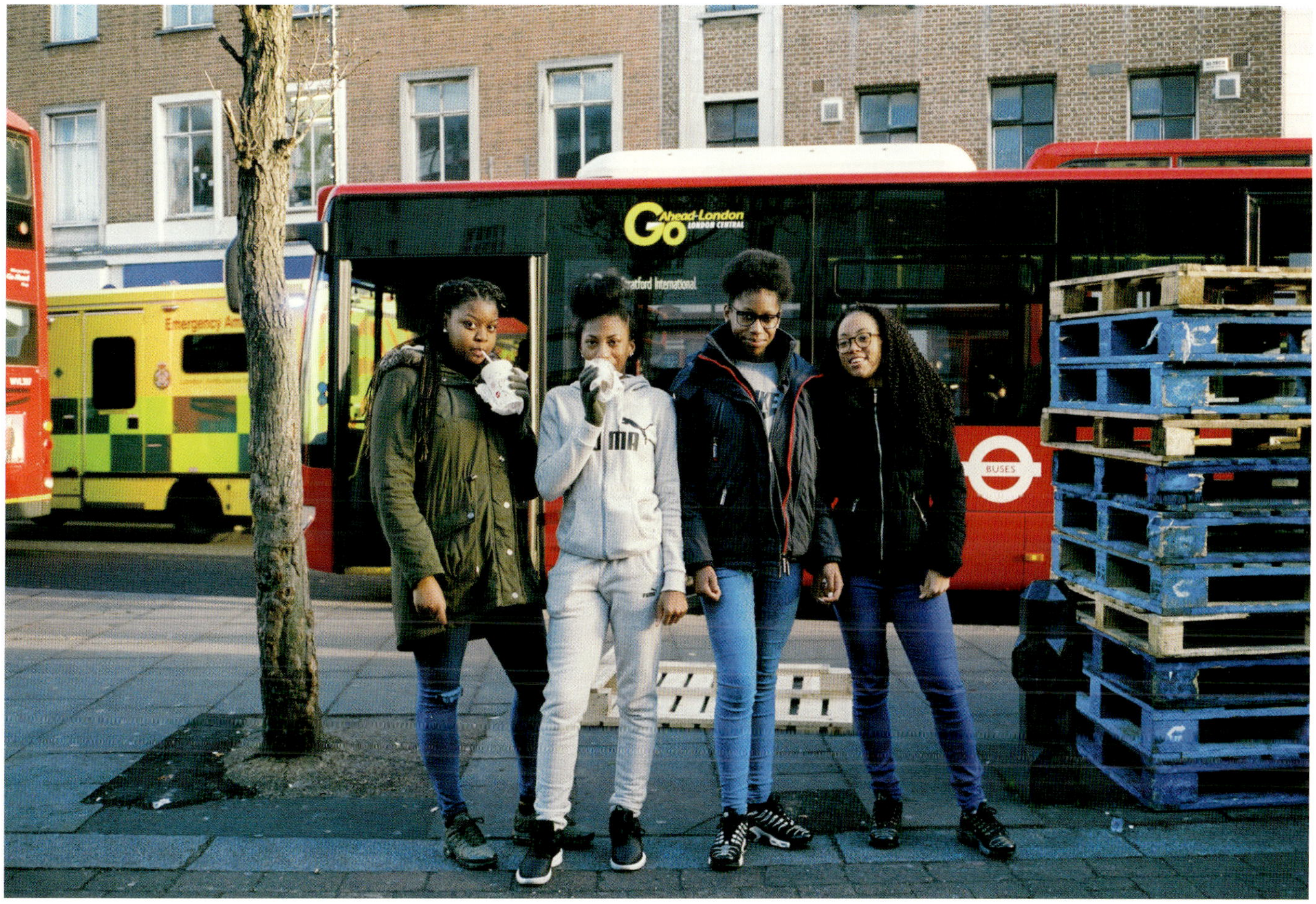
Go Ahead-London
LONDON CENTRAL
BUSES

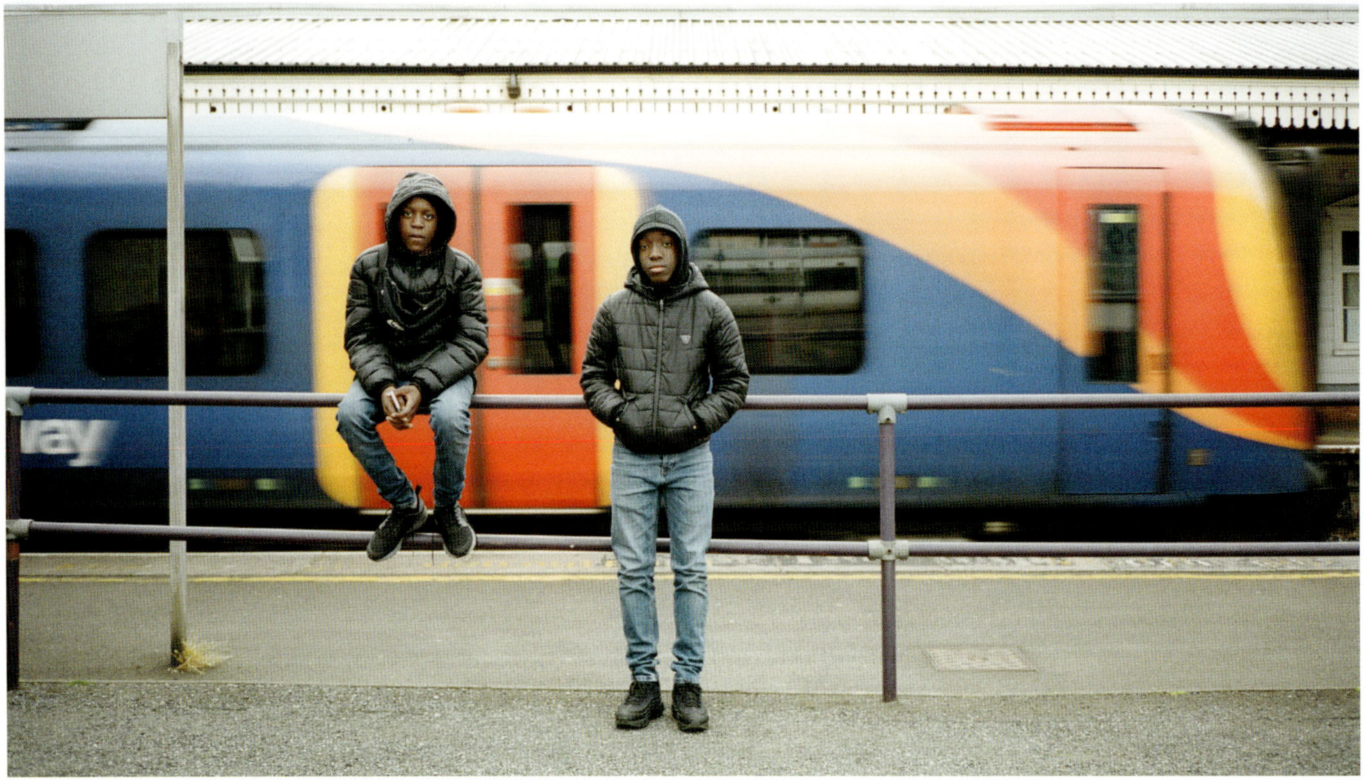

"Gonna be a Mechanical Engineer"

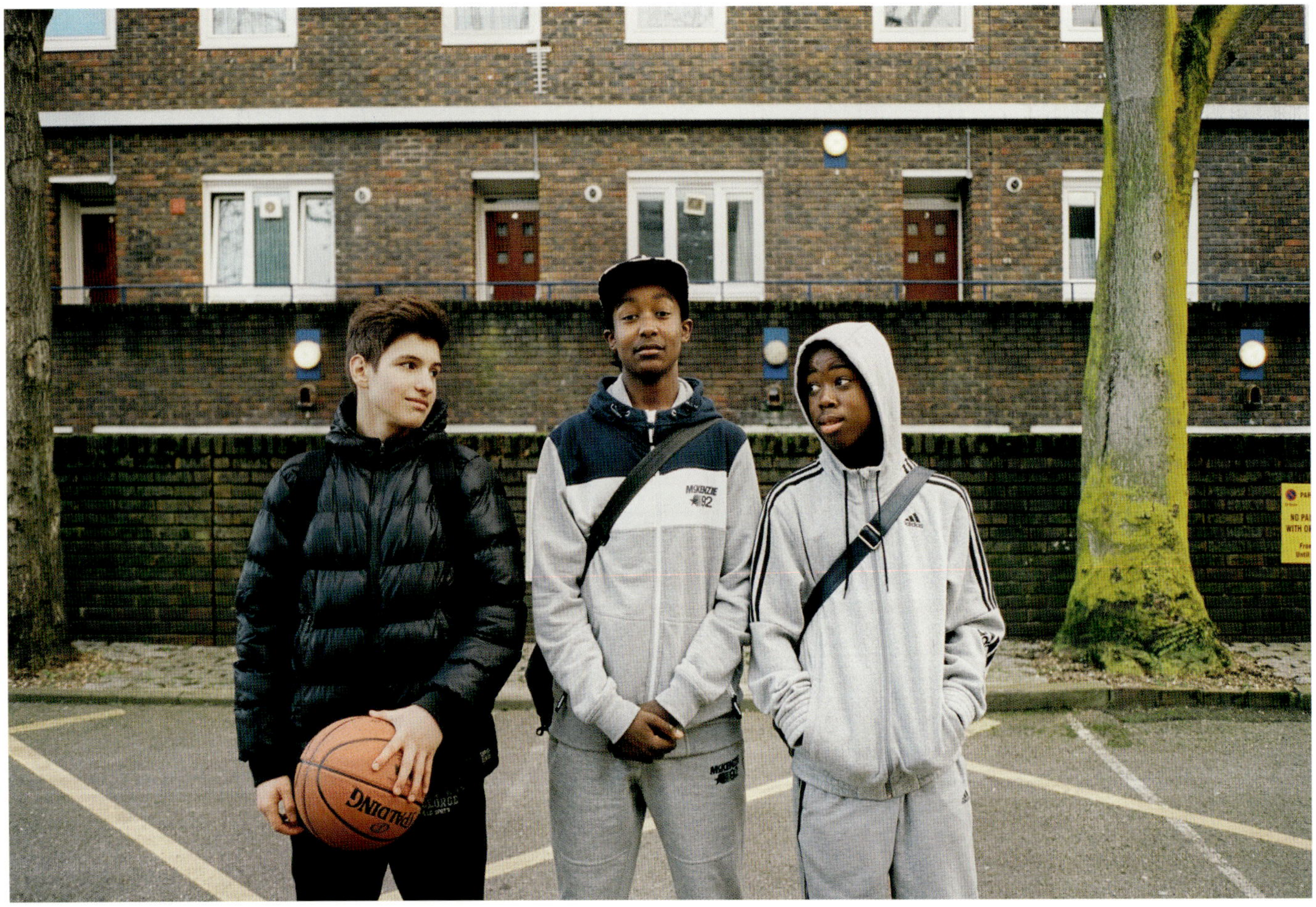

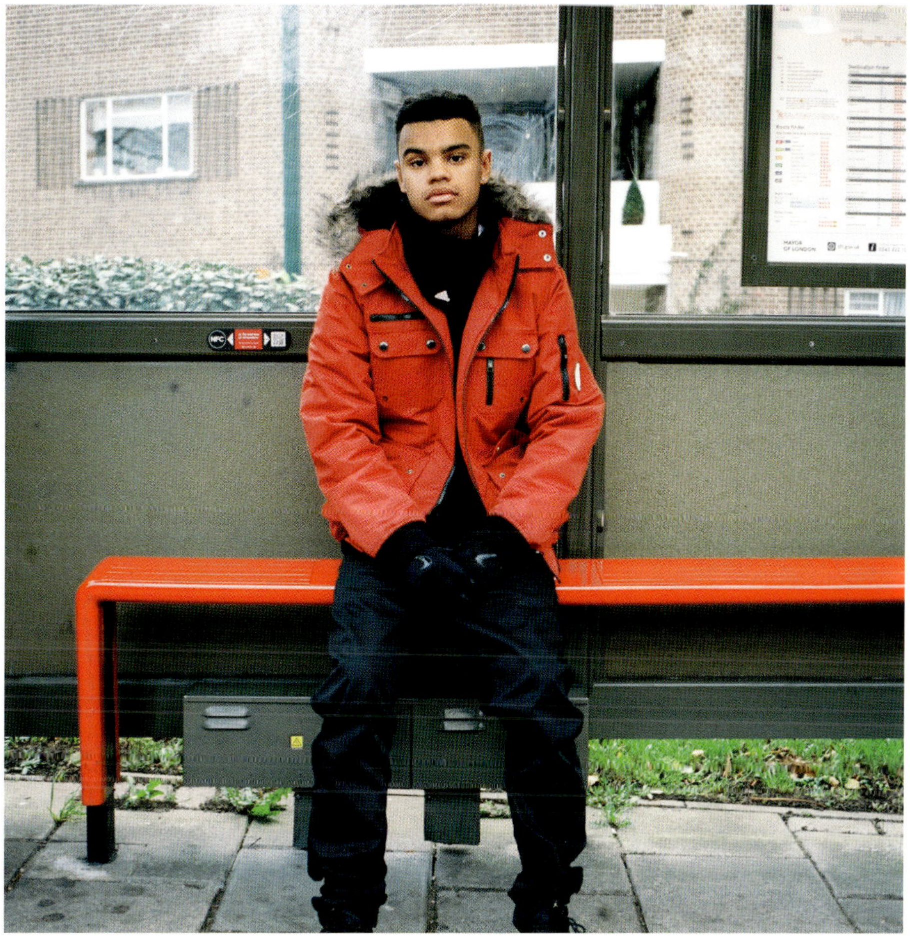

"I'll work for my dad's export company"

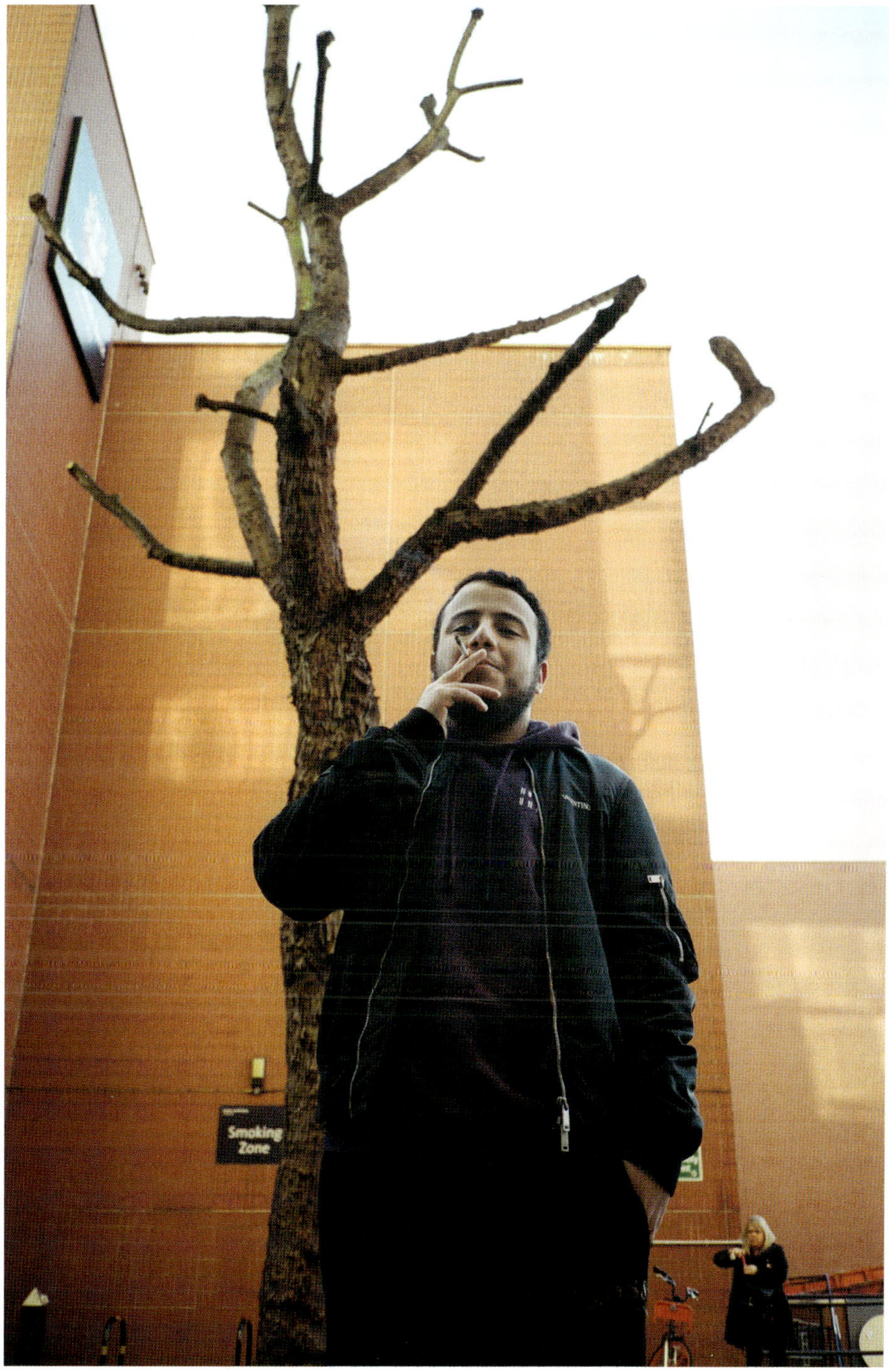
Smoking
Zone

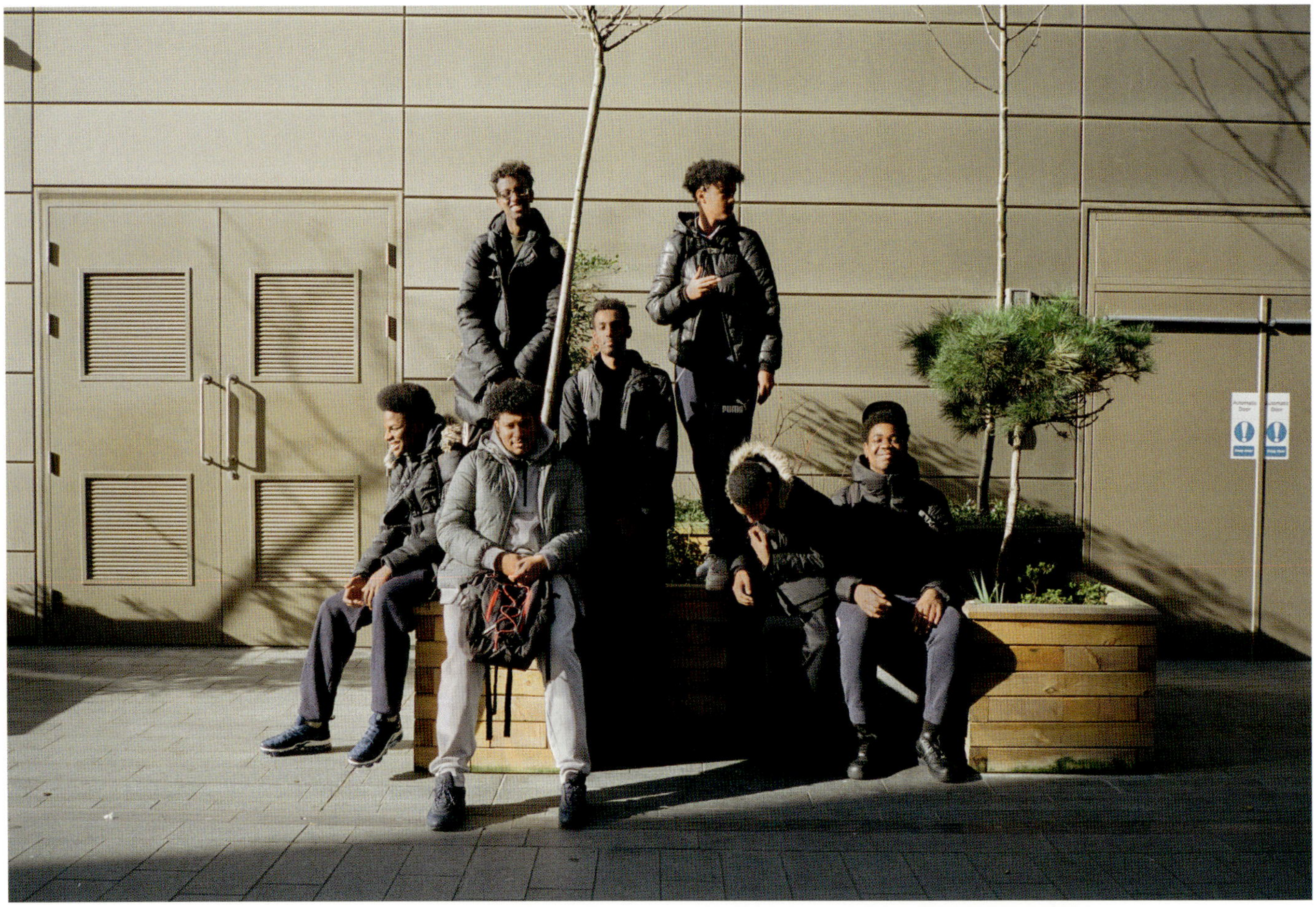

"Oi

don't touch up the trim, man"

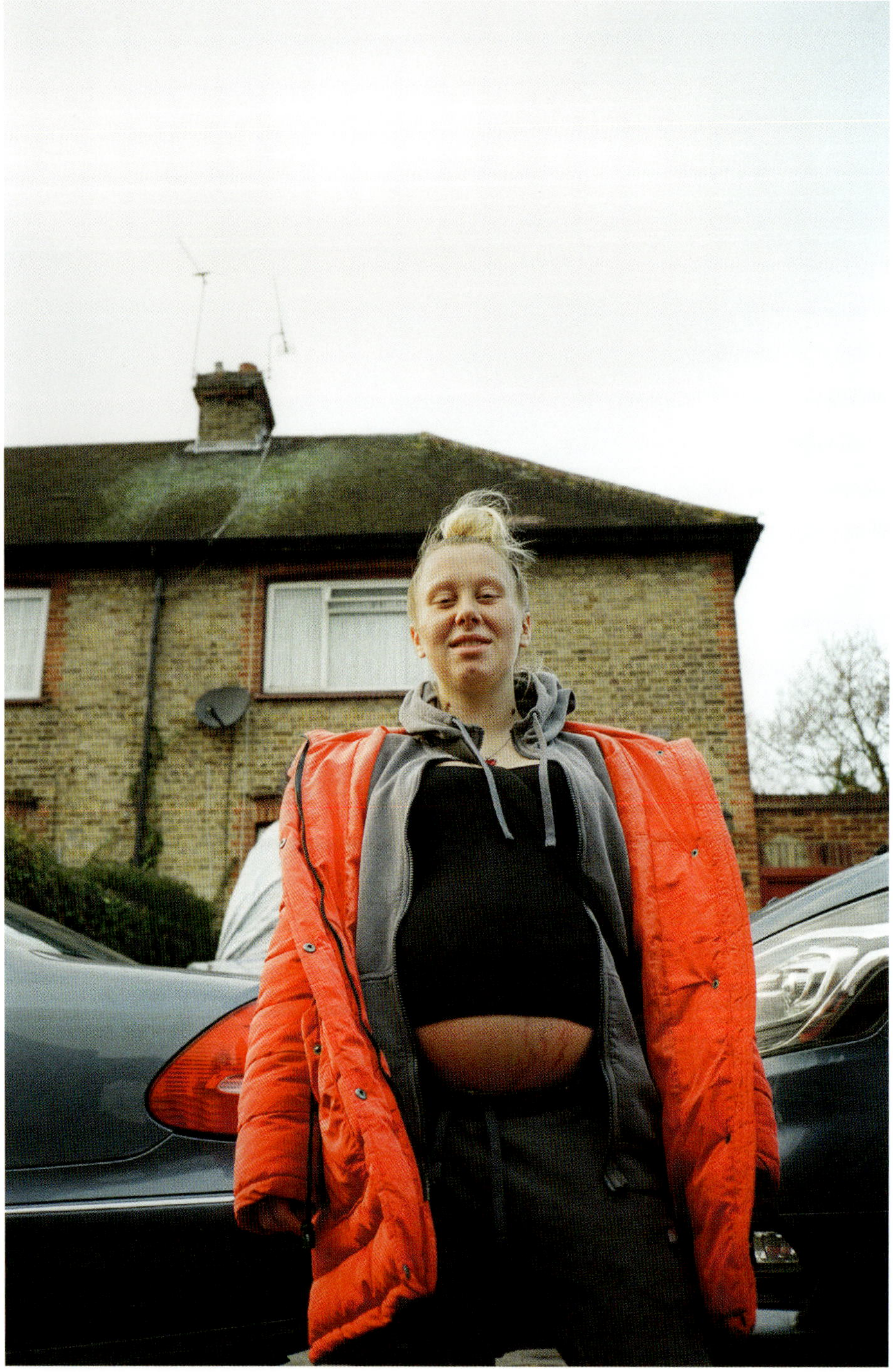

"Can't wait to meet my little baby
Brookie-Cookie"

"The trainers I wear
all depend on the mood I'm in"

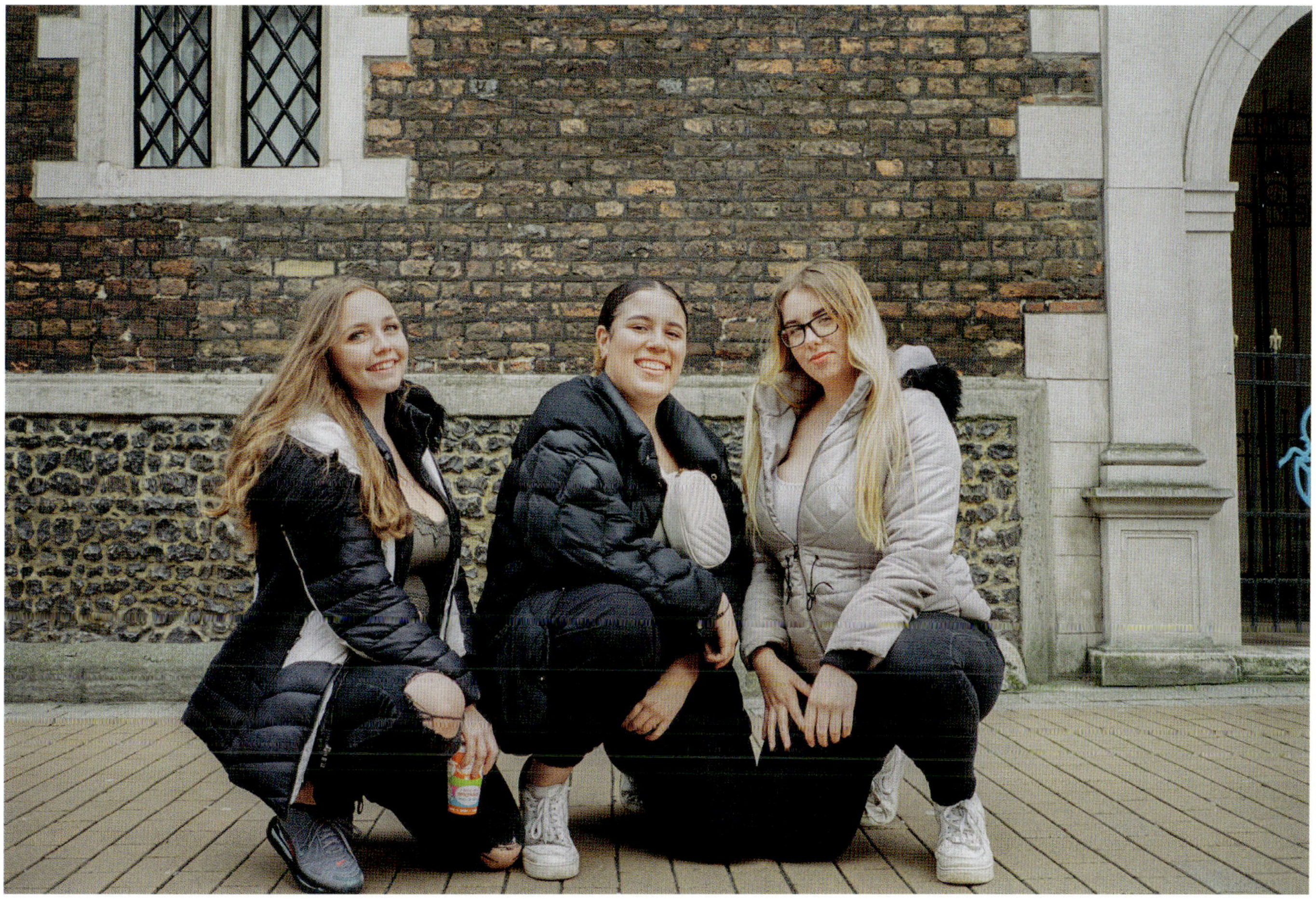

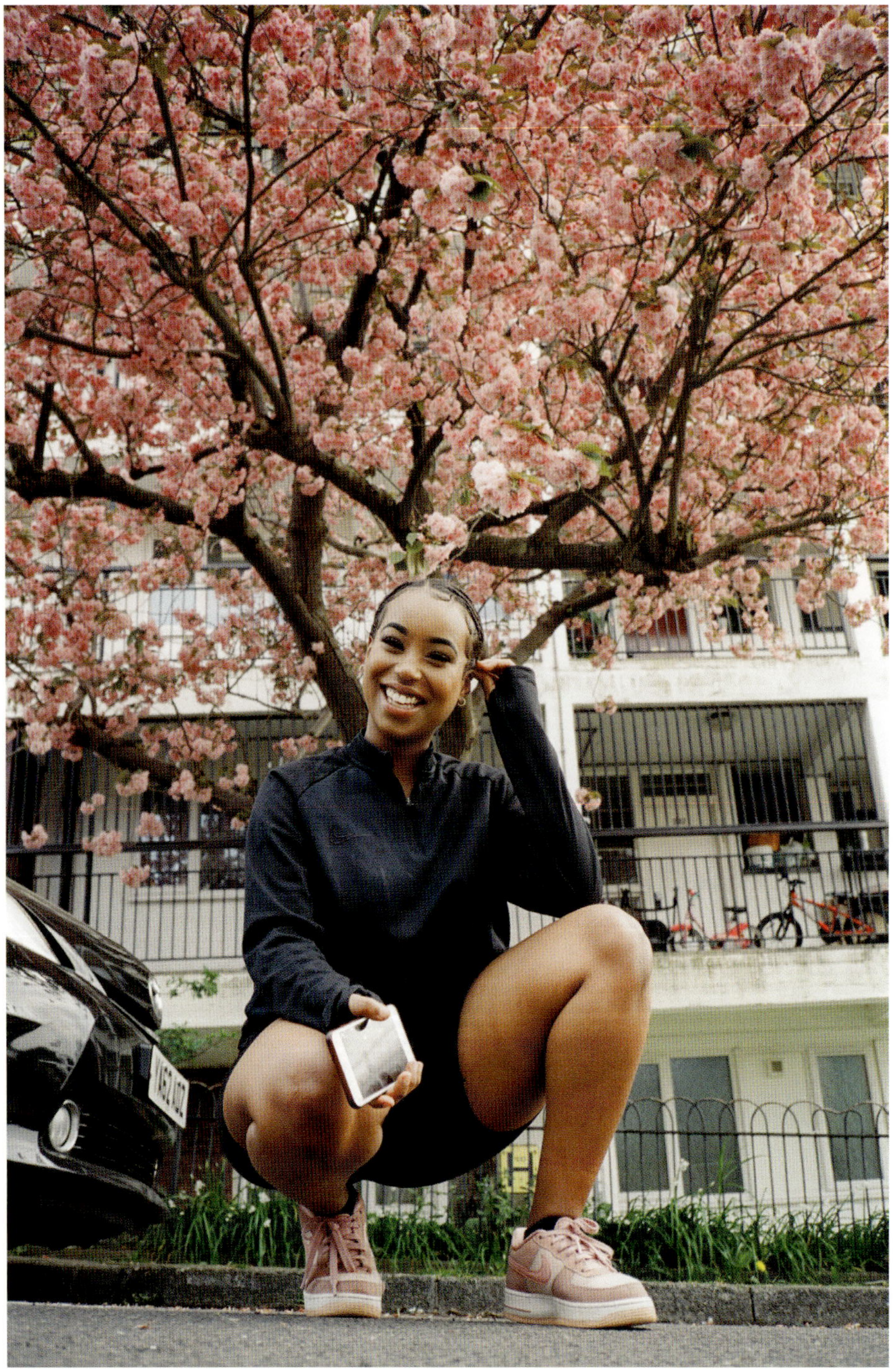

"There's a pandemic,
everything is shutting down,
it's getting kind of weird out here"

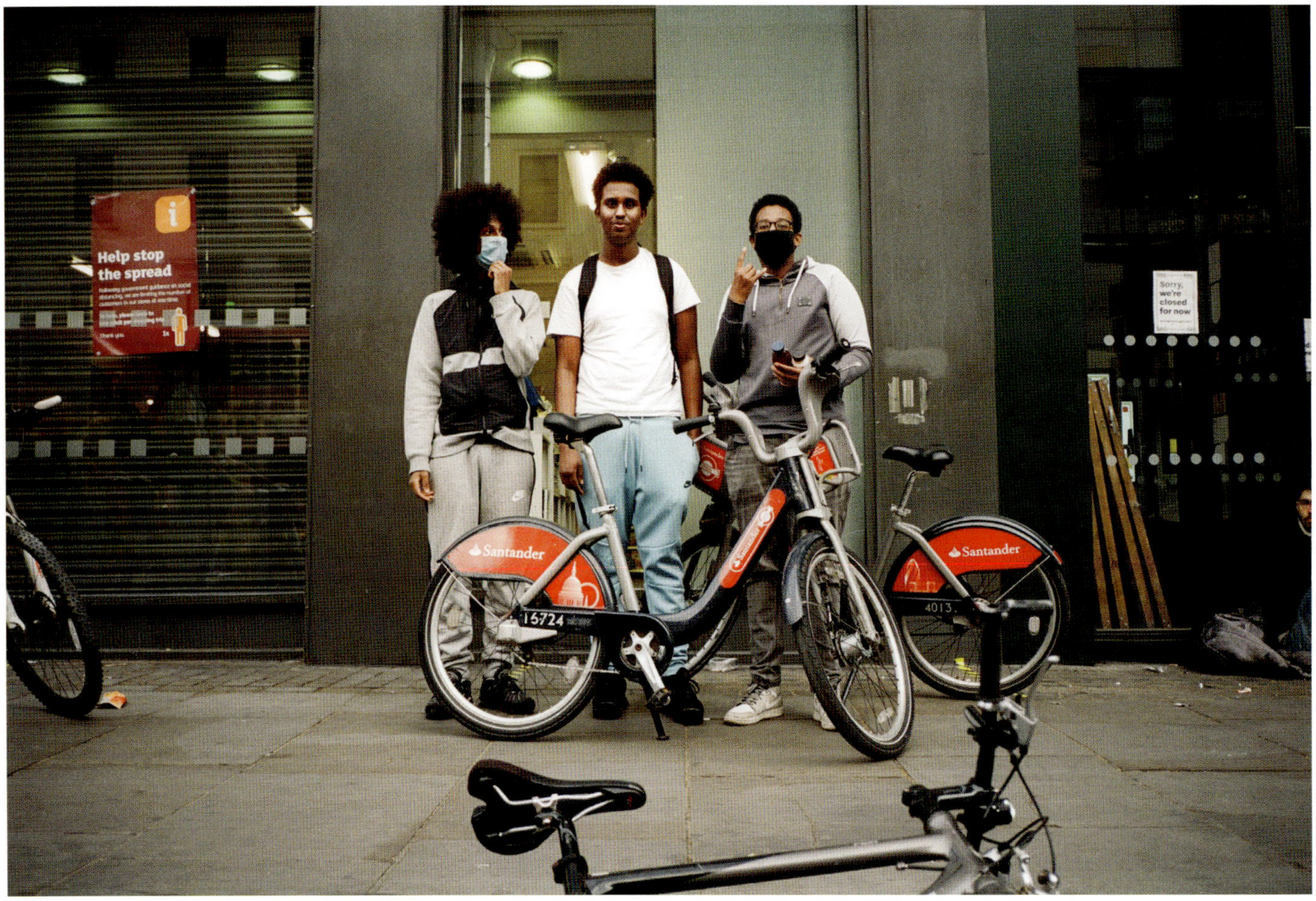
Help stop the spread
Santander
Santander
Sorry, we're closed for now

"Make me Prime Minister"

"Lockdown has my brothers
ganging up on me and Mum,
they keep telling us we're nosy"

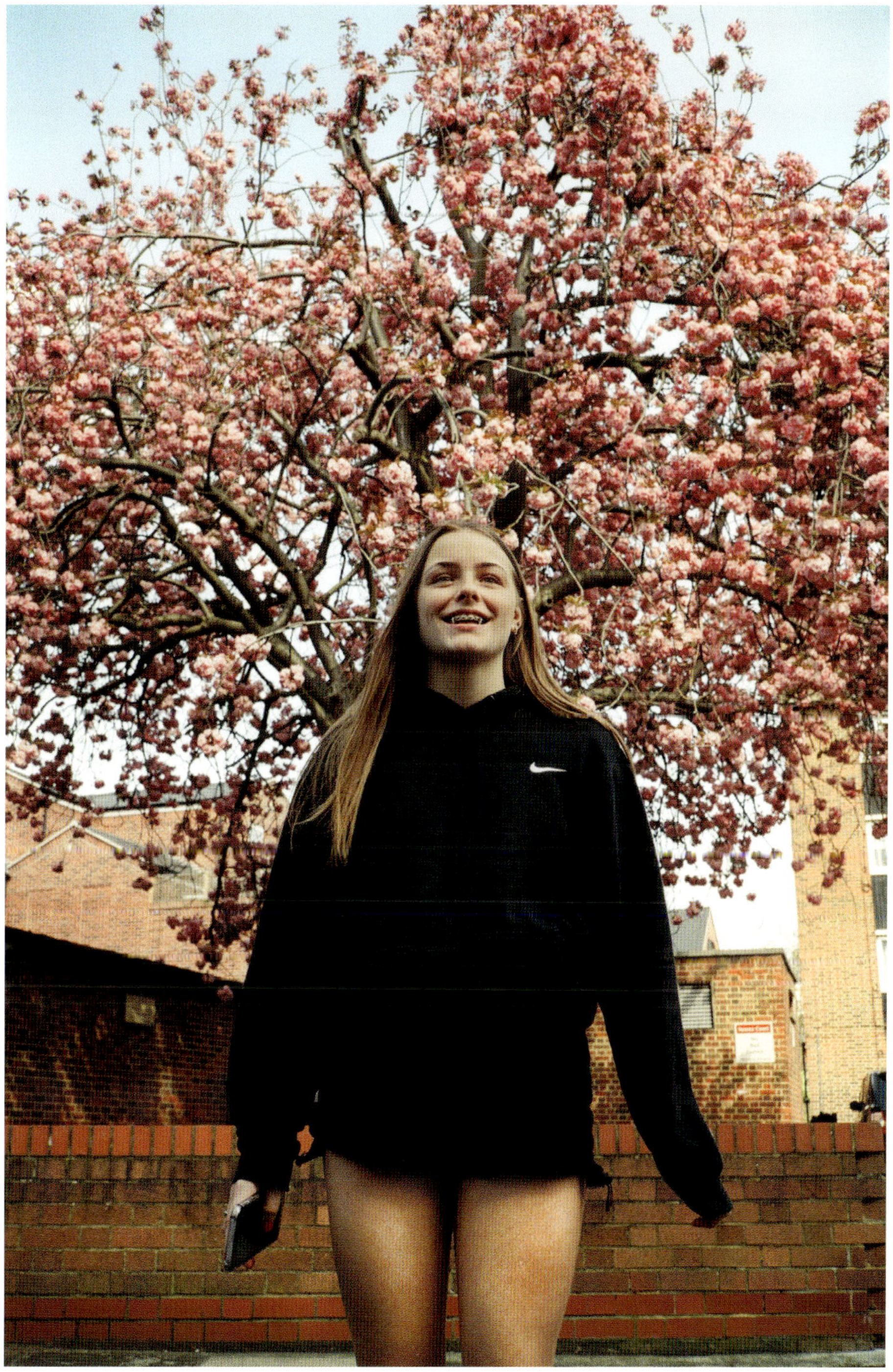

"I'm sorry to hear your mum passed,
I don't know what to say.
My cousin and her grandmother died recently
in Somalia.
Death is always talked about in my family,
it's a religious thing,
family gather to pray around the body,
not sure that's a good thing
whilst Covid's spreading in Somalia"

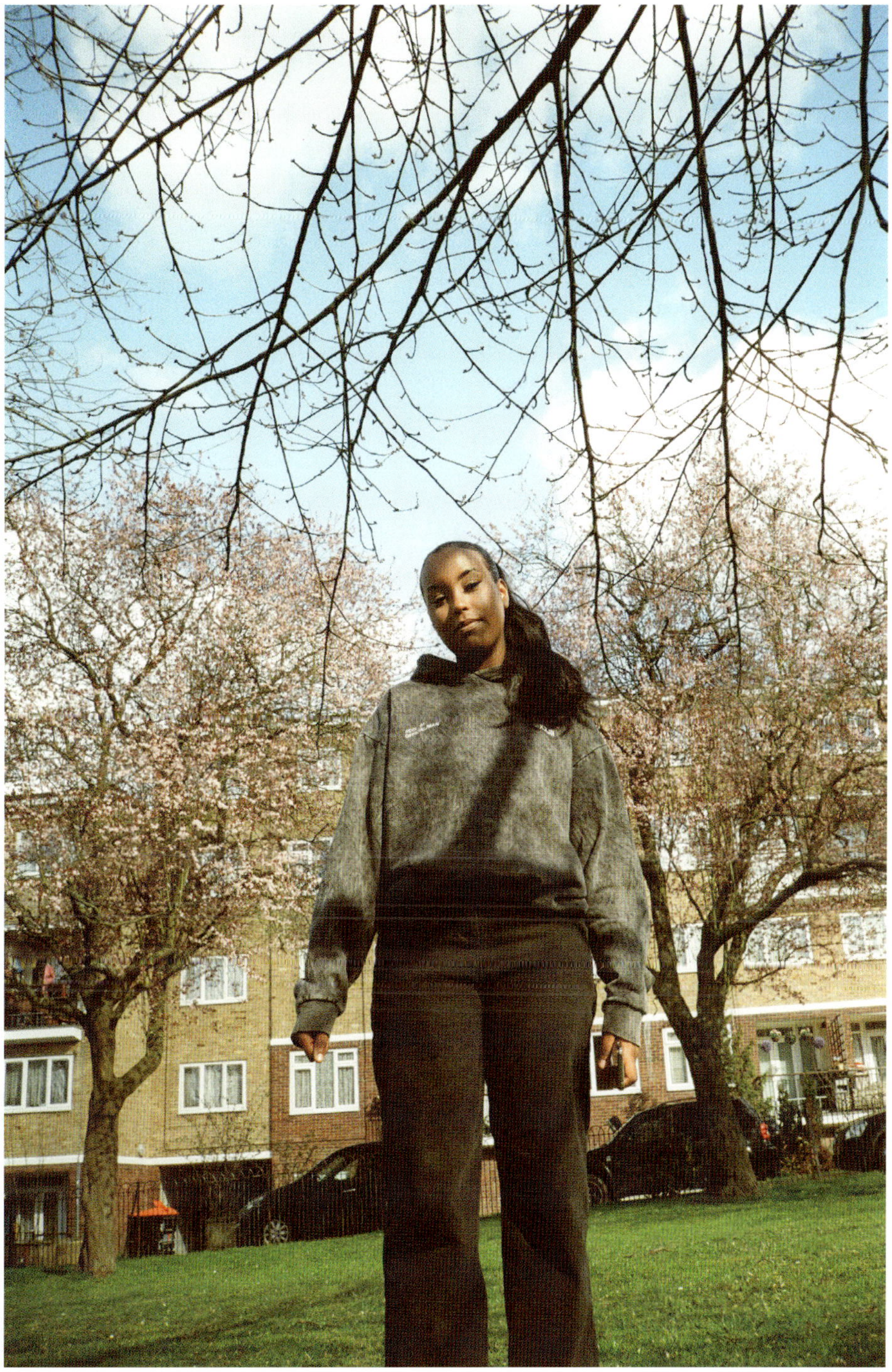

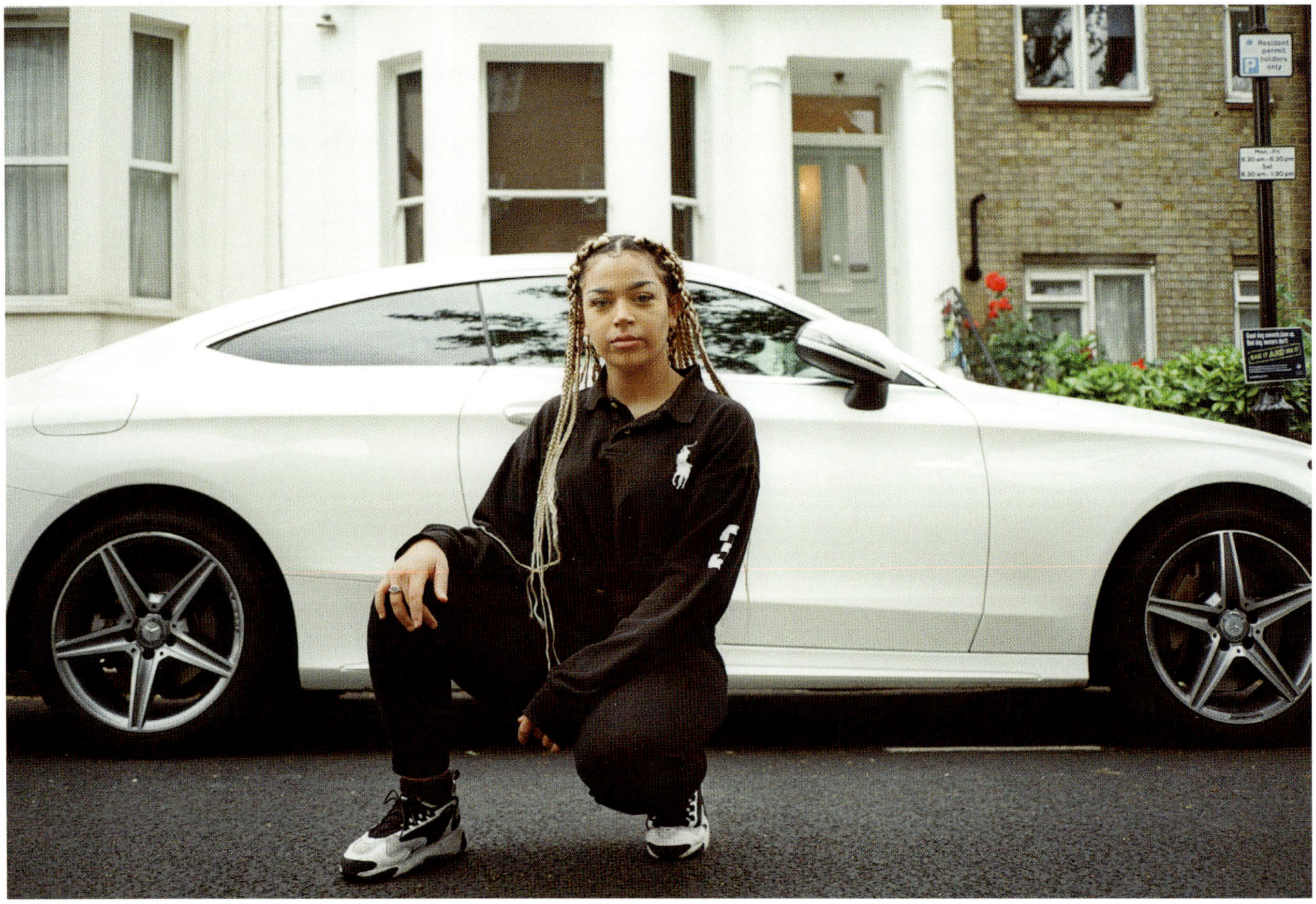
Resident permit holders only
P
Mon - Fri
8.30 am - 6.30 pm
Sat
8.30 am - 1.30 pm

"Lockdown has been good for me,
I'm different now.
But it feels like the world is a mess right now,
when I saw that video, man.
And you know what really annoys me,
some people are saying
'all lives matter',
they just don't get it"

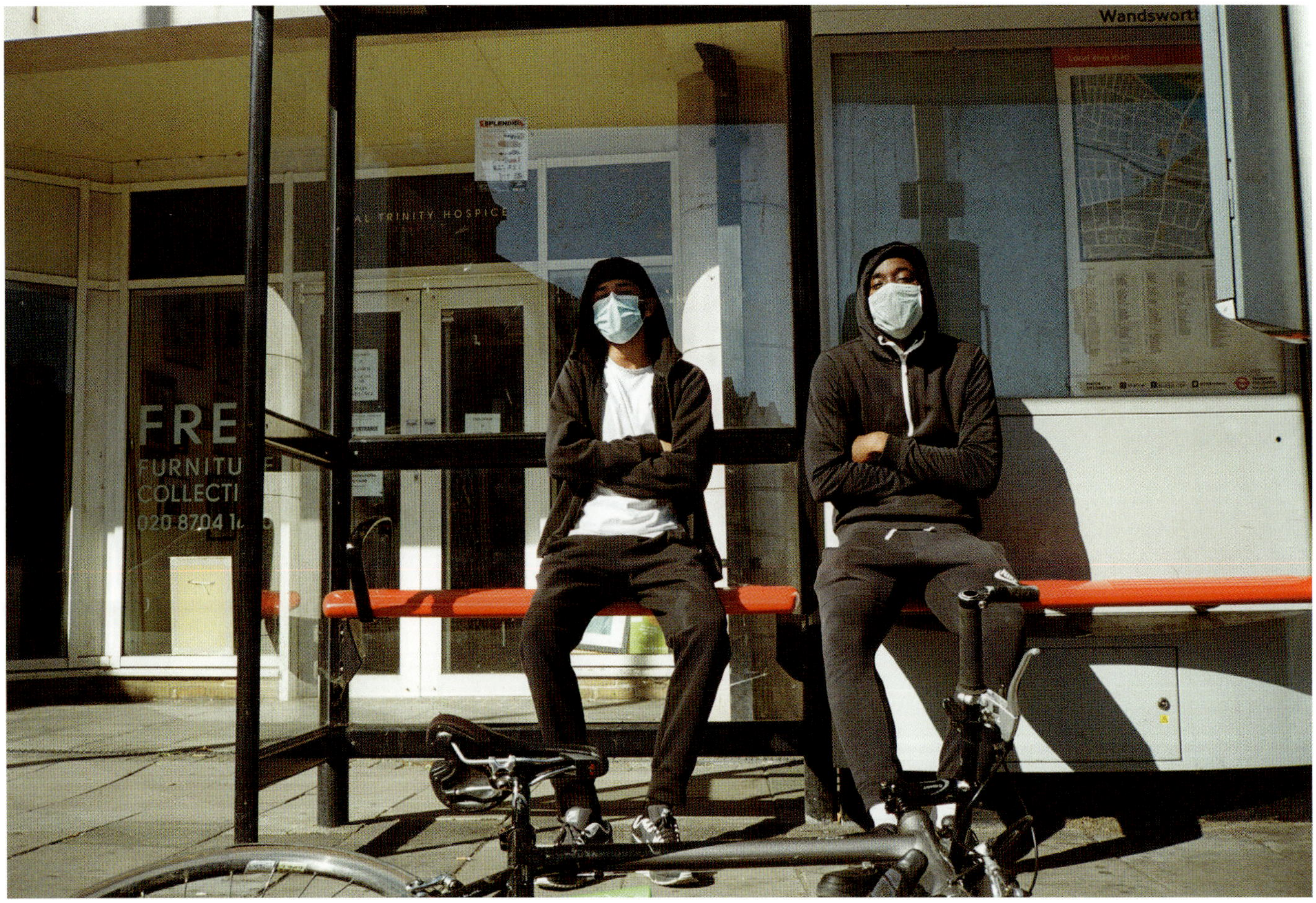
FRE
FURNITU
COLLECTI
AL TRINITY HOSPICE

"Yeah,
I saw the news,
'I can't breathe'.
Officers killing people"

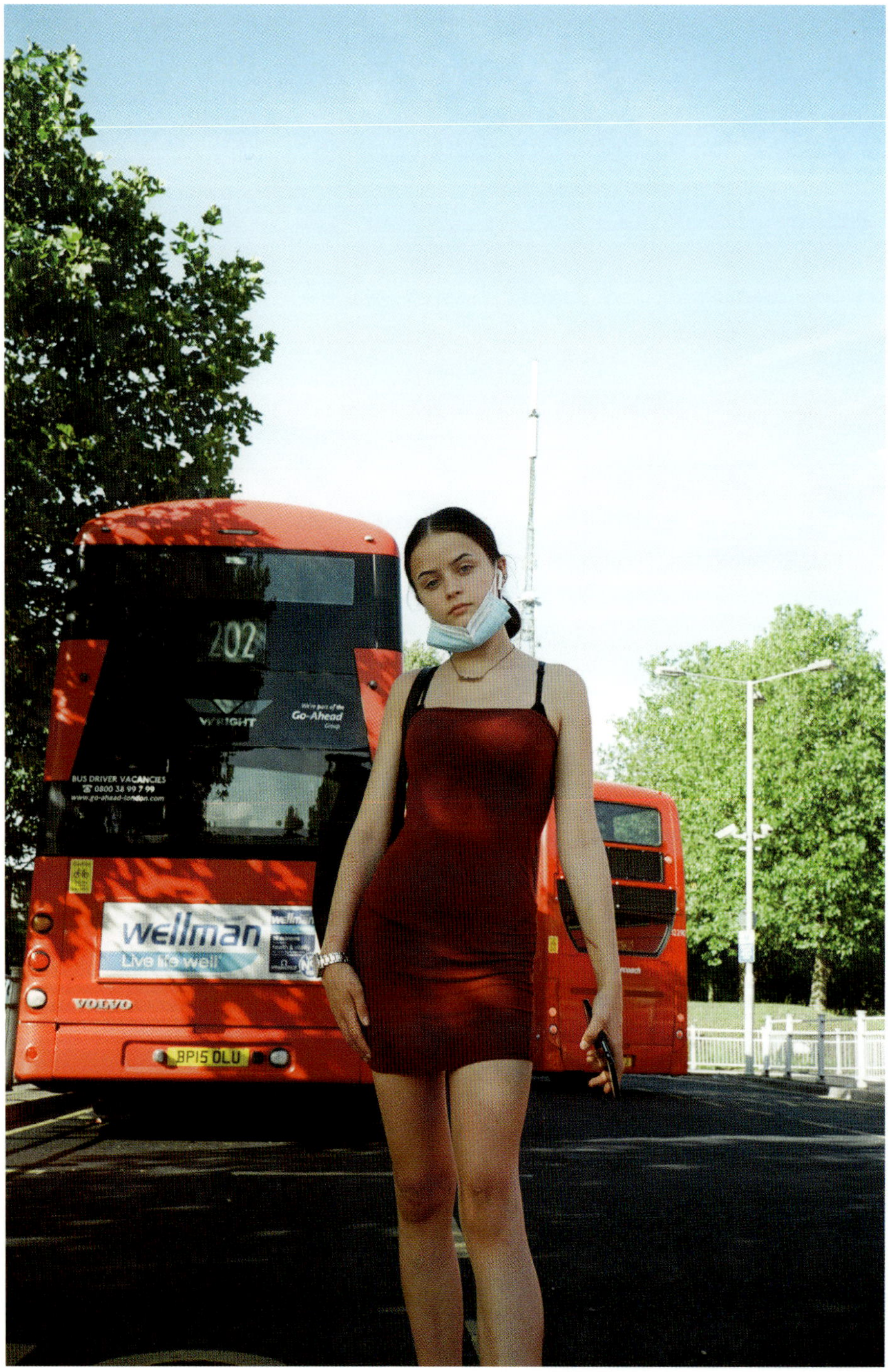
202
WRIGHT
Go-Ahead
BUS DRIVER VACANCIES
wellman
Live life well
VOLVO
BP15 DLU

*"Barbecue on Friday
with my mates,
haven't seen them
for three months"*

"This is the first time
we've been out for weeks,
we're gonna dock the bikes
then head home"

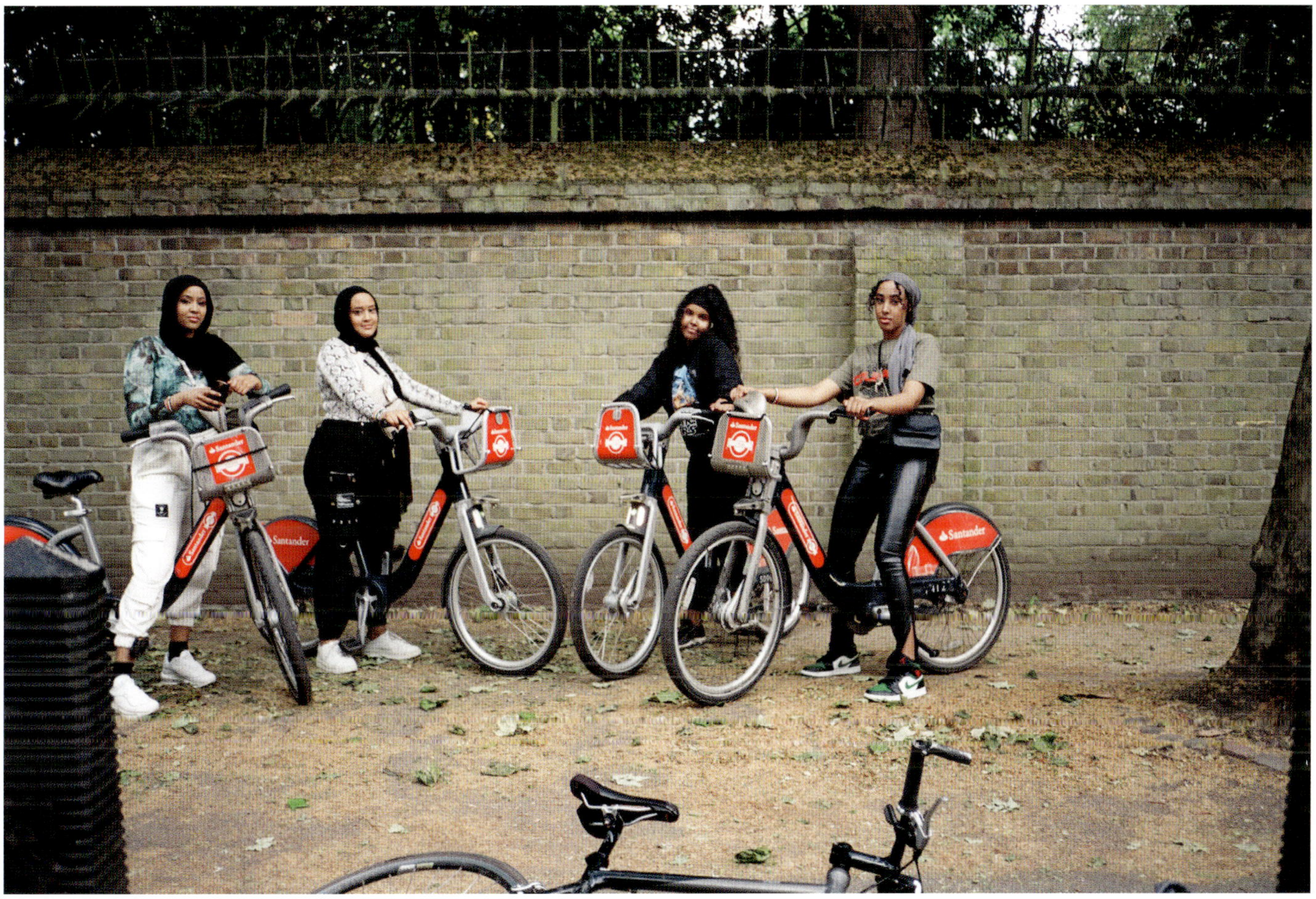
Santander

"There's so much happening right now,
what can I say,
I think the system is broken,
there's so much to change and fix.
For now, right now,
it's so good to be
back out there on the water,
you should see it at sunrise,
there's nothing like rowing,
there's nothing like it"

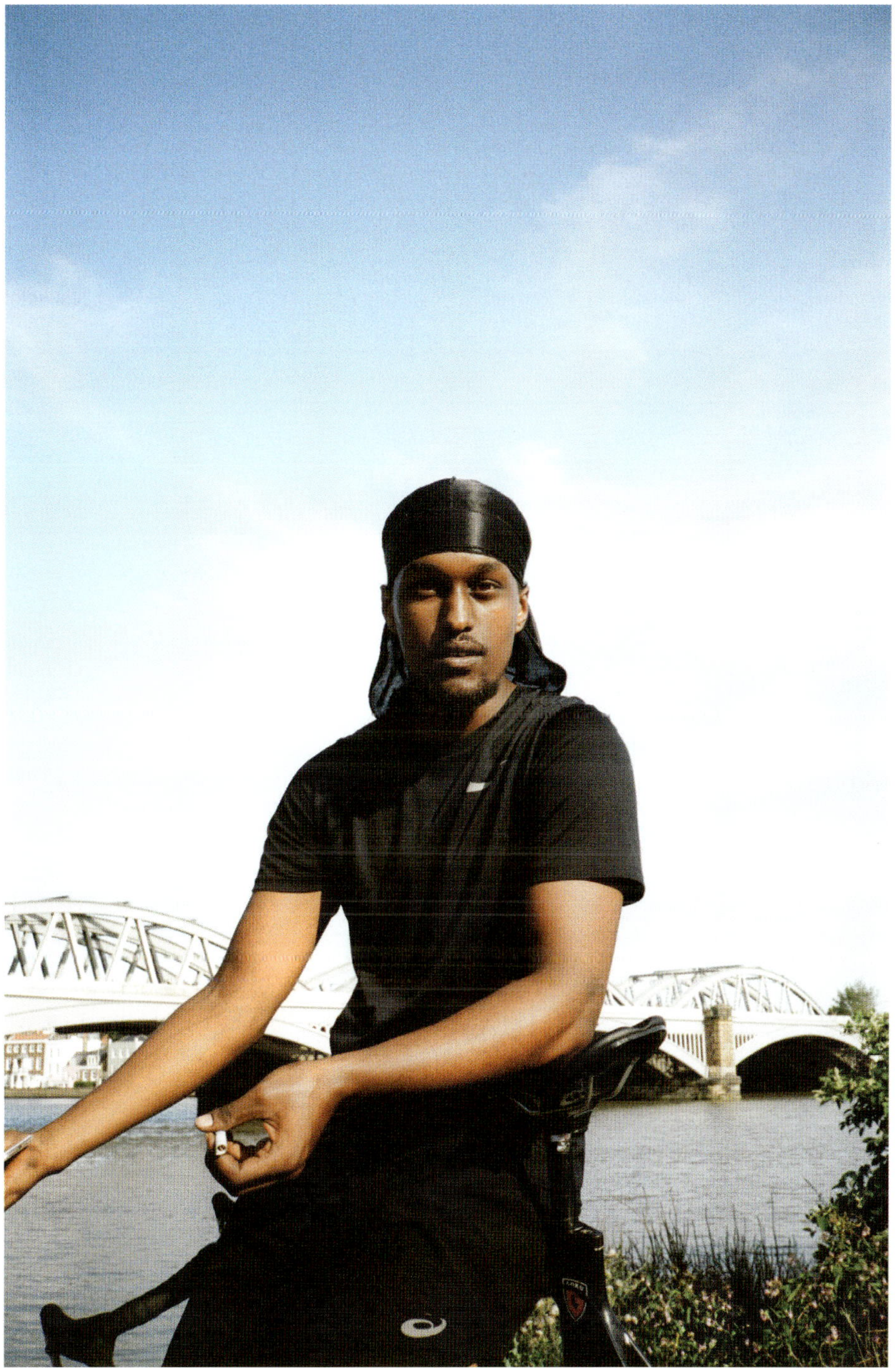

"I'm not photo ready"

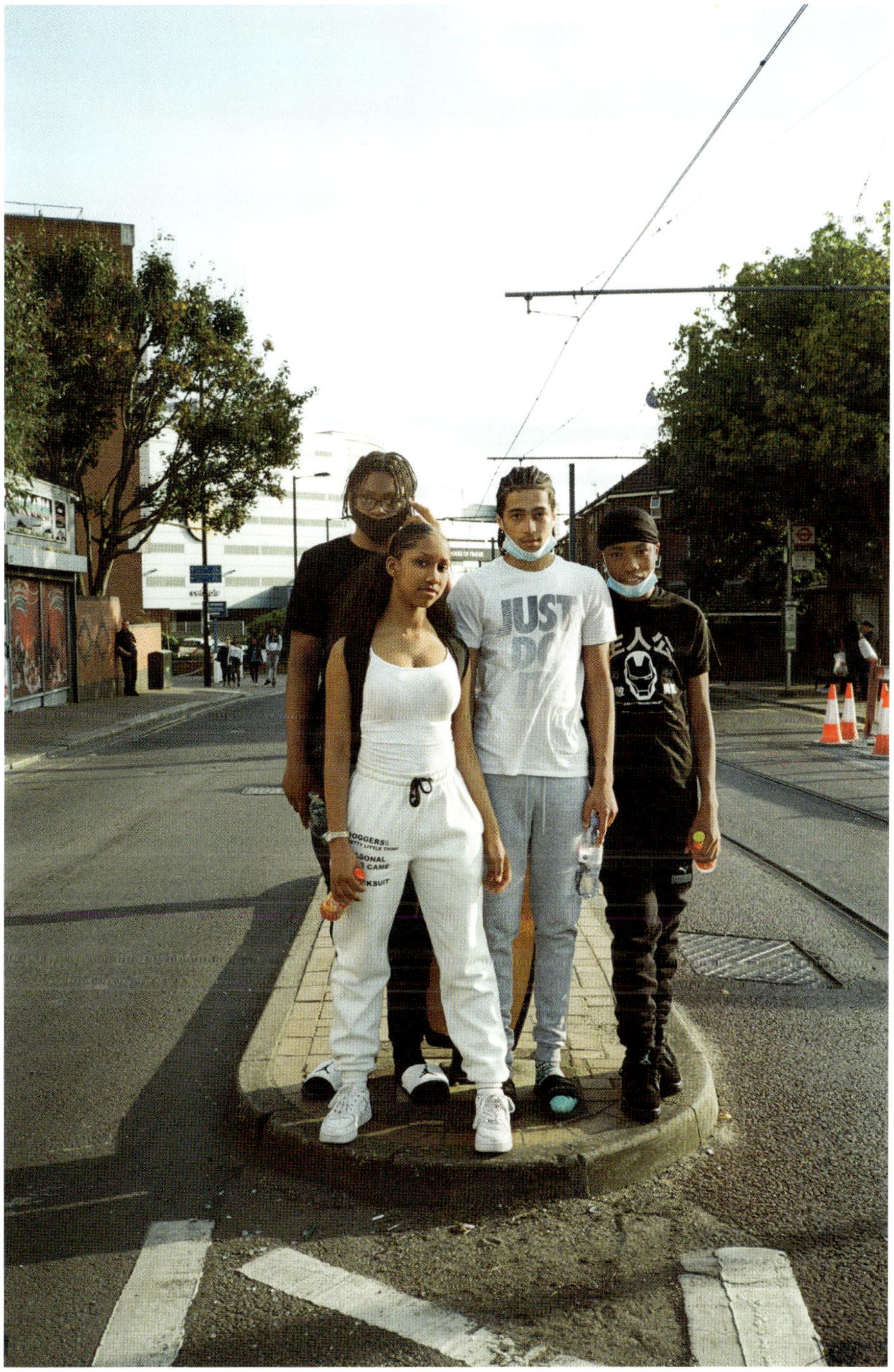
JUST

"So this is little
Brookie-Cookie,
she's a good girl,
we're all doing OK.
Had to take a break from reading
the news today though,
it's too much"

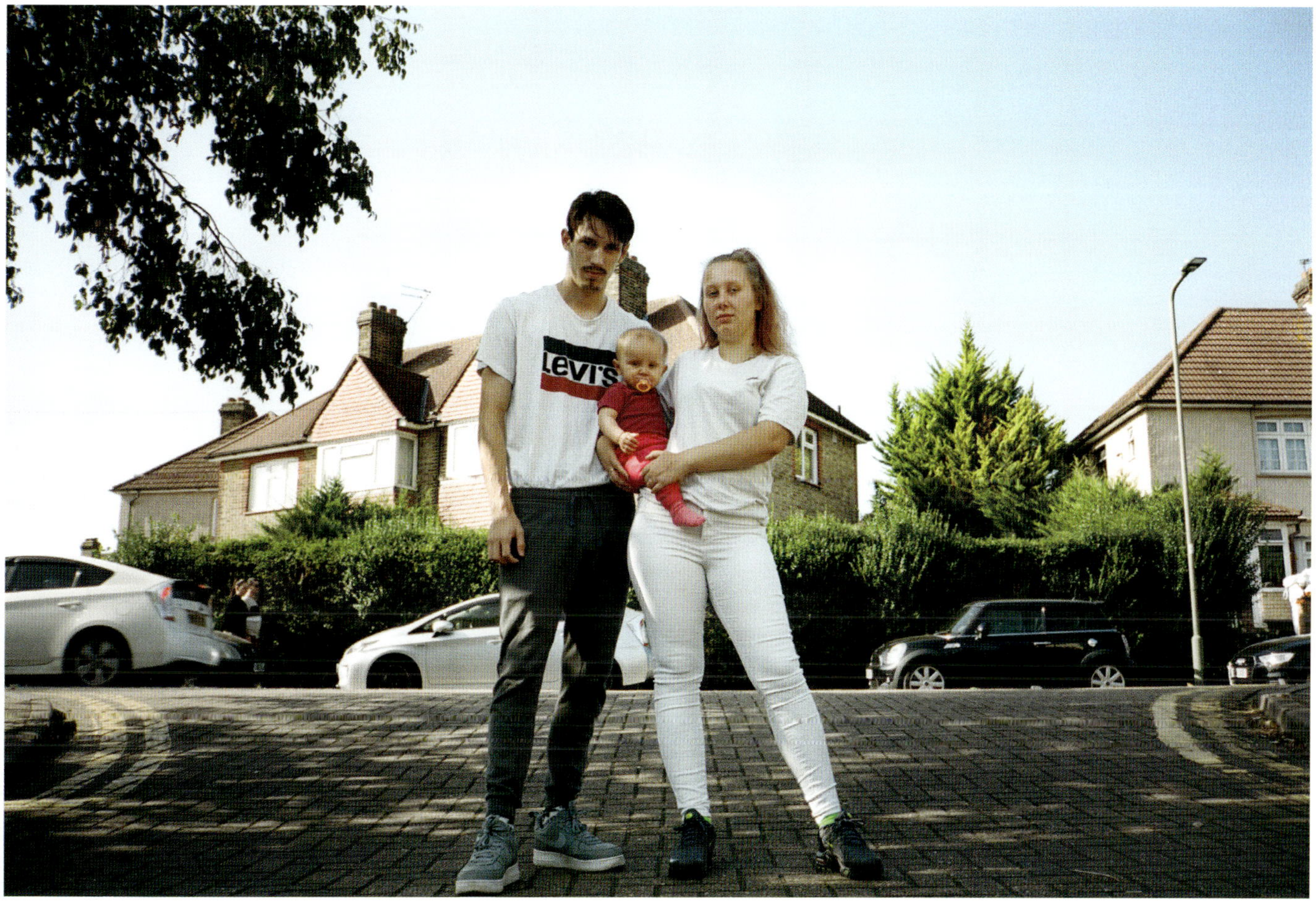
Levi's

"This is my design brand CLB,
'Can't Live Broke'.
I got all the printing machines at home.
School is still shut with this lockdown,
so right now it's all about getting ready.
I'm running my online store,
making music and looking out for my mates"

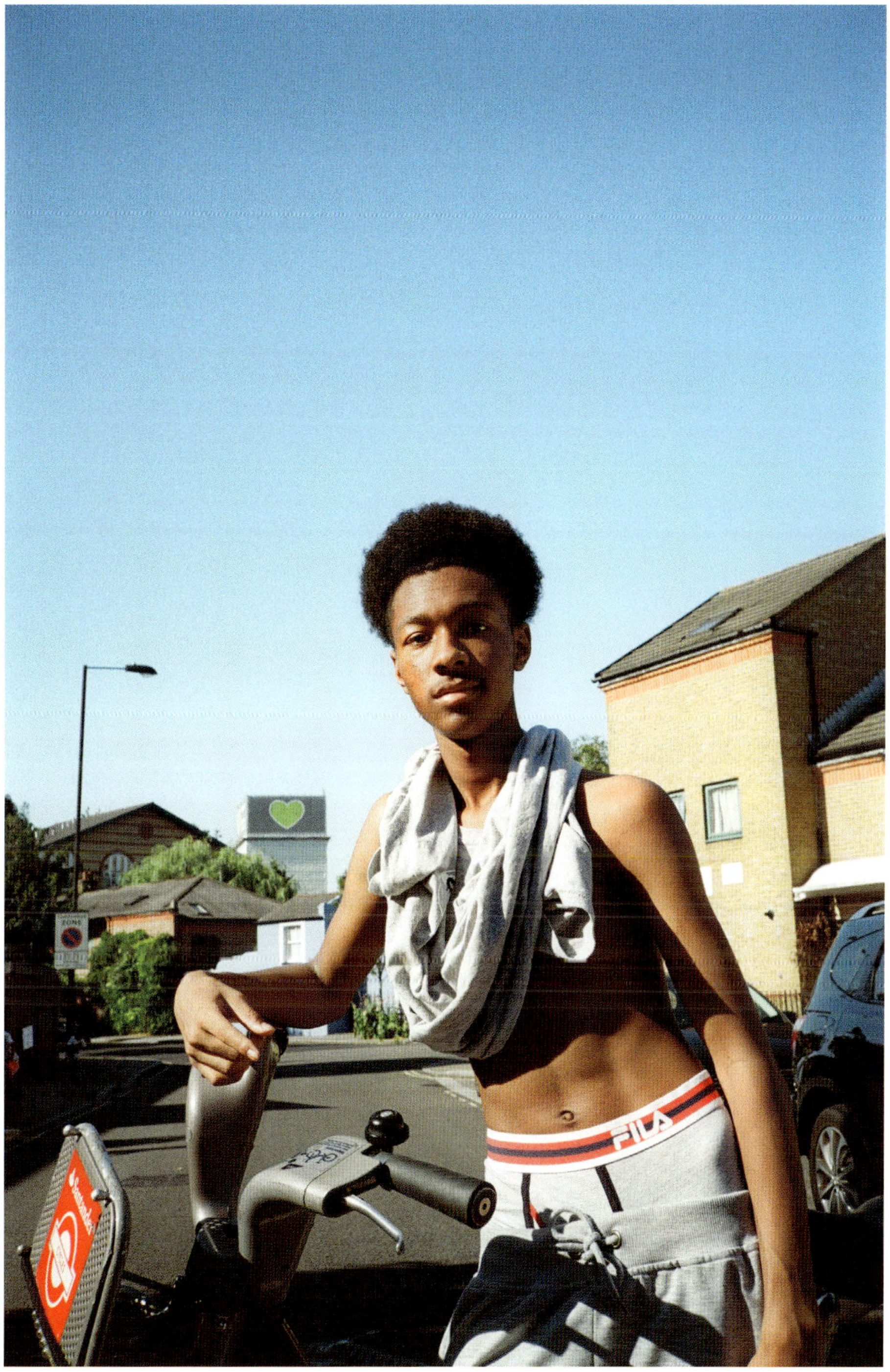
FILA

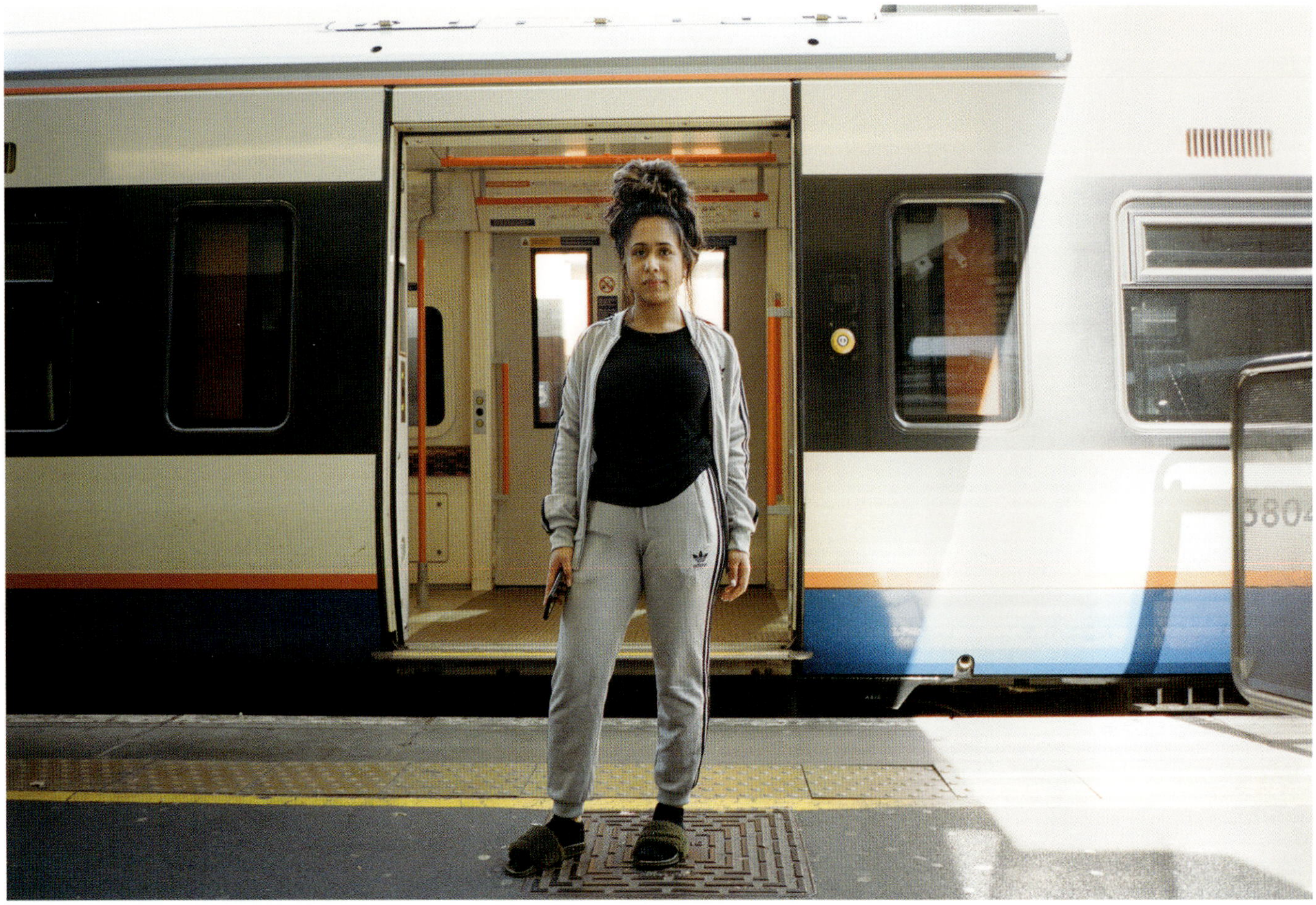

"I'm going to be a Neurosurgeon"

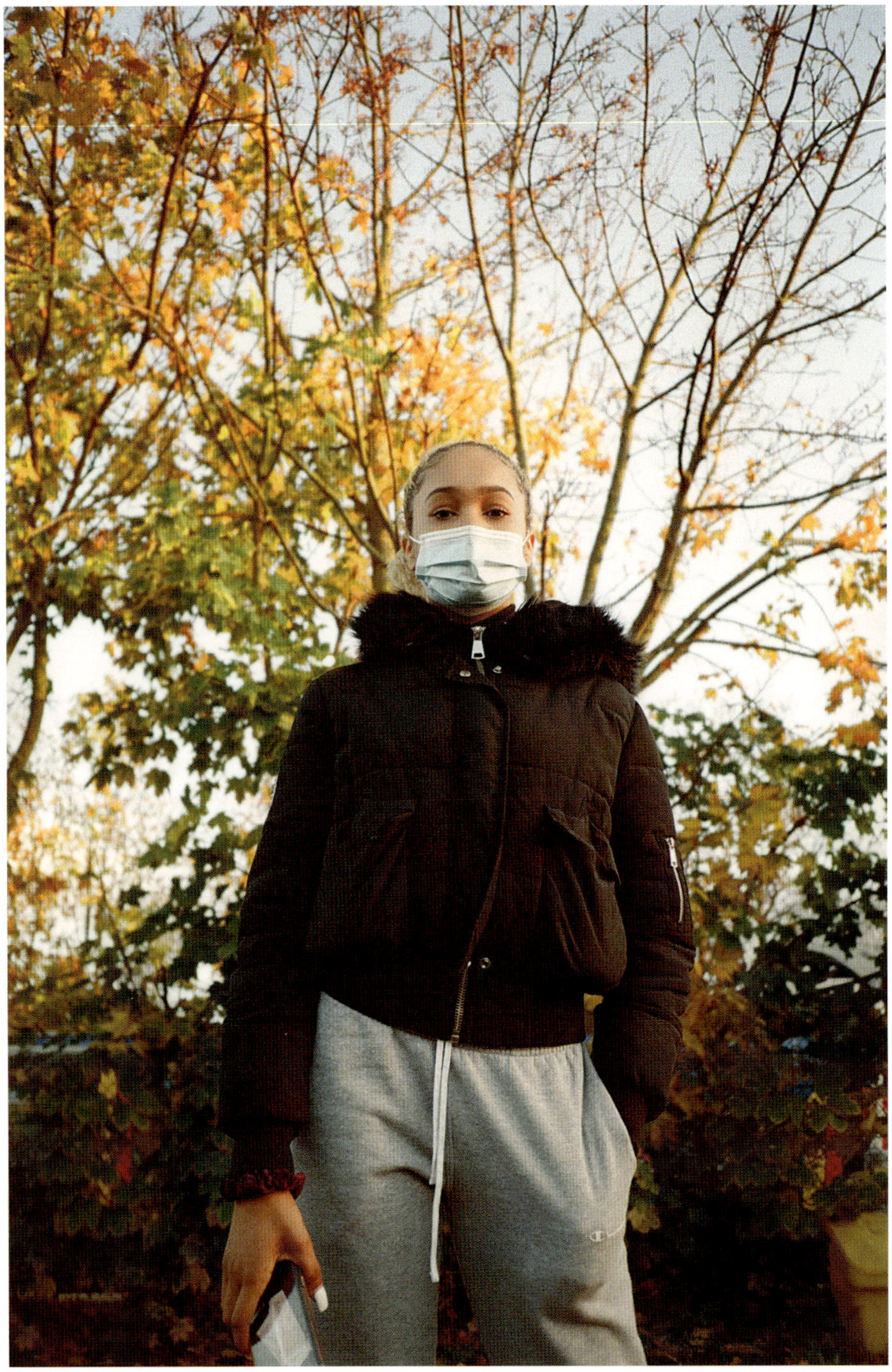

"I like to have cash on me"

"He really misses his boxing"

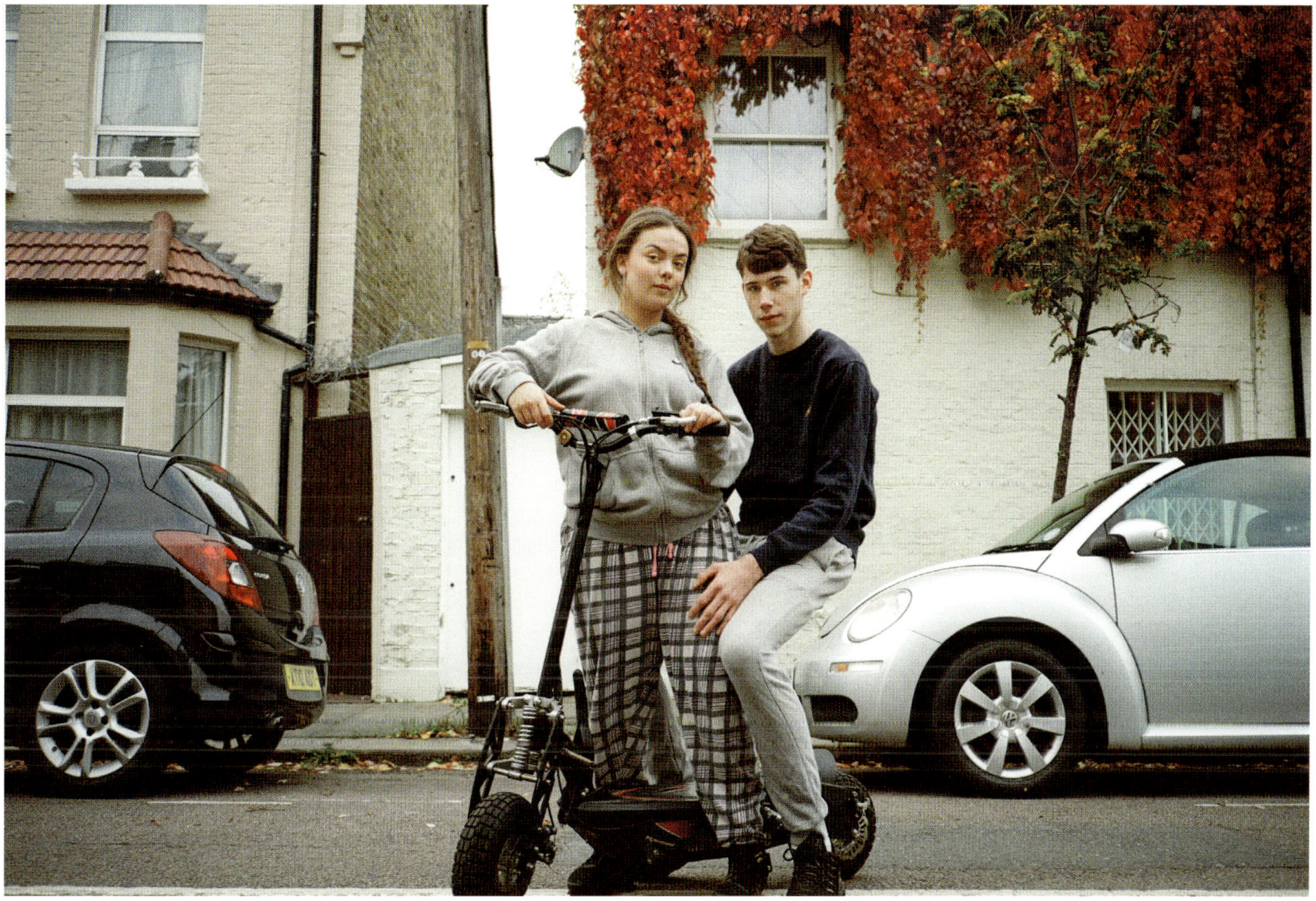

"That's calm"

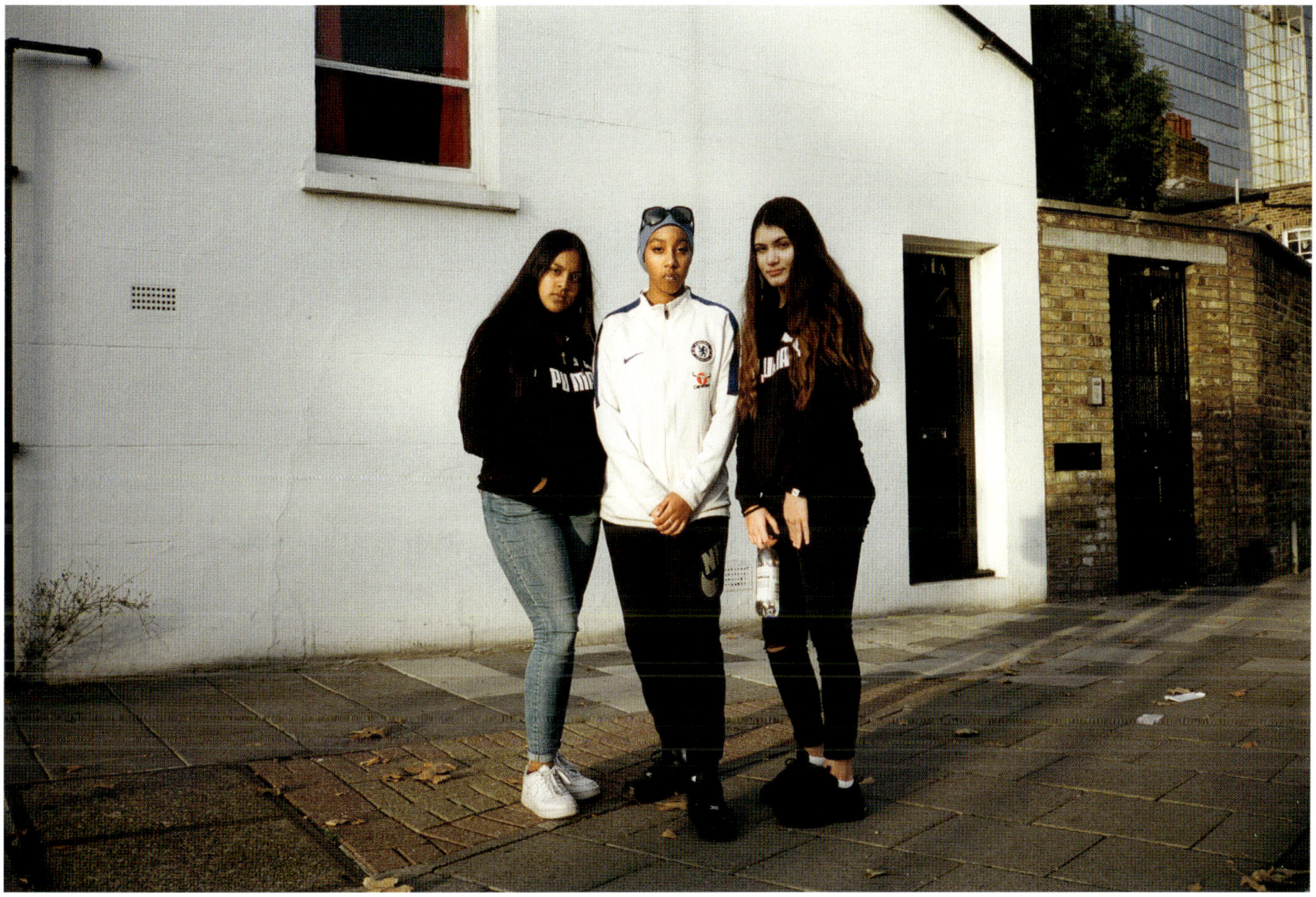

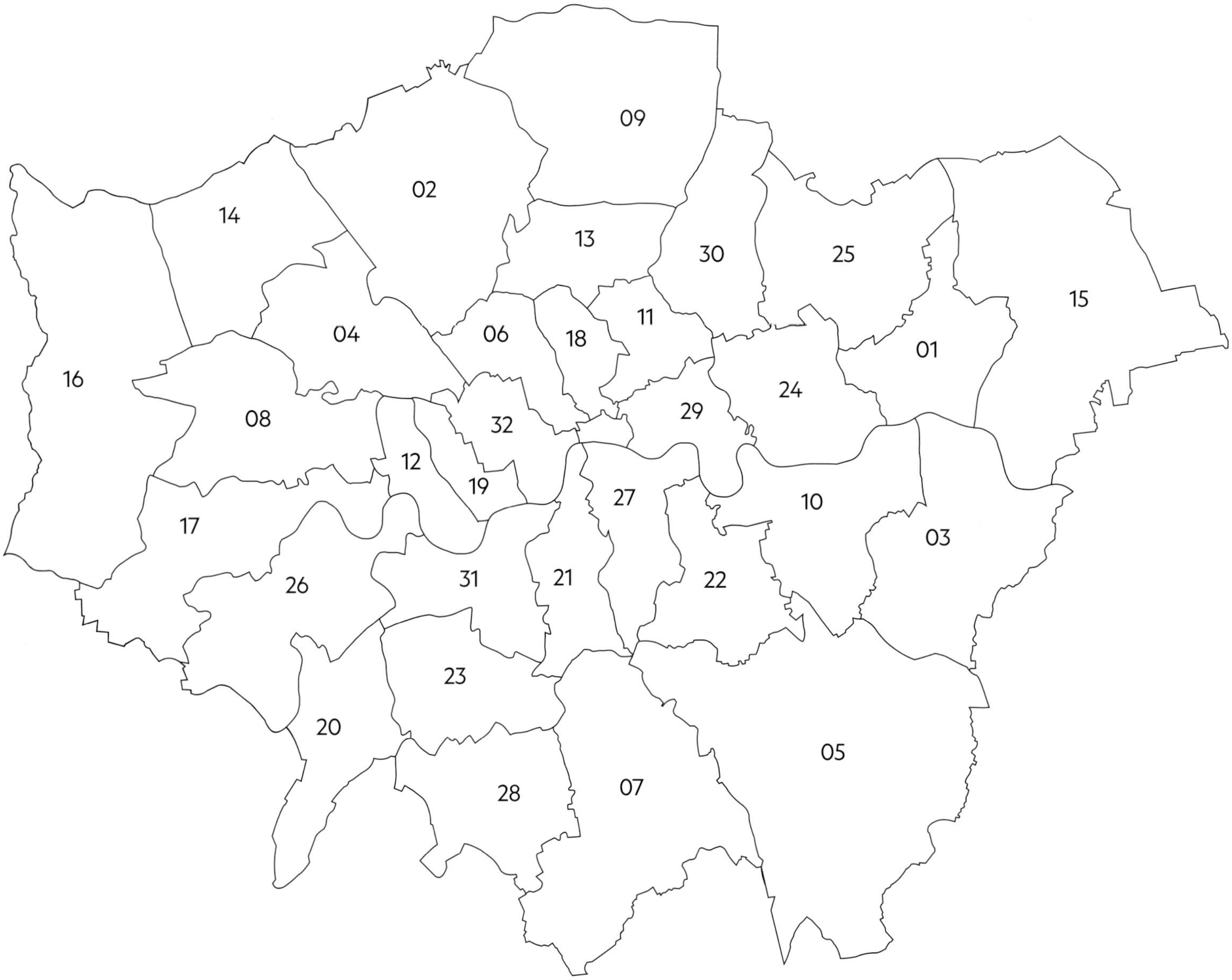
09
02
14
13
30
25
15
04
06
18
11
01
16
24
08
29
32
12
19
27
10
17
03
26
31
21
22
23
20
05
28
07

London, UK

Barking and Dagenham 01
Barnet 02
Bexley 03
Brent 04
Bromley 05
Camden 06
Croydon 07
Ealing 08
Enfield 09
Greenwich 10
Hackney 11
Hammersmith and Fulham 12
Haringey 13
Harrow 14
Havering 15
Hillingdon 16
Hounslow 17
Islington 18
Kensington and Chelsea 19
Kingston upon Thames 20
Lambeth 21
Lewisham 22
Merton 23
Newham 24
Redbridge 25
Richmond upon Thames 26
Southwark 27
Sutton 28
Tower Hamlets 29
Waltham Forest 30
Wandsworth 31
Westminster 32

Q
&
A

Harriet Turney

Seetal Solanki

Where did the idea behind *32 boroughs* begin and what does this book represent?

Initially, the plan was 12 boroughs, just the inner city boroughs. I guess that reflects where popular culture was at, in some ways, at that time.

12 seemed possible over a timeline of one to two years. Hah. That sounds ever so neat and tidy in retrospect. And not quite how it played out.

However, it just so happens I was living in Brent, around 2011/2012, an outer London borough. I shot the first portrait there, and I didn't want to eliminate that portrait, so I became committed to the idea of 32 boroughs.

32 made sense; that way, all of the representative boroughs in and around Greater London could be documented and illustrated throughout this period of pivotal shifts in our society.

You began ideating on *32* around 2011. What was influencing you at that time?

Around this time, popular culture was all things urban: grime, hoodies, tracksuits.

Then the 2011 London riots happened, which created some negative attention, a ghettoisation of a group of people, which had been happening for some time.
I was never going to enhance or add to that narrative.

During 2011 I had also been reflecting on Kehinde Wiley's work and the positive elevation of his subjects, often the underserved communities – subjects that might have been portrayed in an 'urban' or 'ghettoised' context around that time. I wanted to bring that positive, authentic light to the story. Wiley's work showed me it was possible; well, his work is on a whole other level.

Have there been any pivotal points of reference that have shaped your vision and approach for *32*?

Around 2013, Seetal and I went to the screening of Everybody Street, *Cheryl Dunn's film, a documentary about various highly acclaimed New York street photographers. This film pretty much gave me permission to go out there. To look for a narrative in the chaos of life, the chaos of the city.*

To be less intimidated.
To be in the present moment.
On reflection, I would say, it was an exercise in perseverance.
This is something that really stayed with me.

Having documented London over a significant period of time, did you discover any common narratives that stood out to you?

As time went on, the story built, one portrait at a time, one conversation at a time, one borough at a time, one season at a time.

The significance of the seasons and seasonal light emerged gradually and organically in the edit, finding the running thread throughout the story. This became part of my criteria.

This was applied to the compositional structure and sequencing of the portraits in the book artwork.

So the 32 boroughs *story begins/opens with London in the summertime and rolls through the four seasons – autumn, winter, spring, lockdown spring, lockdown summer, emerging from lockdown autumnal golden light.*

I was always on the lookout for the cherry blossom bloom or getting out there if we had snow. These very significant moments within the context of seasonality and shifts throughout the city.

Are there any other people that have been influential in your process of *32*?

In 2017, the first conversation with Jeffrey Boakye took place. He had just published his first book, Hold Tight: Black Masculinity, Millennials and the Meaning of Grime *(Influx, 2017). As you can tell from the book title, it adds another dimension and perspective to the 32 boroughs of London.*

His book was very influential, addressing social codes, masculinity and the scene's energy.

And actually, realness, humour and insight.

It's also the insider/outsider perspective.

So much of this book resonated and felt like it connected to 32.

After shooting these portraits from 2013–17, discovering Hold Tight *was like receiving some kind of reassurance/permission to create such a body of work that represented my home, as well as other people's home.*

I also contacted Ted Polhemus 2016/2017. I had received my first copy of StreetStyle *(Thames & Hudson) in 1994, which gave me a deeper insight into the raw and gritty nature of subcultures within London.*

StreetStyle *helped build the foundations of* 32 *by offering an anthropological lens on the social and communicative importance of style in personal expression. Ted talks about the litmus test of 'street credibility' that is crucial within popular culture; this really stayed with me.*

Ted and I met at the Tate Modern 2017; I gave him a printed proof of 32*. We began a dialogue and friendship; we've been speaking ever since. To be honest, it feels like I've always known him.*

What else has been able to offer you some sense of grounding with *32*?

In 2017, it was exciting to have a proof of the book and see the project taking shape in physical form, not only through a lens.

But I also had a sense something was missing, that there could be more to 32*. This realisation felt like I had constructed something, and then I was tearing it all down.*

2017 was a transformative moment of deconstructing, reconstructing, and starting over. Taking it apart.

This is when I started bringing the quotes into the artwork.

Since 2013, I had been making quick short notes of the conversations that I was having with all of the people I was photographing in and around all 32 boroughs.

Documenting any interesting, funny, real moments that I wouldn't want to forget.

The conversation, exchange, banter really became a reflection of the time and popular culture.

How did you continue to find the stamina to shoot and document *32* over such a considerable amount of time?

The project was shot on film, making each portrait intuitive and decisive. Every stage of the process is considered; thirty-six exposures on a roll of film, C-41 development, scans and prints.

I got a deeper understanding that the project was becoming the boss of me in 2017, when I realised I needed to revisit all of the boroughs – this was never the plan, but now, at the very least, I was looking at another two years.

From this point on, though, there were stronger images, more defined criteria: the light, seasons, subjects, location, settings and details, and a strength emerged from bringing in the dialogue and banter. So, I continued to shoot 2017–21.

This led to further realisation: that 32 could be taking shape as photojournalism work. A pivotal moment.
Slightly new territory.
What did this mean?

How did you go about sharing the stories of London and the people living in this city?

These people's lives are being shown and shared; they didn't ask to be photographed. You have to be respectful, a custodian of their truth – with photojournalism projects, there's a responsibility. To approach the workflow with integrity and respect.

Important as the serious conversations, quotes and statements are, comedy and humour get us through the everyday. That's the reality and truth being spoken right there by the people and for the people.

During 2019–20, Boakye and I were in touch again, and I shared these conversations. This gave him – a teacher who had also grown up in London – the chance to really see 32.
It was the right time for Boakye to write the introduction to 32.

How has *32* shaped you as a person?

2020–21 was a pivotal moment; I continued to shoot with the written introduction in mind and the renewed, strengthening portrait criteria.

We collectively started living/surviving and experiencing historical events.

This became a thread in the storyline; it's also a look at life before, during, and coming out of lockdown.
32 *was an anchor for me.*
Especially during that time.

It's also given me an appreciation for my network, peers and mentors.

Ted Polhemus, Jeffrey Boakye, Seetal Solanki.

These people saw something else in 32, more than I could see.

That was very important; their feedback, insight, critique and perspectives were crucial.

Each portrait has stuck with me. Everyone I meet, I remember each portrait.

Were there any standout moments while you were documenting *32*?

Melissa's three portraits: a few weeks pregnant, heavily pregnant, then a family portrait with baby Brookie-Cookie. Pages 79, 156, 181.

'How's my bally?' The scarecrow in the background happens to be in the same outfit as Rory in the foreground: grey sweats and a black balaclava. Page 42.

Adam's boxing quote about staying up until 4am to watch the Tyson Fury fight. Page 104.

Aquilla, the first early lockdown portrait, on the brink of an apocalypse – her words – the portrait set to beautiful cherry blossom filling the frame. And, of course, Hanna, which was the final portrait I shot. The finality. Pages 160 & 167.

How did you weave the narratives and your experience of *32* and how would you sum it up?

In early 2013, the first portrait in Brent, on the Bakerloo line, overground, approaching Willesden Junction. Page 112.

That was when the project portrait criteria started to emerge.

The tube carriage, London Underground patterned seat covers; the boys didn't move or change their posture/composure for the camera, and the dog's eye contact with the lens. The sunlight, winter branches, blue sky reflections on the windows.

Which leads me to think of the final portrait, 2021. My mum had passed on to the next place. It was too big an event; I mean, this time had been eventful personally and collectively.

For some reason, a final portrait was all I could do and seemed meaningful at a time when grief makes everything seem meaningless.

The closure. The finality. An outlet, trying to find some familiarity and connection, acceptance in the shock and grief.

A final portrait, a ritual to honour and keep the connection to her in some way; as it turns out, that very day, it all just kind of aligned. The light, the seasons, winter to spring, weathered winter branches, new spring shoots, cherry blossom, crisp blue sky, clouds, clear, bright sunlight.

The chat, the honesty. We talked about life, death and humanity.

I kept in touch with a lot of people in the portraits.

This became important throughout the lockdown restrictions. I asked people to create video diaries, stories, anything they liked. A more collaborative effort emerged naturally, which is really the truest nature of 32.

A short film was created, editing and collating the footage made by the people I met and photographed, along with my existing footage.

We gradually built a collage. A story built up over time.

The book and film feel as if you are walking through London in a day, a season, a year.

Acknowledgements

Thank you to everyone photographed for *32 boroughs*, this book is dedicated to you: Melissa, Connor, Brooke, Aquilla, Jade, Aaliyah, Hanna, Pharrell, Niecey, Adam, Zane, Andre, Ishairo, Crystal, David, Jasmin, Paige, Stacy, Dante, Reignor, Denis, Lora, Saab, Khalid, Omar, Corey, Jordan, Terry, Kai, Levi, Reggie, Don, Abraham, Kano, Veronica, Fourad, Dominic, Rory, Joseph, Tafari, Jamal, Darine, Rahma, P.roblem, Baby Q, Ossy, M-Dot, Romeo, Naturel, Alchemico, Bubba, Mozzi, Alz, Chontz, Elliot, Sharna, Leon, Andrew, Lee, Daniel, Joe, Owen, O'Shea, Sharae, Malek, Caine, Danny, Yobel, Ibraham, Georgie, Akim, Raphael, Riaz, Jeremy, Andrew, Mo, Diane, Aaron, Tammy, Sade, Michael, Hannah, Kevin, Samuel, Ricardo, Chris, Erden, Jaafar, Fainur, Sasha, Neil, Jay, Matthew, Kane, Muhammed, Brandon, Hamid, Charlie, Oaksey, Hamza, Yakul, Danna, Hussain, Patrick, Andrei, Stephen, Nicholas, Demetrius, Archer, Leeandre, Sharif, Alfie, Elle, Simon, Ace, Rashad, Fred, Shashi, Ollie, Chloe, Bobby, Georgia, Wesley, Mel, Craig, Raffi, Cody, Brita, Soroya, Kyle, Obamfemi, Cory, Salman, Ellie, Mariam, Shaya, Niba, Aiya, Trina, Musa, Spencer, Anton, Roman, Tyler, Ben, Christine, Samira, Dylan, Sarah, Jonathon, Leo, Jahman, Hanad, Nuno, Joshua, Fiona, Milly, Osman, Reniyah, Leshaya, Tracy, Isobelle, Sophie, Anisa, Hezi, Abby, Tess, Nipsy, Reese, Kenzi, Nathan, Kae, Megan, India, Frankie, Riley, Jafar, Travis, Marcy, Tyrese, Katie, Archie.

I would like to extend a special thank you to Seetal Solanki, Jeffrey Boakye, Ted Polhemus, Jennie Condell, Will Robinson, Karin Fremer.

Thank you to Peter Appleton and the team at Park Communications for printing advice.

This publication has been made possible thanks to the generous support of the following people: Melanie Wilkinson, Ralph McKeown, Terence Anthony, Joe Guest, Connie Farr, Segal Seguleh, Gilly Turney, Lynne Carr, Joni Plews-Bingle, Ingrid Bingle, Candy Plews, Nick Spiers, Emily Payne, Django Beatty, Lisa Bennett, Liam Aylott, Mark Peacock, Chloe Mallett, Heather McMeckan, Ben Arthur, Liz Collins, Bill Hardy, James Deacon, Nathan Thompson, Ursula Lake, John Williams, Richard Damery, Kitty Gale, Charlotte Kew, Jawahir Roble, Arwish Kisoensingh, Jan Taubert, Michael Bone, Dan Jones, Jaye Gilbert, Helen Ramwell, Gabi Besevic-Simpson, Dhanesh Jayaselan, Ellie Smith, Carlos Silva, Paul Reardon, Tara Sharpe, Lee Brown, Sabrina Wisely, Alfio Sambataro, Roxane Feerick, G. Leventhall, Zsofia Farkas, Toks Owoh, Kiera Blakey, Peter Bevan, Ed Whiting, Gordon Steward, Romain Forquy, Chris Zane, Clare Chong, Francesco Tabormina, Jo Paterson, Adama Jalloh, Kaja Jangaard, Mo Yusuff, Barry O'Connell.

32 boroughs

Printed in London by Park Communications in the Borough of Newham

All photographic images C-41 colour processed by Aperture Printing, Rathbone Place, London, UK.

www.32boroughslondon.co.uk

Cataloguing in Publication Data is available from the British Library.

ISBN: 978-1-3999-3562-3

32 boroughs is also supported by Arts Council England and The National Lottery Arts Fund.

LOTTERY FUNDED

Supported using public funding by ARTS COUNCIL ENGLAND

FSC MIX Paper | Supporting responsible forestry FSC® C001785

Park Excellence in sustainable print

Carbon neutral Company